James Joyce and Photography

Historicizing Modernism

Series Editors

Matthew Feldman, Professorial Fellow, Norwegian Study Centre, University of York, UK; and Erik Tonning, Professor of British Literature and Culture, University of Bergen, Norway

Assistant Editor: David Tucker, Associate Lecturer, Goldsmiths College, University of London, UK

Editorial Board

Professor Chris Ackerley, Department of English, University of Otago, New Zealand; Professor Ron Bush, St. John's College, University of Oxford, UK; Dr Finn Fordham, Department of English, Royal Holloway, UK; Professor Steven Matthews, Department of English, University of Reading, UK; Dr Mark Nixon, Department of English, University of Reading, UK; Dr Julie Taylor, Northumbria University; Professor Shane Weller, Reader in Comparative Literature, University of Kent, UK; and Professor Janet Wilson, University of Northampton, UK.

Historicizing Modernism challenges traditional literary interpretations by taking an empirical approach to modernist writing: a direct response to new documentary sources made available over the last decade.

Informed by archival research, and working beyond the usual European/American avant-garde 1900–45 parameters, this series reassesses established readings of modernist writers by developing fresh views of intellectual contexts and working methods.

Series Titles

Arun Kolatkar and Literary Modernism in India, Laetitia Zecchini
British Literature and Classical Music, David Deutsch
Broadcasting in the Modernist Era, Matthew Feldman, Henry Mead and Erik Tonning
Charles Henri Ford, Alexander Howard
Chicago and the Making of American Modernism, Michelle E. Moore
Christian Modernism in an Age of Totalitarianism, Jonas Kurlberg
Ezra Pound's Adams Cantos, David Ten Eyck
Ezra Pound's Eriugena, Mark Byron

Ezra Pound's Washington Cantos and the Struggle for Light, Alec Marsh
Great War Modernisms and The New Age Magazine, Paul Jackson
Historical Modernisms, Jean-Michel Rabaté and Angeliki Spiropoulou
Historicizing Modernists, Edited by Matthew Feldman, Anna Svendsen and Erik Tonning
James Joyce and Absolute Music, Michelle Witen
James Joyce and Catholicism, Chrissie van Mierlo
Jean Rhys's Modernist Bearings and Experimental Aesthetics, Sue Thomas
John Kasper and Ezra Pound, Alec Marsh
Judith Wright and Emily Carr, Anne Collett and Dorothy Jones
Katherine Mansfield and Literary Modernism, Edited by Janet Wilson, Gerri Kimber and Susan Reid
Katherine Mansfield: New Directions, Edited by Aimée Gasston, Gerri Kimber and Janet Wilson
Late Modernism and the English Intelligencer, Alex Latter
The Life and Work of Thomas MacGreevy, Susan Schreibman
Literary Impressionism, Rebecca Bowler
The Many Drafts of D. H. Lawrence, Elliott Morsia
Modern Manuscripts, Dirk Van Hulle
Modernist Authorship and Transatlantic Periodical Culture, Amanda Sigler
Modernist Lives, Claire Battershill
Modernist Wastes, Caroline Knighton
The Politics of 1930s British Literature, Natasha Periyan
Reading Mina Loy's Autobiographies, Sandeep Parmar
Reframing Yeats, Charles Ivan Armstrong
Samuel Beckett and Arnold Geulincx, David Tucker
Samuel Beckett and the Bible, Iain Bailey
Samuel Beckett and Cinema, Anthony Paraskeva
Samuel Beckett in Confinement, James Little
Samuel Beckett and Experimental Psychology, Joshua Powell
Samuel Beckett's German Diaries 1936–1937, Mark Nixon
Samuel Beckett's 'More Pricks than Kicks', John Pilling
Samuel Beckett and the Second World War, William Davies
T. E. Hulme and the Ideological Politics of Early Modernism, Henry Mead
Virginia Woolf's Late Cultural Criticism, Alice Wood

James Joyce and Photography

Georgina Binnie-Wright

BLOOMSBURY ACADEMIC
LONDON • NEW YORK • OXFORD • NEW DELHI • SYDNEY

BLOOMSBURY ACADEMIC
Bloomsbury Publishing Plc
50 Bedford Square, London, WC1B 3DP, UK
1385 Broadway, New York, NY 10018, USA
29 Earlsfort Terrace, Dublin 2, Ireland

BLOOMSBURY, BLOOMSBURY ACADEMIC and the Diana logo are trademarks of
Bloomsbury Publishing Plc

First published in Great Britain 2022
This paperback edition published 2023

Copyright © Georgina Binnie-Wright, 2022

Georgina Binnie-Wright has asserted her right under the Copyright, Designs and
Patents Act, 1988, to be identified as Author of this work.

For legal purposes the Acknowledgements on pp. xiii–xiv constitute an extension
of this copyright page.

Cover design: Eleanor Rose

All rights reserved. No part of this publication may be reproduced or
transmitted in any form or by any means, electronic or mechanical, including
photocopying, recording, or any information storage or retrieval system,
without prior permission in writing from the publishers.

Bloomsbury Publishing Plc does not have any control over, or responsibility for,
any third-party websites referred to or in this book. All internet addresses given
in this book were correct at the time of going to press. The author and publisher
regret any inconvenience caused if addresses have changed or sites have ceased
to exist, but can accept no responsibility for any such changes.

A catalogue record for this book is available from the British Library.

A catalog record for this book is available from the Library of Congress.

ISBN:	HB:	978-1-3501-3696-0
	PB:	978-1-3503-2870-9
	ePDF:	978-1-3501-3697-7
	eBook:	978-1-3501-3698-4

Series: Historicizing Modernism

Typeset by Integra Software Services Pvt. Ltd.

To find out more about our authors and books visit www.bloomsbury.com
and sign up for our newsletters.

For my parents

Contents

Illustrations	x
Editorial Preface to *Historicizing Modernism*	xii
Acknowledgements	xiii
Abbreviations	xv
Introduction	1
1 Photography and paralysis in *Dubliners*	25
2 That 'spoof of visibility': stereoscopic 'realism' in *Stephen Hero to Finnegans Wake*	51
3 'it simply wasn't art in a word': Leopold Bloom, photography and artistic and erotic debate	81
4 James Joyce's 'Photo girl[s]'	111
Coda: 'A photograph […] may be so disposed for an aesthetic end'	145
Notes	150
Works Cited	179
Index	197

Illustrations

0.1 Théodore Maurisset, La Daguerreotypomanie (Daguerreotypomania), 1839. Digital image courtesy of the Getty's Open Content Program.   3

0.2 Julia Margaret Cameron, Alethea, 1872. Digital image courtesy of the Getty's Open Content Program.   9

0.3 Carola Giedion-Welcker, Joyce at Platzspitz, Zürich, 1938. Courtesy of the Zürich James Joyce Foundation.   16

1.1 Pierre Petit, Priest Holding a Crucifix, Standing, c. 1865–70. Digital image courtesy of the Getty's Open Content Program.   30

1.2 Lafayette Photography, James Joyce at Age 6 ½, with his Parents John and Mary Jane, and his Maternal Grandfather, John Murray, 1888. Courtesy of Lafayette Photography, Dublin.   44

2.1 Unknown Photographer, On the Banks of the Liffey, Dublin, Ireland, c. 1859–64. Digital image courtesy of the Getty's Open Content Program.   53

2.2 London Stereoscopic Company, Woman Seated, Pulling on Her Stocking, c. 1865. Digital image courtesy of the Getty's Open Content Program.   62

2.3 London Stereoscopic Company, A Ghost, c. 1865. Digital image courtesy of the Getty's Open Content Program.   66

3.1 Unknown Photographer, Draped Female Nude, c. 1855. Digital image courtesy of the Getty's Open Content Program.   88

3.2 Lafayette Photography, Queen Alexandra, 1902. Courtesy of Lafayette Photography, Dublin.   95

4.1 Unknown Photographer, Kodak, 89 Grafton Street, Dublin, 1928. Courtesy of the George Eastman Museum. Used with permission from the Eastman Kodak Company and the estate of Sam Campanaro.   116

4.2 Lewis Carroll, Saint George and the Dragon, 1875. Digital image courtesy of the Getty's Open Content Program.   119

4.3 Herbert Bell, Amateur World Tour Album, Taken with Early Kodak Cameras, Plus Purchased Travel Photographs by Various Photographers, c. 1880–90. Digital image courtesy of the Getty's Open Content Program.   125

4.4 Mario Circovich, James Joyce, 1914. Courtesy of the Zürich James Joyce Foundation. 129
5.1 Carola Giedion-Welcker, Joyce at Platzspitz, Zürich, 1938. Courtesy of the Zürich James Joyce Foundation. 149

Editorial Preface to *Historicizing Modernism*

This book series is devoted to the analysis of late nineteenth- to twentieth-century literary modernism within its historical contexts. *Historicizing Modernism* therefore stresses empirical accuracy and the value of primary sources (such as letters, diaries, notes, drafts, marginalia or other archival materials) in developing monographs and edited collections on modernist literature. This may take a number of forms, such as manuscript study and genetic criticism, documenting interrelated historical contexts and ideas, and exploring biographical information. To date, no book series has fully laid claim to this interdisciplinary, source-based territory for modern literature. While the series addresses itself to a range of key authors, it also highlights the importance of non-canonical writers with a view to establishing broader intellectual genealogies of modernism. Furthermore, while the series is weighted towards the English-speaking world, studies of non-Anglophone modernists whose writings are open to fresh historical exploration are also included.

A key aim of the series is to reach beyond the familiar rhetoric of intellectual and artistic 'autonomy' employed by many modernists and their critical commentators. Such rhetorical moves can and should themselves be historically situated and reintegrated into the complex continuum of individual literary practices. It is our intent that the series' emphasis upon the contested self-definitions of modernist writers, thinkers, and critics may, in turn, prompt various reconsiderations of the boundaries delimiting the concept 'modernism' itself. Indeed, the concept of 'historicizing' is itself debated across its volumes, and the series by no means discourages more theoretically informed approaches. On the contrary, the editors hope that the historical specificity encouraged by *Historicizing Modernism* may inspire a range of fundamental critiques along the way.

Matthew Feldman
Erik Tonning

Acknowledgements

As with many other Joyceans, the idea behind this project first took shape in Katy Mullin's modern literature seminars at the School of English, University of Leeds. I am indebted to Katy for her PhD supervision and for recognizing the career pathway that I might subsequently enjoy. I feel privileged to have been welcomed into a community of James Joyce scholars, from the editors of the *James Joyce Broadsheet* and members of the University of Leeds' *Finnegans Wake* reading group, to those that I have spent time with in Dublin, Rome, Trieste and Zürich. My PhD thesis was examined by Richard Brown and Keith Williams, whose comments helped me to reshape this project. Keith and Cleo Hanaway-Oakley kindly sent digital copies of their work to me and I have learnt much from sharing conference panels with them. Sincere thanks are due to series editors, Matthew Feldman, David Tucker and Erik Tonning, and to this book's anonymous reviewer whose feedback has always been rigorous and kind.

This project has been predominantly completed during the global Covid-19 pandemic, with writing begun in 2020. Without the generosity of archivists and scholars in providing digital access to images and texts, its completion would not have been possible. I am grateful to Ronan Crowley and John O'Hanlon for sending detailed answers to email queries. Glenn Johnston facilitated virtual access to his New York collection of photographs of Joyce during an enjoyable Zoom call. Glenn Fisher, Chairman and Editor of the Crimean War Research Society provided comments on the Crimean War, which enabled me to develop work on Roger Fenton in Chapter 2. Writing on Triestine photography in Chapter 4 was inspired by attending John McCourt and Laura Pelaschiar's Trieste Joyce School and was supported by The James Joyce Italian Foundation's Giorgio Melchiori Scholarship, 2014. Material on Joyce's 'Photo girl[s]' was first published in the *Journal of Modern Literature* and has subsequently undergone revision.

During a brief hiatus in travel restrictions in 2020, I spent three weeks at the Zürich James Joyce Foundation. Thanks are due to Fritz Senn, Frances Ilmberger, Ruth Frehner, Silke Stebler and Ursula Zeller for their scholarship and support of my visit, as well as to Rolf Utzinger, Tiana Fischer, Arianna Autieri, Rahel Huwyler and my host and friend, Sara Moran. Lauren Lean and

Jesse Peers at the George Eastman Museum, New York located the 1928 image of Kodak's Grafton Street, Dublin store shown in Figure 4.1. Despite every effort, it has not been possible to identify this image's photographer. This photograph was a gift from the estate of Sam Campanaro to the George Eastman Museum and I am thankful to Laura Zigarowicz of the Eastman Kodak Company and Sam's daughter, Vickijo Campanaro for providing image permissions and details. It was a welcome delight to discover that Vickijo has a long-standing interest in Joyce. Gwen O Gorman and Kristina Hadju at Lafayette Photography, Dublin, helped to obtain digital copies of the photographs shown in Figures 1.2 and 3.2. Third Parties must contact Lafayette Photography regarding alternative Usage and Licensing of these images. Alison Fraser at the University at Buffalo provided virtual access to Joyce's photographic postcard sent to Sylvia Beach referenced in this project's Coda. The Getty Open Content Program has made available without charge all digital images to which they hold the rights or that are in the public domain to be used for any purpose without cost. This is an invaluable resource for scholars and, as an Independent Scholar, has enabled me to contextualize references to photography without financial burden.

I completed my postgraduate studies with Emma Trott and Ragini Mohite, who made this a hugely enjoyable experience. Ragini has answered my many questions about the publishing process with endless patience whilst publishing her own book. Throughout my doctoral degree, Jenny Durrant provided a much-needed European hub for visits. My sister and new nieces have been a further, welcome source of distraction. My mother-in-law has helped to turn our house into a home whilst we have been working, wedding planning and writing. For everything, I am indebted to my parents, both of whom returned to Master's degrees at retirement and continue to inspire me. Lastly, to my husband, Chris, thank you for always believing that this book was possible.

Abbreviations

References to the publications listed below appear throughout this volume as abbreviations followed by page number, unless otherwise specified.

D	Joyce, James, *Dubliners,* ed. by Terence Brown (London: Penguin, 1992).
FW	Joyce, James, *Finnegans Wake,* ed by John Bishop (London: Penguin, 1999). References given as page number plus line number.
JJ	Ellman, Richard, *James Joyce,* revised edn (New York: Oxford University Press, 1982).
LI	Joyce, James, *Letters of James Joyce, Vol. I,* ed. by Stuart Gilbert (New York: Viking Press, 1966).
LII	Joyce, James, *Letters of James Joyce, Vol. II,* ed. by Richard Ellmann (New York: Viking Press, 1966).
LIII	Joyce, James, *Letters of James Joyce, Vol. III,* ed. by Richard Ellmann (New York: Viking Press, 1966).
OCPW	Joyce, James, *Occasional, Critical and Political Writing,* ed. by Kevin Barry (Oxford: Oxford University Press, 2000).
P	Joyce, James, *A Portrait of the Artist as a Young Man,* ed. by Jeri Johnson (Oxford: Oxford University Press, 2000).
SH	Joyce, James, *Stephen Hero,* ed. by Theodor Spencer, John Slocum and Herbert Cahoon (New York: New Directions Publications, 1963).
SL	Joyce, James, *Selected Letters of James Joyce,* ed. by Richard Ellmann (New York: Viking, 1975).
U	Joyce, James, *Ulysses: The Corrected Text*, ed. by Hans Walter Gabler, Wolfhard Steppe and Clause Melchor (New York: Random House, 1986). References appear as episode number plus line number.

Introduction

In 1903, in his only critical exploration of photography, James Joyce wrote, 'Can a photograph be a work of art?'[1] His answer followed four pages later, that whilst a photograph 'may be so disposed for an aesthetic end [...] it is not a work of art!'[2] He continues this theme in *Ulysses* (1922), where he depicts Leopold Bloom considering, 'Marble could give the original, shoulders, back, all the symmetry, all the rest. [...] Whereas no photo could because it simply wasn't art in a word' (*U* 16.1451–55). Lacking the 'three conditions of art: the lyrical, the epical and the dramatic' (*OCPW* 103), Joyce's negation of photography's inherent, aesthetic value initially appears to belie the importance of this visual medium to his literature. Yet only one year later in 1904, he published 'Eveline' in the *Irish Homestead*, a story in which the framing and subject of the 'yellowing photograph of the priest' (*D* 30) proves intrinsic to his portrayal of Dublin's paralysis. The duality of the photograph and its ability to invoke innovation and stasis lends itself to Joyce's ambition in *Dubliners* (1914) to 'betray the soul of that hemiplegia or paralysis which many consider a city' (*LI* 55), with hemiplegia the paralysis of one side of the body. Through an exploration of Joyce's manuscripts and photographic and newspaper archival material, as well as the full range of his major works, this project sheds new light on Joyce's personal and professional engagement with photographs, photographic devices and photographically informed techniques.

Roland Barthes describes the 'Photograph as a motionless image', arguing that 'this does not mean only that the figures it represents do not move; it means that they do not *emerge*, do not *leave*: they are anesthetized and fastened down, like butterflies'.[3] As in Barthes's claim, this sense of paralysis is essential to Joyce's literary portrayal of photography. Alfred Stieglitz published New York's *Camera Work* journal (1903–17) and spearheaded the early-twentieth-century photo-secession movement, in which he advocated for photography to be considered a fine art. With modernist photographic experimentation reaching its peak in the 1920s–30s, its more stylistic investigations arrive too late for *Dubliners'* late-nineteenth-century setting. Instead, in Joyce's earlier work, he engages with more conventional photographic portraits and popular advertorial images before making use of celebrity snapshots, pornography and stereoscopic technology in *Ulysses* and *Finnegans Wake*. In this latter work, Joyce merges Victorian photographic practices, predominantly inspired by his knowledge of Lewis Carroll's photography, with George Eastman's Kodak Girls, moving from young girls behind to in front of the camera to demonstrate the medium's hemiplegic potential.

Photography [*photos* (φωτός), light + *graphos* (γραφή), writing] has its origins in experimentation with optics and light dating back to the fifth century BC. The camera obscura was a darkened room with a pinhole at one side. Through use of the sun's rays, an inverted image of the exterior scene could be projected onto the opposite, interior wall, rendering the outside 'revealled by Oscur Camerad' (*FW* 602.230). After becoming interested in lithography in the early 1800s, a printmaking process using oil-based crayon and water, French scientist and artist, Nicéphore Niépce sought to transfer these scientific principles to the camera obscura to 'fix' the projected image. Niépce used a pewter plate coated with asphalt and residue of lavender oil as a photosensitive agent, terming this process and its reliance on light, heliography [*helios* (ἥλιος), sun + *graphos* (γραφή), writing]. He produced the first known heliographic image *c.* 1826, which he titled, 'View from the Window at Le Gras'. The exposure time would have taken several days. Often also later referred to as the shutter speed, the exposure time was the duration for which the plate was exposed to light and the subject required to remain still to prevent the image from becoming blurred.

Following Niépce's death in 1833, Louis-Jacques-Mandé Daguerre was hailed as the sole inventor of photography at the medium's 1839 launch before an audience of the French Academy of Sciences. Only seven months later, the audience also contained the French Academy of Fine Arts. Despite this claim to singularity, Daguerre had previously worked with Niépce, and British scientist, William Henry Fox Talbot had been experimenting with the positive-negative photographic process. In an 1839 essay, Daguerre described his technology as 'not merely an instrument which serves to draw Nature; on the contrary it is a chemical and physical process which gives her the power to reproduce herself'.[4] He credited his silver plate daguerreotypes to Niépce's 'incomplete' experiments.[5] In *The Pencil of Nature* (1844–6), Fox Talbot similarly stressed the interrelationship between photography and nature, recognizing 'the inimitable beauty of the pictures of nature's painting which the glass lens of the Camera throws upon the paper'.⁶ Fox Talbot concluded his essay, 'I think the year 1839 may fairly be considered as the real date of the birth of the Photographic Art, that is to say, its first public disclosure to the world'.⁷

Such was the public appetite for daguerreotypes that in December 1839, French lithographer, Théodore Maurisset produced the lithograph, 'La Daguerreotypomanie (Daguerreotypomania)' shown in Figure 0.1 attesting to their popularity. His lithograph includes reference to 'Potences à louer pour mm les graveurs [gallows for hire for the engravers]' and 'épreuve retourné 13 minutes [proofs returned in 13 minutes]'. The satirical suggestion of death for engravers and the rate of the production of prints reveal the speed at which photography came to be embraced by the public. Daguerre and Fox Talbot's photographic inventions differed from one another. Daguerre created a single image on a silver-coated copper plate, which could only be reproduced through rephotographing the original image. His daguerreotype plates were extremely sensitive and had to be placed in protective viewing cases to avoid air getting in and tarnishing the images. Talbot invented his calotype technique in the 1830s and patented this in 1841. By combining gallic acid and silver nitrate solution, he was

Figure 0.1 Théodore Maurisset, La Daguerreotypomanie (Daguerreotypomania), 1839. Digital image courtesy of the Getty's Open Content Program.

able to accelerate the chemical reaction involved in rendering the image visible after this had been exposed to light in a camera. In 1843, Anna Atkins published the first book to be photographically illustrated, *Photographs of British Algae: Cyanotype Impressions*, Part I. As a keen botanist, Atkins used the cyanotype, cyan blue photographic printing process invented by Sir John Herschel in 1842 to produce her photographic negatives of individual algae. Although Atkins owned a camera, her algae images are photgrams, camera-less images. She produced these by placing specimens on coated, light-sensitive paper, which she then exposed to light. A fixer solution was added to preserve the resulting image.

Cameras were used in wartime photography shortly after the medium's 1839 public launch during the Mexican-American War (1846–8). By the Crimean War (1853–6), technological developments had reduced the photographic exposure time to under twenty seconds. Women were later involved in wartime photography, including Scottish photographer, Christina Broom, who took up photography in 1903 and Olive Edis, a British practitioner who captured images in 1900–1955. Broom was a pioneer of women's press photography and became a 'semi-official photographer for the Household Brigade'.[8] Her images include photographic portraits of royalty, though she is now best known for her photographs of First World War soldiers and London suffragettes. Edis was the first woman to be allowed to photograph scenes at France and Flanders in the First World War and captured snapshots of women in working, wartime roles at home and abroad. She reopened her photographic studio at 68 Castle Street, Farnham, Surrey, after the end of the First World War. Her professional trajectory demonstrates the potential for women to independently manage photographic businesses, albeit with her first studio designed by her uncle, who was an architect. This was a career pathway often aided by familial connections and support, as in Milly Bloom's paternal links to photography in *Ulysses*, where Bloom thinks, 'Now photography. Poor papa's daguerreotype atelier he told me of. Hereditary taste' (*U* 8.173–74). Whether the 'Tulloch-Turnbull girl' (*FW* 171.31) is working for a studio is never substantiated but the presence of women wartime and press photographers prior to Joyce's composition of I.7 of the *Wake* reveals the professional opportunities available to women.

The Photographic Society of Ireland began holding monthly meetings in the 1850s, as well as an annual exhibition, which by the 1890s included awards, lectures, programmes of music and lantern displays.[9] The public could gain access to an evening exhibition event for six shillings.[10] In winter 1906, the Society was praised by the *British Journal of Photography* for an upcoming programme of talks on 'lantern use, carbon printing, photography in general [and] microscopic photography', as well as their exhibition of papers, demonstrations and a lantern lecture on 'High-Speed Photography' from a Japanese speaker.[11] Commercial portrait photography was available in Dublin from 1840. Obtaining a portrait became increasingly popular from 1865, after over 170 photographers exhibited their work at Dublin's International Exhibition of Arts and Manufacturers. Before the exhibition, fewer than twenty professional photographers appeared in Dublin's street directories but 'by the end of 1865 the number had risen to over thirty'.[12] Despite competition from amateur photographers, photography remained a viable career choice and between 1901 and 1911, the number of Irish residents listing their occupation as within the photographic industry increased from 766 to 972.[13] As acknowledged by Rose Teanby, census records must be treated with caution, since professional female photographers often had their occupation obfuscated after marriage or had only their first occupation listed if they had originally trained in a different field.[14]

In the late nineteenth century, William Lawrence's photographic studio was one of Dublin's most commercial enterprises. Part of the appeal of visiting Lawrence's studio lay in the excitement surrounding its displays of 'celebrity images from royalty, clergy and politicians, to opera singers, entertainers and political agitators'.[15] Lawrence's main competition came from James Stack Lauder, who began operating under the professional name Jacques Lafyette in 1880. Joyce immortalizes Lafayette's as 'Dublin's premier photographic artist' in *Ulysses* (*U* 16.1435–36) and was photographed at his studio in his 'man-o'-war suit' in childhood (*D* 187), prior to his 1888 departure to Clongowes Wood College.[16] By 1898, Lafayette's success in Dublin, Glasgow, Manchester and London was such that he acquired the additional photographic businesses Lauder Brothers and 'E J Stanley, Photographers, of Dublin', amalgamating these into 'Lafayette Limited'.[17] In the early 1900s, a dozen cartes de visite could be purchased from Lafayette's for twenty-one shillings.[18] A dozen, larger cabinet prints cost double the price.[19] The studio produced albumen and silver gelatin prints, as well as more expensive mezzotint portraits.[20] Given their popularity, visitors to Lafayette's would have also been photographed by other staff members and not only by Stack Lauder.

The albumen print process was invented by Lois Désiré Blanquart-Evrard in 1850 and used throughout the second half of the century. By placing a glass negative onto a sheet of paper coated in albumen egg white and silver nitrate, and exposing this to light, the photographer could reproduce their image in albumen print form. In 1871, English physician Richard Leach Maddox invented the silver gelatin dry plate process. Gelatin plates could be used without a portable darkroom, revolutionizing photographic practices. Joyce owned a copy of *Thom's Official Directory of Great Britain and Ireland: for the Year 1904*. This details twenty-two photographic studios in Dublin, including 'J. Lafayette, 30 Westmoreland Street' and 'Kodak Co. (ltd.), 89 Grafton Street'.[21] A single business located at 40 Capel Street is recorded under the heading 'Photo-Lithographer, Photo Engraver, and Photo-Mechanical Printers' and three businesses appear under 'Photographic Apparatus Manufacturers'.[22] Given Joyce's desire for historical accuracy and his multiple references to Grafton Street, occurring five times explicitly in *Ulysses* and implicitly more, he would have known of Dublin's Kodak branch, using this and his copy of Otto Jespersen's *Growth and the Structure of the English Language* (1912) to inform his Wakean references to the Kodak camera and popular photography.[23]

The earliest known colour photograph was produced in 1861 by Scottish physicist, James Clerk Maxwell, who combined images taken using red, green and blue filters into one, recognizable colour composite. The French pioneers of cinematic technology, Auguste and Louis Lumière invented their autochrome process in the late 1890s, which involved adding colour to a single, photographic plate. The Lumière brothers presented their findings to the French Academy of Sciences in 1904. *Punch* magazine satirically responded, 'The secret of photographing in colours has again been discovered. We were getting afraid that this year was going to be an exceptional one.'[24] Reproducing colour photographs remained expensive. Joyce appeared in colour on the front cover of the 8 May 1939 edition of New York's *Time* magazine in an image captured by Gisèle Freund. Colour photographs did not feature regularly in newspapers until the 1950s. Given the costs involved in producing these images, hand colouring and retouching of photographs remained popular throughout the nineteenth and early twentieth centuries. This task was typically performed by photographers' assistants, who were often female. The number of women working in this capacity rose so sharply that in 1900, the *British Journal of Photography* revealed 'women form the majority, and the men are a small and fast-disappearing minority'.[25] Male assistants would have still usually taken charge of the darkroom development of photographs, given the chemicals involved.[26]

Developments in photographic and printing practices increasingly enabled Irish residents to view photographs in the popular presses. The use of photography in newspapers and magazines brought transformative, international scenes to the general public. Pictures were taken by new photojournalists or were sent into newspapers by readers, often as part of competitions with monetary prizes.

In 1904, the *Daily Mirror* became Britain's first illustrated daily newspaper. The *Mirror*'s photographic images enhanced the publication's popularity, which by 1910 had a daily readership of 900,000.[27] The paper featured an array of photographs, such as 1904 images of comedian Mr Dan Leno and a 1910 front cover snapshot taken in court of Mr Bradley, an ex-footman brought into disrepute after allegedly falsely receiving £60,000 from his employers.[28] As Eloise Knowlton has noted, whilst photographs could be printed in newspapers, 'Dublin's daily news organs did not incorporate photographs, or indeed engravings or advertising logos, until the mid-teens.'[29] Early editions of the *Freeman's Journal* contained advertisements for photographic studios and articles on visual practices. On 20 November 1914, the *Freeman's Journal* printed their first photograph, showing 'National volunteers for the Irish Brigade off to the Great War'.[30] Joyce had access to this newspaper after his departure from Dublin in 1904 and included a 'photo cut from Dublin Freeman [sic]' in a Parisian letter to Robert McAlmon dated August 1921, along with the comment, 'I.O.U.' (*LI* 170).

Pictorialist photography rose to prominence in the late 1880s but had largely peaked by around 1910. The art photography movement was pioneered by figures such as Julia Margaret Cameron, whose work was later published in Stieglitz's *Camera Work* journal.[31] Pictorialists saw the camera as an artistic tool capable of elevating the aesthetic status of the photographic medium. Cameron photographed Alice Pleasance Liddell (APL) in August and September 1872. Liddell was the inspiration for Lewis Carroll's *Alice* books, as explored in Chapter 4 of this project. Charles Lutwidge Dodgson, better known as Lewis Carroll, began experimenting with photography in the mid-1850s whilst studying at Christ Church College, University of Oxford. He asked his uncle Skeffington Lutwidge 'to get me some photographic apparatus, as I want some occupation here [other] than mere reading and writing'.[32] Given that he was engaging with the medium in its relative infancy, he initially turned to the wet collodion process credited to Frederick Scott Archer in 1851.[33] This required the photographer or studio assistant to coat a glass photographic plate with chemicals designed to form silver iodine. The wet plate was then placed in a camera and exposed to light, rendering the photographic negative visible after developer and fixer solutions had been added.

Carroll's early photographs were of landscapes, family friends and children, including Liddell and her family, who he had known since her father, Dr Henry Liddell's 1855 appointment as Dean of Christ Church College. He initially rented a photographic studio at Badcock's Yard, Oxford, but his interest in photography was such that by 1872, he commissioned a purpose-built, glass-structured studio on the roof of his college accommodation in the grounds of the Great Quadrangle, Tom Quad. Carroll developed his images in the darkroom of his flat, doing so until 1880 when he ceased photography to devote more time to his writing and theatrical adaptations. Photography informed Carroll's writing as well as the images he produced and he published essay, 'Photography Extraordinary' in 1855, and poems 'Hiawatha's Photographing' and 'A Photographer's Day' in 1857 and 1860, respectively. He composed 'Photography Extraordinary' in the same year in which he began experimenting with photography, producing a satirical account of a 'mechanical' camera capable of rivalling 'novel-writing' by capturing 'the workings of [...] [the] mind'.[34] In 'Hiawatha's Photographing', Carroll satirizes Henry Wadsworth Longfellow's epic poem 'The Song of Hiawatha' (1855), the latter work which appears as 'hiarwather' in *Finnegans Wake* (*FW* 600.08). Had Joyce read *Phantasmagoria and Other Poems* at Shakespeare and Company bookstore in Paris, as is possible given their ownership of this work, he would have been able to access 'Hiawatha's Photographing' as this was printed in this collection.[35]

In Cameron's albumen silver print of Liddell shown in Figure 0.2, her work contains the soft focus and ethereal qualities essential to pictorialist photography. Cameron combined romanticism with classical, pictorial tropes focused on beauty and aestheticism, rather than documentary-style realism. Stieglitz used his quarterly photographic journal, *Camera Work* to promote photography as a fine art and devoted a special issue to Cameron in 1913. Terming his fine art, photographic movement, photo-secession, he strove to emphasize the medium's pictorial qualities and highlight the 'evolution of the photographic art'.[36] The impact of the First World War on subscriptions to the journal and the cost of printing photographs meant that their 1 June 1917 edition was their last. Stieglitz moved away from pictorialism and dedicated the final issue of *Camera Work* to American street photographer Paul Strand, with whom he pioneered the straight photography movement in which practitioners used a sharp focus to capture images of previously ignored or neglected street scenes. Throughout the late nineteenth and early twentieth centuries, Eugène Atget documented Paris buildings and architecture with unflinching, documentary realism. Residing in Paris in the same street as Man Ray, Atget saw his work promoted by surrealist visual innovators and Ray's former darkroom assistant, Berenice Abbott, who photographed Joyce in 1926 and 1928.

Man Ray was a proponent of camera-less photograms, which he termed 'rayographs'. By placing objects onto photosensitized paper and exposing

Figure 0.2 Julia Margaret Cameron, Alethea, 1872. Digital image courtesy of the Getty's Open Content Program.

them to light, he produced reproductions of objects that he subsequently printed onto gelatin silver paper. He also engaged in commercial photography but is best known for his contributions to surrealist and Dada movements, including experimentation with fragmentation, illustrating surrealist texts with photography and photographing leading, avant-garde figures. Joyce was familiar with Ray's work and was photographed by him as publicity for *Ulysses* in 1922. In a 1935 essay, André Breton emphasized the importance of psychology on photography, arguing that surrealism 'allowed certain artists to set down stupefying photographs of their thoughts and their desires on paper or canvas'.[37] Joyce acknowledges the interrelationship between the camera and the subconscious in *Finnegans Wake*, where he combines reference to "alices, when they were yung and easily freudened' with '*in camera*', a play on photography and the Latin legal terminology for a private jury session in which press and public are absent (*FW* 115.22–23). Tristan Tzara and Ray's involvement in Dadaism saw them promote experimentation with 'photographic materials and processes' in order to drive their 'anti-art aesthetic'.[38] To reveal the 'superficiality' of mass-produced imagery, they used techniques such as photomontage, the process of combining individual photographs to create a new image.[39] Joyce alludes to Dada in *Finnegans Wake*, where Mr Hunker is 'too dada for me to dance' (*FW* 65.17). Here the word 'dada' invokes both modernist experimentation and the paternal motif heavily associated by Joyce with his literary 'Photo girl[s]', as discussed in Chapter 4 of this book.

'I am so glad you like my picture'

In *c*. 1885, Joyce was photographed in an elaborate ruff collar in his first known studio session.[40] Measuring only 6.4 cm × 9.5 cm, the image would have been a small carte de visite mounted on cardboard, involving use of a specially designed, multi-lens camera. The photograph could have been taken at Lafayette's since Joyce later visited the studio with his parents and maternal grandfather. In 1888, they were photographed at Lafayette's to mark Joyce's impending departure to Clongowes Wood College.[41] The later images are larger than those captured in 1885, as one of Joyce by himself measures approximately 14 cm × 19.3 cm.[42] The size of the larger image determines that this is a cabinet print. Since they cost double the price of cartes de visite from Lafayette's, the Joyces evidently deemed their son's schooling worthy of this higher cost.[43] Joyce sent a childhood image to his partner, Nora Barnacle, on 23 December 1909, joking 'Darling, I am so glad you like my picture as a child. I was a fierce-looking infant, was I not?' (*LII* 279). He was likely referring to the *c*. 1885 photograph, given his sterner expression. Joyce moved from a flirtatious engagement with photography during his early relationship with Nora to a more reflective response to the medium in his final decade, writing to his son, Giorgio, 'I will look for a photograph of Mama but she says that they are all bad. [...] I see a lot of paternal pride in your letter. I too have known that joy in the years that were' (*LIII* 360).

The geographical location of Dublin's photographic studios along 'the main commercial thoroughfares' led to this being referred to as 'the photographer's mile'.[44] Joyce's brother, Stanislaus recalls how, after 'passing a photographer's studio with his brother and noting the *embonpoint* of the ladies pictured in the window', he had remarked of their ample curves, 'It's like the briskets hanging in a butcher's shop' (*JJ* 134). Joyce transfers this comment to *Ulysses*, where Leopold Bloom looks 'away thoughtfully with the intention of not further increasing the other's possible embarrassment while gauging her symmetry of heaving *embonpoint*', after showing his photograph of Molly to Stephen Dedalus (*U* 16.1466–68). John Stanislaus Joyce's former sweethearts may have been photographed at Dublin's 'photographer's mile'. Their images stood on the family's piano, until the children's governess, Mrs 'Dante' Hearn Conway persuaded May Joyce that 'it was downright improper to keep the photographs in the drawing-room where the children [...] could see them'.[45] Joyce's mother later regretted her decision to burn the photographs, reflecting that 'they were all nice-looking girls'.[46] Her decision to dispose of the photographs in this manner recalls Molly's actions in *Ulysses*, where she remembers having 'burned the half of those old Freemans and Photo Bits leaving things like that lying about' (*U* 18.600–01).

Joyce was photographed after his 31 October 1902 graduation from Royal University, later University College Dublin.[47] He had the image mounted on card giving the photographer's details as Paul Darby, 147 Boulevard Saint-Germain, Paris. Since Joyce was photographed at the Photo-Cartes studio at 28 Boulevard Poissonnière, Paris, in 1902 (*JJ* viii), he would have been able to visit Darby's atelier to obtain reproductions of his existing Dublin images, as the two studios were located less than two miles apart. A reprint by Darby exists of Constantine Curran's 1904 photograph of Joyce standing in front of a Dublin greenhouse.[48] Joyce purchased multiple reproductions of his graduation photograph, the varying dimensions of the images revealing differences in the ways in which these were rephotographed and mounted. By 1903, Joyce's financial situation in Paris was so dire that he could not meet his 'hotel bill' (*SL* 18). Upon first arriving in the city in December 1902, he had at his 'disposal a position in the Ecole Berlitz, beginning at 150 francs a month (£7-10-0)' and private tuition at '20 or 25 francs a month', along with paid, written engagements (*SL* 10–11). These roles likely contributed to his freer, earlier engagement with photographers' studios. Joyce continued to have his portrait taken professionally across Europe and was photographed in Zürich by Alex Ehrenzweig in 1915 and by Wilhelm Pleyer and Camille Ruf in 1916.[49]

Following his departure from Dublin on 8 October 1904, Joyce exchanged multiple photographs with his family and friends. Those of his son, Giorgio acted as a partial aid in repairing his relationship with his father. In a letter dated 16 May 1909, John Stanislaus Joyce reveals, 'My feelings have undergone a change towards you, hastened by the receipt of the photos of your son whose *strong likeness* to you at his age brought vividly back to my mind, memories which I try strenuously to avoid' (*LII* 228). Despite this, his father deemed his collection lacking, writing in the same letter, 'I would be glad to have a *good photo* of Georgie when you have one done, as also of yourself and Stannie. I am writing him' (*LII* 228). Joyce received a photograph from Stanislaus during his internment in Austria in the First World War, informing Michael Healy on 2 November 1915, 'I thank you for your inquiries about my brother. He sent me his photograph last week. He has a long full beard and looks like the late Duke of Devonshire' (*LI* 85). This interchange of images was a regular occurrence and Joyce posted 'a photo' of himself to Frank Budgen from Zürich in July 1919 in what was likely intended as a reciprocal exchange (*LI* 128). The image could have been one of those taken by his friend, Ottocaro Weiss in 1915 or that captured by Swiss photographer, Ruf. Writing again to Budgen in early February 1920, Joyce asked, 'When is your photo coming? Or when yourself?' (*LII* 458). By 28 August 1937, he had at least received from Budgen 'the photo of yourself and daughter which is certainly she and you. Our compliments to the mother as well' (*LIII* 404).

Joyce's relationship with his children was frequently mediated via photography. On 9 September 1935, he wrote to his daughter, Lucia, 'By chance some days ago I wrote to Zurich for the photograph which the young Salzburger took of your hand. This morning it arrived and I enclose it in this letter' (*LI* 381). He wrote again to Lucia on 29 September 1935, 'I enclose a few rather wretched photographs and, by the way, you will receive from Mrs Curran (just now in London) a new camera which, I hope, will prove useful and enjoyable' (*LIII* 374). This was not the family's first camera, as Lucia took photographs during their holidays to Saint Malo in 1924 and Ostend in 1926.[50] As Xavier Tricot has noted, her actions as a photographer are evident in the images in which she is substituted with her family members as the subject. Lucia had received her new camera by 17 October 1935, as Joyce advised:

> We received your post cards and the two photographs also, of you and of Miss Weaver. Thank you. Miss Weaver is always the same and as for you, you look as if you did not care in the least about the *terrestrial globe,* absorbed as you are in

your reading and swinging. If only all the inhabitants of the above mentioned rolling ball were so peaceful!

(*LIII* 377)

Brenda Maddox describes these images as portraying a 'sullen but attractive girl in a hammock [...] a very stern Miss Walker, an unsmiling Miss Weaver [...] and a very unhappy young woman with a mass of wavy hair'.[51] Lucia is likely to have taken the photographs of Miss Walker and Miss Weaver, but besides Joyce's reference to Miss Weaver as 'always the same', his reply focuses solely on his daughter (*LIII* 377). In his 17 October 1935 letter, he concluded, 'If your picture is indicative of your state of health you must be much, much better' (*LIII* 378), his positive interpretation of the photograph negating Lucia's serious psychological issues.

Joyce engaged with photography as a means of publicity and revealed in an 8 November 1916 letter to Harriet Shaw Weaver, 'I shall send photographs, one for the *Egoist* and one for Mr Huebsch' (*LI* 98). These images were used as marketing material for *A Portrait of the Artist as a Young Man* (1916). Requests for pictures did not always prove successful and Richard Ellmann records how in 1934, 'Joyce was unexpectedly receptive when the Honorable Mrs. Reginald (Daisy) Fellowes, a well-known figure in society with literary pretensions, announced that she wanted her group *Les Amis de 1914* to hold a celebration in Joyce's honor' (*JJ* 668). Having set up the event, Mrs Fellowes:

> cut through this folderol by suddenly appearing at Joyce's door and pushing in with a photographer at her heels. Her intention was to be photographed alone with Joyce, but Joyce insisted that Léon, who was present, join the group, added Eugene Jolas who appeared during the preparations, and even drew the buxom concierge into the picture in spite of Mrs. Fellowes's protests. 'This is wonderful; we can have a family group,' he said.
>
> (*JJ* 668)

Nora was displeased with the resulting images, as these showed only Joyce and Mrs Fellowes, the others having been purposefully cropped out (*JJ* 668). Joyce wrote to Giorgio in 1935 advising, 'When I find a lady who is content with her own picture I will send a bouquet to the pope' (*LIII* 360), yet he acknowledged his 'very profound objection' to his 'own image' (*LI* 215). His comments hint at the reluctance of the 'national apostate' to be photographed by the Tulloch-Turnbull girl in *Finnegans Wake*, as addressed in Chapter 4 of this project, who is similarly 'cowardly gun and camera shy' (*FW* 171.31–34).

Joyce's failing eyesight impacted on requests for photographs during the 1920s–30s, decades in which he lived in Paris and in which modernist experimentation with photography was at its peak. Improvements in flash lighting in the late 1880s led to a reduction in the amount of smoke that was produced during a sitting but Joyce would still have found flash technology challenging. Assisting Man Ray at a photographic shoot in 1922, Gisèle Freund recalls:

> His eyes being bad, his poses were 'very stiff' and finally, unable to bear the lights, he dropped his head in his hands and refused to go on; it was then that Ray took the photograph which he subsequently sent to Beach.[52]

In 1926, Joyce's eyesight prevented him from posing under Berenice Abbott's bright studio lights and she was forced to take her photographic equipment to his apartment at 2 Square Robiac, Paris.[53] Freund first considered photographing Joyce after meeting him at a 1936 Parisian party hosted by Adrienne Monnier, where she 'dared to speak to him about it'.[54] He was initially reluctant, pleading 'his work, his health, his poor eyesight'.[55] After eventually securing two photoshoots with Joyce in 1938 and 1939, Freund took 'over a hundred fresh exposures', with both sessions arranged to promote *Finnegans Wake*.[56] Freund produced images of Joyce for a photo-essay with *Life* magazine at their first meeting and, at their second, photographed him in colour for *Time* magazine. Freund's portraits also appeared in the 13 May 1939 issue of British photojournalistic magazine, *Picture Post*, to accompany an article on Joyce.[57]

Freund was aided in her requests to photograph Joyce by his belief in superstitions. Following her taxi crashing after their first meeting, she accused him of putting 'some kind of a bad Irish spell on them'.[58] She reports that 'Joyce gasped, and I knew I had guessed rightly. [...] Contrite, he begged me to return the next day so he could pose again'.[59] With Freund's film from the first shoot surviving intact, she acquired two sets of colour portraits of Joyce. He was 'so pleased' with the images that he advised her to go to England to photograph 'Wells, Shaw, Elizabeth Bowen, V. Sackville-West, and Virginia and Leonard Woolf', informing her, 'Tell them you did my portrait and I am very happy with it. Say I told you to do theirs. They won't refuse.'[60] Joyce was correct, and his endorsement of Freund aided her transition into photographing London's literary scene. Her visual archive attests not only to her skills with the camera but to the vibrant nature of Parisian culture. A snapshot of Joyce, Monnier and Sylvia Beach at Shakespeare and Company bookstore shows the group in front of the shop's well-known assortment of photographs of celebrated figures; these include images by Freund, Abbott and Ray of Samuel Beckett, F. Scott Fitzgerald, Katharine Mansfield and Joyce, amongst other artists.[61] Ray was so unhappy at Beach distributing prints of his photograph of Joyce for free that he 'raised his fee to compensate for not being paid royalties'.[62]

After becoming a grandfather in 1932, Joyce entered a new period of interplay with photography. In a 20 November 1934 letter to his son, Giorgio and wife, Helen Joyce, he told the couple, 'The photos of Stevie are not good. Take a few more. I should like to have a group taken' (*LIII* 328). Since the new parents' time was split between America and Europe, Joyce was keen that his grandson did not forget him. Writing again to Giorgio the next day, he asked, 'Did the little man recognize me when he saw the photograph? I suppose he speaks with an American accent. If so (curse this fountain pen!) I will resign myself. I greet you, young man!' (*LIII* 332). Joyce's frustration at his lack of images is apparent in his letter of 19 February 1935, in which he demands 'Why don't you send me a photograph of Stevie? I asked several times' (*LIII* 345). He repeated his appeal on 26 February 1935, telling Giorgio and Helen simply, 'Send us a photograph' (*LIII* 347). Joyce received the snapshots on 19 March 1935, replying, 'Photos just arrived. They are very good. The little boy is very good-looking. Giorgio in the paper has exactly the same pose as I have in Silvestri's picture' (*LIII* 352). Joyce was referring to Tullio Silvestri's 1914 oil on paper portrait, evidencing his continued acknowledgement of the interrelationship between photography and art, as explored in Chapter 3 of this project.

Joyce was not averse to photography's humorous potential and on 20 September 1928, he asked Weaver, 'Did Miss Beach send you photos he took of us and his letter in which he said that his wife, under the influence of reading me, had announced that she was terribly sick of bluggage' (*LI* 267). A month later, he playfully mocked John McCormack, telling her '[he] has been three times in the Trianons this last week and you will see by the enclosed photograph that the regional dishes are agreeing with him' (*LI* 272). He deemed the 1938 photograph taken by his friend and art-historian, Carola Giedion-Welcker in Figure 0.3 his 'favourite portrait', joking, 'At last a view of myself I can look at with some pleasure' (*LII* 418). In 1940, the Italian minister of education appeared in a photograph alongside an instalment of the *Wake*, posing as if 'seated at a table with one hand clasping his forehead, his eyes closed and an expression of exhausted bewilderment on his face' (*LI* 412–13). Rather than take offence, Joyce thought the photograph 'rather amusing' and

Figure 0.3 Carola Giedion-Welcker, Joyce at Platzspitz, Zürich, 1938. Courtesy of the Zürich James Joyce Foundation.

joked to Mary Colum, 'the pained look in the photograph will soon give place to the first of many similar [? Smiles]' (*LI* 412–13).

Joyce recognized that photography could be 'disposed for an aesthetic end' (*OCPW* 104) and the medium enabled him to share art with others. He carried painted portraits of his family members across multiple countries and households until his final arrival in Zürich in 1940.[63] John Stanislaus Joyce bequeathed 'the family portraits' to his son 'in the spring of 1913' (*JJ* 332), after declaring, 'I know *you* will set proper value on them when I am dead and gone' (*LII* 291). Joyce added art to this collection, which came to include Tullio Sillvestri's c. 1913–14 portrait of Nora and Patrick Tuohy's 1924 painting of Joyce.[64] In 1927, he commented upon the 'coincidence that for several years he had been carrying in his pocket photographs of the portraits by Tuohy of his father, himself, and – James Stephens' (*JJ* 592). As with Bloom's 'slightly soiled photo' (*U* 16.1465), the portability of the photographs of the portraits enhanced their appeal and allowed him to readily display these to others. In a letter dated 14 August 1927, Joyce revealed that he had lost one of the photographs but had decided to have another 'photograph taken (of the portrait)' (*LI* 257). Joyce ensured that his 1935 oil portrait by Émile Blanche was also photographed, with this image now housed with Sylvia Beach's Papers at Princeton University Library.[65] In a 1938 sitting with Freund, Joyce 'posed with George and Stephen in front of Tuohy's portrait of his father, to make "Four Generations of Joyces"' (*JJ* 715). Painted portraits exist of Joyce's great-grandmother, Anne McCann and his paternal grandmother, Ellen O'Connell but with Lucia having been institutionalized and Nora not appearing in the image, there is a noticeable absence of female, family lineage given Joyce's interest in women and photography.

James Joyce and visual culture

In 2009, Sean Latham acknowledged, 'we are only just beginning to understand the importance […] of photography and the ways in which its narrative and temporal structures intersect with Joyce's writing'.[66] Over ten years later, despite multiple works considering Joyce's literature and photography, there is still much work to be done. One of the first critics to devote attention to this subject was R. Brandon Kershner in his essay 'Framing Rudy and Photography' (1998–9). Detailing 'the appearance of Rudy as a photograph' in *Ulysses*'s 'Circe' episode, Kershner argues:

> Rudy's elaborately detailed appearance in his materialization at the end of 'Circe' as he takes on definition like a photographic plate within the developing solution, is in part a testament to the load of significance that the personal photograph in all its richness and rarity was expected to bear.[67]

Kershner expands on this topic in his later monograph, *The Culture of Joyce's 'Ulysses'* (2010), which includes a rich analysis of Bloom and Rudy's relationship alongside the intricacies of Victorian memorial photography.[68] In *Advertising and Commodity Culture in Joyce* (1998), Garry Leonard brings Irish photography and photographic advertising material to Joyce's literature via Lacanian theory.[69] For Leonard, 'Commodity culture is modern, in part, because it relies on technological advances in visual presentation, such as photography, and improved methods of printing, such as lithography.[70] He combines critical theory and materialist approaches and uses the erotic postcard as a means of approaching Joyce's depiction of 'pleasure' and 'pornographic scenarios'.[71]

In 'Joyce and Consumer Culture' (2004), Jennifer Wicke explores visual and commodity culture, outlining how:

> Every aspect of mass culture and media technology makes an appearance across the spectrum of Joyce's writing, from newspapers, magazines, gramophones, silent films, newsreels, telephones, telegraphy, and photo studios in the earlier works to radio and even an intimation of television in *Finnegans Wake*.[72]

Wicke reads photography through a materialist lens but her argument that Milly's 'prettiness is a commodity used to lure young men on vacation to have a snapshot made of themselves standing on the beach with her' does not fully acknowledge the professional spaces offered to women by photography.[73] This project recognizes Milly's aesthetic function, as noted by Wicke, but combines this with archival excavation to highlight women's professional and amateur roles with the camera. Eloise Knowlton takes a historicist approach in her essay, 'Showings Forth: *Dubliners*, Photography, and the Rejection of Realism' (2005), in which she acknowledges 'that Joyce's early work owes something to photography is an idea that seems easily and obviously true'.[74] She combines archival excavation with photographic theory, arguing that the narrator in 'Araby' is 'Not just a camera, the boy is a "detective camera," who can "penetrate wherever there is life worth seeing"'.[75]

In 'Visual Clockwork: Photographic Time and the Instant in "Proteus"' (2006), Louise E. J. Hornby uses the 'discursive status of the photographic instant' to aid understanding of 'modernist epistemologies of sight and time' and draws comparisons between Eadweard Muybridge's 1870's motion studies and the 'Proteus' episode of *Ulysses*.[76] Hornby's essay exposes the influence of stereo cards on Joyce's writing, particularly her reading of the 'flatness' of photographic images as 'a critical factor in Stephen's description of the modality of sight'.[77] Graham Smith devotes a chapter to Joyce in '*Light that Dances in the Mind': Photographs and Memory in the Writings of E.M. Forster and His Contemporaries* (2007).[78] Smith considers the broad range of Joyce's literature and provides a brief introduction to photographs taken of the author. Alongside suggesting that the stories in *Dubliners* can be viewed 'as a collection of daguerreotypes or [...] an album of snapshots of Dublin and its inhabitants', he concludes by recognizing 'Photographs and photography may be secondary elements in the vast tapestry of Joyce's work but they are not inconsequential'.[79]

Stephen and the stereoscope have received much critical attention, with Philip Sicker's recent monograph *'Ulysses', Film and Visual Culture* (2018) contributing significantly to this topic and to the broader field of Joyce and visual culture.[80] Sicker conclusively demonstrates that Joyce's portrayal of sight in *Ulysses* is informed by optical breakthroughs, such as 'photography, chronophotography, and such proto-cinematic attractions as the mutoscope and kinetoscope'.[81] He further explores the impact of street photography on Bloom's actions as a modernist *flâneur*.[82] Modernist photographers experimented with artistic and proto-cinematic techniques and photography cannot be considered in isolation. John McCourt's edited collection, *Roll Away the Reel World: James Joyce and Cinema* (2010) brings cinematicity to the forefront of Joycean study, with contributors including Cleo Hanaway-Oakley, Keith Williams and Katherine Mullin, who expose the literary significance of Joyce's involvement with the 1909 opening of Dublin's first dedicated picture house and respond to *Ulysses*'s proto-cinematic techniques.[83]

Knowledge of Joyce and cinematicity has been substantially enhanced by Cleo Hanaway-Oakley's *James Joyce and the Phenomenology of Film* (2017) and Keith Williams's *James Joyce and Cinematicity: Before and After Film* (2020).[84] Hanaway-Oakley uses *Ulysses* as a case study to bring the phenomenology of film 'into dialogue with literary modernism studies'.[85] Recognizing that Merleau-Ponty, the phenomenologist she predominantly draws upon 'could not have influenced Joyce directly', she instead seeks to 'uncover parallel philosophies latent within early cinema spectatorship, within early films themselves and within Joyce's texts and the experience of reading'.[86] Williams uses rigorous archival research to showcase the influence of pre- and post-cinematic culture on Joyce's writing, from *Stephen Hero* to *Ulysses*. This includes work dedicated to the magic lantern and stereoscopic technology and a coda on *Finnegans Wake*, in which he argues that the latter text's inclusion of television, radio and photography expands Joyce's 'overall mediacultural imaginary'.[87] He further engages with photography, noting that 'just as individual photographic frames acquire aesthetic value as part of a dynamic flow of images in film, Joyce integrated many of the epiphanic moments he records [in his "Paris Notebook"] into *Portrait*'s dynamic structure'.[88]

Critics have long recognized Joyce's knowledge of Lewis Carroll and the author's presence in *Ulysses* and *Finnegans Wake*.[89] Responding to Joyce's 1927 comment, 'I never read him till Mrs Nutting gave me a book' (*LI* 255), James S.

Atherton determines that this book was Carroll's *Sylvie and Bruno*.[90] For Atherton, Joyce's combination of Alice, Iseult, Christine Beauchamp and Swift's two Stellas in the *Wake* allows him to create 'a symbol of the Virgin [....] [and] constantly changing personalities in the same character'.[91] Hugh Kenner devotes a chapter to 'Alice's Chapelizod' in *Dublin's Joyce* (1956), in which he investigates Carroll's influence on *Dubliners* and *Ulysses* and the impact of his 'romantic night-world' on the *Wake*.[92] Kenner emphasizes the importance of Carroll's young girl friends on Joyce's depiction of Humphrey Chimpden Earwicker's (HCE's) 'incestuous infatuation with his daughter Iseult' and argues that he transfers 'Dodgson's ambivalent relations with Isa to the *Wake* almost unaltered as HCE's incestuous infatuation with his daughter Iseult'.[93]

In genetic analysis of Joyce's manuscript notebooks, Viviana Mirela Braslasu reveals the ways in which Belle Moses's biography of Carroll informs 'The Hen' episode in I.5 of the *Wake*.[94] Braslasu recognizes that Joyce may have taken the description of the 'national apostate' as 'camera shy' from Moses's account of Carroll but does not devote substantial attention to his photography.[95] Connections between Lucia Joyce and the *Wake*'s young, dancing girls have been well-evidenced, most recently by Genevieve Sartor, who highlights the influence of Lucia's dance training and her work with 'Les Six de rythme et couleur' female dance troupe on Joyce's composition of the *Wake*.[96] Images of Lucia dancing in costume taken by Berenice Abbott in 1928 showcase her dance skills, yet they also hemiplegically attest to the stasis of the image and the way in which the camera paradoxically captures the subject in flight.

In the last decade, significant critical attention has been dedicated to Irish photographic culture. In their edited collection, *Visual, Material and Print Culture in Nineteenth-Century Ireland* (2010), Ciara Breathnach and Catherine Lawless argue that 'non-textual sources are essential to the study of nineteenth-century Ireland'.[97] This is a view shared by Justin Carville in his article on 'Popular Visual Culture in Ireland' (2007), in which he notes:

> The questions at stake around colonial and postcolonial identity, modernism and modernity [are] played out not in the canon of Irish art, but in the visual displays, mass spectacles, popular tourist travelogues and commemorative ephemera of the late nineteenth and early-twentieth centuries.[98]

Carville and visual historians, Kevin Rockett and Emer Rockett have revealed the importance of Joyce and Ireland's photographic archives. In 'With His

"Mind-Guided Camera": J. M. Synge, J. J. Clarke, and the Visual Politics of Edwardian Street Photography' (2012), Carville proposes that 'In the canon of Irish cultural history, it is Joyce who has predominantly been identified as having the most affinity with the mechanical sensorium of this emerging technological modernity'.[99] Rockett and Rockett further explore Joyce's literary use of photographic techniques in *Magic Lantern, Panorama and Moving Picture Shows in Ireland, 1786-1909* (2011), where they write:

> The following May [1898] the Mutoscope Palace opened in Dublin at 29 Grafton Street with a programme of films of Pope Leo XIII, but to read this as indicative of the general content of mutoscope films would be unwise, as is clear not just from the promotional material's reference to pantomime and that 'the little ones enjoy it immensely', but also from James Joyce's *Ulysses*.[100]

They recognize the value of Katherine Mullin's archival work on the mutoscope in this area, with the mutoscope an early moving-picture device using photographic flip cards.[101] As in many of the texts dedicated to Joyce, Rockett and Rockett posit magic lantern shows and cinematic technology as key to his literature, leaving space for additional work on Joyce and photography.

A schema

As Latham notes, given the 'array of [...] print artefacts' circulated in Joyce's lifetime, 'One major task that clearly beckons is the critical examination of this so-called "ephemera", the visually dense material that made up so much of the city's life.'[102] This project responds to this call and draws upon photographs and the representation of photography in newspapers, archival holdings and Joyce's letters and manuscripts to inform close reading of his major works. Intrinsic to this study is the idea that Joyce portrays photography in his writing as hemiplegic. He imbues the medium's more innovative, technological aspects with a sense of stasis and/or sexual innuendo, rather than rendering photography wholly progressive. This project analyses *Stephen Hero, A Portrait of the Artist as a Young Man, Dubliners, Ulysses* and *Finnegans Wake*, texts in which Joyce's explicit and implicit use of photography speak to concerns with hemiplegia and paralysis. Texts are explored in which there are direct references to photography and *Chamber Music* (1907), *Exiles* (1918), *Pomes Penyeach* (1927) and *Giacomo Joyce* (1968) are not featured. Not all photographs are critically addressed, including sailor D. B. Murphy's 'picture postcard' of a 'group of savage women in striped loinclothes' in *Ulysses* (*U* 6.472–76). Joyce's depiction of the 'savage women' is likely to have been influenced by the Edwardian vogue for sending picture postcards and trends in ethnographic photography but this topic has received excellent critical attention from Stephen Watt.[103] More recently, Catherine Flynn's *James Joyce and the Matter of Paris* (2019) also considers photopostcards, focusing on the three sent by Joyce from Paris in 1902.[104] Flynn uses these photographic postcards to demonstrate the 'fundamental importance' of Joyce's Parisian writing on his 'work as whole' and the 'challenges Paris presented to his art'.[105]

This project combines close reading with a historicist approach, informed by the material images and photographic technology to which Joyce and his protagonists could have had access. Where possible, his published works and developments in photography are considered chronologically. There is overlap between his composition of *Stephen Hero*, *A Portrait* and *Dubliners* and this project first considers photographic portraits in *Dubliners*, before moving to an exploration of stereoscopic technology spanning *Stephen Hero* to *Finnegans Wake*. Each chapter looks back to the 1839 birth of photography in the context of particular visual innovations, covering: portraiture; stereo cards and projectors; debates between photography, art and eroticism; and women's roles behind and in front of the camera. With *Finnegans Wake* published 100 years after photography's 1839 launch, this project focuses on photographic movements relevant to Joyce's references to this medium.

Chapter 1, 'Photography and paralysis in *Dubliners*' explores the interplay between photography and paralysis via close reading of four of *Dubliners*' short stories: 'Eveline', 'A Little Cloud', 'Grace' and 'The Dead'. With 'Eveline' first published in *The Irish Homestead* in 1904 and 'The Dead' composed in 1907, this chapter reveals how his collection is indebted to photography in more traditional forms, popular in the late nineteenth century. Through an examination of Joyce's intention to 'betray the soul of that hemiplegia or paralysis which many consider a city' (*LI* 55), this chapter presents *Dubliners* as a microcosm for Joyce's wider concerns with photography and paralysis. For Tristan Tzara, writing in Man Ray's *Les Champs délicieux* (1922), an album dedicated to his 'rayograph' camera-less images, the photographer who 'switched on his thousand-candle-power lamp [...] had discovered what could be done by a pure and sensitive flash of light'.[106] Joyce portrays photographic portraits as capable of inspiring creativity and epiphany but lacking the modernistic 'pure and sensitive flash of light' needed to conquer 'palsy' in those remaining in Dublin.[107]

Chapter 2, 'That 'spoof of visibility': stereoscopic 'realism' from *Stephen Hero* to *Finnegans Wake*', examines politically charged photographs alongside consideration of stereoscopic technology in *Stephen Hero*, *A Portrait of the Artist as a Young Man*, *Ulysses* and *Finnegans Wake* (I.5, II.3 and III.1). In *Stephen Hero*, composed between 1904 and 1906 but published posthumously, 'the name beneath Ibsen's photograph never failed to reawaken his sense of wonder' (*SH* 82). At Belvedere College, 'two photographs' are situated on the 'hall table', 'one of the Tsar of Russia, the other of the Editor of the Review of Reviews' (*SH* 112). The 'Tsar's photograph' and the 'two photographs in frames' reoccur in *A Portrait* (*P* 163), where Joyce depicts Stephen commenting on the Tsar's quality of a 'besotted Christ' (*SH* 112–13; *P* 163). His young protagonist refuses to sign MacCann's petition supporting Czar Nicholas's pursuit of 'universal peace' (*P* 166) but experiences the intrusion of politics and nationhood in his sexual encounters, where 'his senses, stultified only by his desire, would note keenly all that wounded or shamed them; [...] a photograph of two soldiers standing to attention or a gaudy playbill' (*P* 86).

In his depiction of Stephen Dedalus's concerns with stereoscopic theories, and his use of erotic and phantasmagoric imagery in *Stephen Hero* to the *Wake*, Joyce was writing during a century in which the stereoscope had fallen in and out of favour. This chapter argues that Joyce imbues Stephen with the ability to engage with photography from a position of aesthetic and critical detachment, encouraged by his interest in stereoscopy. Stephen's focus on Emma Clery's body in near-fragmented form and later hallucinatory visions in *Ulysses*'s 'Circe' episode reveal a culture in which penny-in-the-slot stereoscopes and supernatural stereo cards combined visual distortion with the promise of 'almost life-like reality'.[108] This chapter concludes by examining allusions to the stereopticon and anaglyph technology in I.5 and III.1 of the *Wake*, with brief reference to Buckley, the Crimean War and the daguerreotype in II.3. Joyce's Wakean use of stereoscopy reveals his continued interest in visual manipulation and the importance of the device's 'tantalising purchase on the real' to his depiction of rumour and transgression.[109]

Chapter 3, "it simply wasn't art in a word': Leopold Bloom, photography and artistic and erotic debate', approaches photography and art in *Ulysses* via Bloom's consumption of photographic images and his concept of himself as 'a bit of an artist in his spare time' (*U* 16.1448–49). In combining historicist research with close reading, this chapter exposes how Bloom's engagement with photography is underpinned by a preoccupation with the female form, where it is 'woman [who] is beauty of course' (*U* 18.559–60). In 1903, Joyce determined that a photograph was 'not a work of art' (*OCPW* 104). He returns to this theme in *Ulysses* (1922), where Bloom thinks of wife, Molly's curves, 'Marble could give the original, shoulders, back, all the symmetry [...] Whereas no photo could because it simply wasn't art in a word' (*U* 16.1451–55). Tracing the interrelationship between photography and art via Bloom's photograph of Molly, the Lafayette photographic studio and the photography of nude, female models in *Ulysses* and *Finnegans Wake* (II.2) reveals Joyce's hemiplegic use of the medium. Photography for Bloom both aids his sexual fantasies and signals a marital and aesthetic lack. This chapter devotes attention to Gerty MacDowell in *Ulysses*'s 'Nausicaa' episode and uses the *Lady's Pictorial* to contextualize Joyce's references to Lafayette's and the 'art' of photographic retouching.

Chapter 4, 'James Joyce's 'Photo girl[s]'' shares the prior chapter's concerns with photography and female sexuality but explores women's amateur and professional photographic roles via *Ulysses'* Milly Bloom and the *Wake*'s Tulloch-Turnbull girl. In examining Milly in relation to Triestine female photographers, Marion and Wanda Wulz, who inherited their father's studio in 1928, new light is shed on Irish and Triestine photographic culture and the relationship between female photography and familial duty. Writing within the context of George Eastman's Kodak Girls, Joyce moves from the statically framed women of *Dubliners* to the increasingly free spirited and dogged, young female photographer. Yet whilst photography offered women new and dynamic professional spaces, Joyce acknowledges its paradoxical function and underscores the technological innovation of his 'Photo girl[s]' with erotic and consumer appeal (*U* 1.685). Despite his encouragement of Lucia's use of the camera, Joyce denies his 'Photo girl[s]' an active, narrative voice. He posits their camerawork and importance to their family units against their fleeting, textual interspersions, which are mediated via others, predominantly men. This chapter concludes by addressing the importance of Lewis Carroll's photography of young girls to Joyce's portrayal of rumour and transgression in the *Wake*, moving from behind to in front of the camera. In doing so, this project demonstrates Joyce's literary preoccupation with photography and paternal relationships, as in 'Photo's papli, by all that's gorgeous' (*U* 14.1535–36). This project's Coda reiterates this text's central purpose: to showcase Joyce's hemiplegic portrayal of photography through close reading and archival excavation. In highlighting new areas for exploration, it closes by asking what next for Joyce and visual culture, whilst acknowledging the challenges of conducting historicist, archivally informed work during the global Covid-19 pandemic.

1

Photography and paralysis in *Dubliners*

Photography commands a particular relationship with paralysis in *Dubliners* (1914), informed by the medium's technological possibilities by the late nineteenth century. In 1839, the daguerreotype process of permanently fixing an image had an initial exposure time of twenty to thirty minutes. By the 1870s, a photograph could be captured in less than a second, thanks to Richard L. Maddox's gelatin dry plate process. This enabled photographic plates to be pre-prepared and removed the need for them to be developed immediately after exposure. These innovations proved critical to the later taking of instantaneous photographs with handheld cameras and to the development of professional and amateur photographic markets. Against the backdrop of James Joyce's early-twentieth-century composition of *Dubliners* and his depiction of photographs and photographically informed techniques, advancements in visual culture were such that by 1900, George Eastman's Kodak Box Brownie camera was retailing for five shillings. The 'amateur photographer' with his 'portable camera' was 'ubiquitous' in Dublin.[1]

In 'The Sisters', written first and retaining its original place at the collection's opening, the date is given as 'July Ist, 1895' (*D* 4). Joyce based the Conroy family photograph on an 1888 image from his childhood and given Gabriel Conroy's age in 'The Dead', the fictional portrait can be dated to the late nineteenth century, one of the earliest to feature in his short stories. *Dubliners* exists at the cusp of visual modernism, with Alfred Stieglitz launching his *Camera Work* journal advocating for the medium's 'pictorial' qualities in 1903 and Tristan Tzara not releasing his 'Dada Manifesto' until 1918, in which he conversely claimed, 'All pictorial or plastic work is useless'.[2] Stieglitz acknowledged the interplay between photography and paralysis in his journal. The first issue features a poem by Roman Catholic priest and poet, Father John B. Tabb entitled 'From a Photograph', in which he alludes to the camera's ability to frame the subject 'In Light's Captivity'.[3] The medium's potential for entrapment is key to *Dubliners*, where Joyce presents photography as hemiplegic, hemiplegia being the paralysis of one side of the body. In his short stories, he uses photographic portraits and techniques to inspire epiphanic 'pure and sensitive flash[es] of light' whilst simultaneously reinforcing domestic and emotional stagnation.[4]

Dubliners features three photographic portraits, 'the priest whose yellowing photograph hung on the wall' in 'Eveline' (*D* 30), 'Annie's photograph' in 'A Little Cloud' (*D* 78) and the image of Mrs Conroy 'pointing out something [...] to Constantine' in 'The Dead' (*D* 187). In 'Grace', Joyce includes 'one of Pope Leo's poems [...] on the invention of the photograph' (*D* 167) and alludes to the 'magic lantern' (*D* 171). His use of the visual medium is not confined to explicit references to photography. Instead, his characters also engage in what Susan Sontag termed 'photographic seeing', a kind 'of dissociative seeing' contributing to 'estrangement from rather than union with nature'.[5] For Tristan Tzara, writing in Man Ray's *Les Champs délicieux* (1922), an album dedicated to his 'rayograph' camera-less images, the photographer who 'switched on his thousand-candle-power lamp [...] had discovered what could be done by a pure and sensitive flash of light'.[6] This 'pure and sensitive flash of light' and possibility of awakening from 'palsy' underscore Joyce's literary engagement with photography. In 'Eveline', 'A Little Cloud', 'Grace' and 'The Dead', he presents this medium as capable of inspiring thoughts of exile and a turn towards the 'familiar' (*D* 30). Detailing his compositional intention in an August 1904 letter to Constantine Curran, Joyce described how 'I call the series *Dubliners* to betray the soul of that hemiplegia or paralysis which many consider a city' (*LI* 55). With hemiplegia a mono-sided paralysis, his intention to expose the soul of Dublin's paralysis still allows for instances of vitality and semi-artistic awakening. Photography frequently encourages his protagonists' creative senses but with Joyce deeming the photograph 'not a work of art' in 1903 (*OCPW* 104), prior to his composition of *Dubliners*, the possibility of this medium leading to prolonged and meaningful change is rendered negligible.

As in 'A Little Cloud' in Little Chandler's reference to Lord Byron's poem, 'On the Death of a Young Lady' (1802), from which he quotes '*Not e'en a Zephyr wanders through the grove*' (*D* 79), at the turn of the century photography was frequently associated with classical and artistic tropes. This was apparent at the 1894 Dublin Photographic Convention, where Lafayette's photograph, '*An Evening Zephyr*' depicting a 'beautiful female figure (life size)' was praised as illustrative of the lines from Irish poet, Thomas Moore's *Sacred Songs* (1816), 'Hark! 'tis the breeze of twilight calling'.[7] Lafayette was the professional name used by James Stack Lauder, who had worked as a Dublin photographer since 1880.

Joyce was photographed at Lafayette's as a child and later immortalized 'Lafayette of Westmoreland street, Dublin's premier photographic artist' as responsible for Leopold Bloom's photograph of his wife, Molly in *Ulysses* (1922) (*U* 16.1435–36).[8] Portrait photography was available in Dublin from 1840 and became increasingly popular from 1865. In 1902, a dozen cartes de visite cost twenty-one shillings at Lafayette's.[9] Excluding the photograph of the 'priest' in 'Eveline', which could have also been taken in 'Melbourne' (*D* 30), the cabinet portraits and cartes de visite depicted in *Dubliners* are likely to have been taken at Dublin's 'photographer's mile', where Lafayette's and William Lawrence's photographic studios were located.[10]

Joyce initially published 'The Sisters' and 'Eveline' in *The Irish Homestead* in August and September 1904, respectively. Writing to Grant Richards on 5 May 1906, he further outlined his aim 'to write a chapter of the moral history of my country and I chose Dublin for the scene because that city seemed to me the centre of paralysis' (*SL* 83). In his composition of his short stories, he sought to awaken Dublin's citizens from 'palsy' and encourage 'the first step towards the spiritual liberation of my country' (*SL* 88). His use of photography supports this cause, as when Eveline thinks after viewing the 'yellowing photograph' of the priest, 'She had consented to go away [...] Was that wise?' (*D* 30). That the image can generate these moments is less surprising when considering what in 1980, Roland Barthes would term the photograph's *studium* and *punctum*.[11] Barthes described the *studium* as a general interest in a particular photograph 'without special acuity' and the *punctum* as that which 'disturb[s] the *studium* [...] that accident which pricks me (but also bruises me, is poignant to me)'.[12] The image's '*punctum*', very often 'a "detail" or "partial object"' can be 'ill-bred' or in good taste, acting as a 'lightning-like [...] power of expansion'.[13] Joycean epiphany is tied to literary production, containing this *punctum* or sense of bruising.

In *Stephen Hero* (1944), roughly composed between 1904 and 1906 and published posthumously, Joyce presents an epiphany as 'a sudden spiritual manifestation, whether in the vulgarity of speech or of gestures or in a memorable phase of the mind itself' (*SH* 188). The photograph is capable of generating artistic and spiritual manifestation, but it is also a static form, unable to embody the rhythmic movement that Joyce viewed as integral to sculptural art (*OCPW* 104). In *Stephen Hero*, Stephen is described as saying to Cranly, 'No esthetic theory [...] is of any value which investigates with the aid of the lantern of tradition' (*SH* 189); instead, the 'modern spirit [...] examines its territory by the light of day' (*SH* 167). Joyce invokes the proto-cinematic magic lantern in 'Grace', where Mr Kernan exclaims 'I bar the magic lantern' (*D* 171). His protagonist in his short story ultimately chooses 'tradition', rather than a 'light' that is able to combat 'palsy'.[14] Approaching 'Eveline', 'A Little Cloud', 'Grace' and 'The Dead' in the historicist context of their photographs, and their references and allusions to photography, exposes Joyce's hemiplegic interaction with this visual medium, which is capable of encouraging creativity but lacks the aesthetic gravitas needed for sustained 'spiritual liberation' (*SL* 88).

'outside she heard a melancholy air of Italy'

The first photograph in *Dubliners* appears in 'Eveline', where 'during all those years she had never found out the name of the priest whose yellowing photograph hung on the wall' (*D* 30). The photographic portrait of the priest could have been a carte de visite measuring approximately 6.4 cm × 9.5 cm or a larger cabinet card at 14 cm × 19.3 cm. Given Joyce's awareness of Lafayette's and his visit to this studio, the priest's photograph may have been taken there, particularly since Lafayette also captured multiple images of religious figures. Eveline's family finances are dependent upon her brother, Harry having 'sent up what he could', her weekly battle to get her father to 'give her the money' to feed the family and the 'seven shillings' she earns per week (*D* 31). Her wages are less than the 'Twelve and six a week' earnt by Milly Bloom as a photographer's assistant, who does not have to share her earnings with her family (*U* 4.425). The priest had been a 'school friend' of her father and, as money is scarce, the photograph could have been gifted to the family (*D* 30). Religious figures and photographic artists were quick to engage with this new visual medium, the former posing for smaller cartes de visite, stereo cards and picture postcards, amongst other printed forms and the latter taking photographs of religious pilgrimages and staging biblical re-enactments. In 1908, Lafayette's published 'photographs of the catholic bishops of Ireland which were presented by the Irish hierarchy to Pope Pius X'.[15]

Art photographers experimenting with religious iconography include Julia Margaret Cameron, who produced an 1864 photographic series entitled 'Fruits of the Spirit' depicting the nine Christian virtues. This was not well-received in Ireland and responding to its display at the 1865 Dublin Exhibition, the *British Journal of Photography* decried, 'we can only express our astonishment that any one should suppose himself or herself capable of conveying in a series of photographs [...] the full, deep import of the words of Holy Scripture'.[16] The photograph in 'Eveline' is evidently more conventional in being situated next to the 'print of the promises made to Blessed Margaret Mary Alacoque' (*D* 30) and Joyce imbues this with a sense of devotion and familial duty. The promises on the 'print' of the 'Blessed Margaret Mary Alacoque' would have included space for family signatures. This feature is largely redundant, since Eveline's mother and brother Ernest have died and her older brother Harry is 'nearly always down somewhere in the country' (*D* 31).[17] Eveline briefly mentions 'the two young children who had been left to her charge' but there is little emotional engagement and Joyce does not define their relationship with one another. Instead, the focus is on her repetition of ensuring they 'went to school regularly and got their meals regularly' (*D* 31).

Joyce devotes attention to childhood in *Dubliners* via his compositional structuring of the stories in childhood, adolescence, maturity and public life. Despite this, he does not depict any photographs of the text's younger protagonists, bar the image of the absent Constantine in 'The Dead'. Since Joyce was photographed in his youth, independently and with his family, his decision to avoid portraying active, family portraits reinforces the sense of sterility he creates between absent and present family members. The photographs that are portrayed paradoxically highlight what is lacking, the 'priest' having managed to emigrate to Australia whilst Eveline considers but ultimately rejects departure with Frank.[18] The description of the priest's photograph as 'yellowing' reveals its age and suggests a level of deterioration also present in 'Araby', where the former tenant of the house 'a priest, [who] had died in the back drawing-room' had left behind books including *The Memoirs of Vidocq*, whose 'leaves were yellow' (*D* 21). The 'yellowing' of the image reveals that this is an albumen print, a photographic printing process invented by Louis Désiré Blanquart-Evrard in 1850. Albumen prints were coated in egg white mixed with sodium chloride or ammonium chloride, leaving them prone to yellowing deterioration. This use of chemicals rendered the image susceptible to a yellowing or brown tone, as in the photograph in Figure 1.1.

The albumen print remained in popular usage until *c.*1890, when it was surpassed by the gelatin dry plate process. The silver sulphide in the gelatin print could also yellow but this process was more apparent in albumen prints, suggesting the earlier photographic process in 'Eveline' and dating the image of the priest to *c.* 1870–90. His photograph occupies a position as one of 'those familiar objects from which she had never dreamed of being divided' but Eveline had 'never found out' his name (*D* 30). Whilst 'familiarly' and 'familiarity' are used elsewhere in *Dubliners,* the word 'familiar' appears only three times, again when Eveline looks 'round the room, reviewing all

Figure 1.1 Pierre Petit, Priest Holding a Crucifix, Standing, *c*. 1865–70. Digital image courtesy of the Getty's Open Content Program.

its familiar objects' (*D* 29) and later in 'Grace', when Joyce writes, 'Gradually, as he recognised familiar faces, Mr Kernan began to feel more at home' (*D* 172). In each of these instances, what is purported to be familiar is inherently deceptive, Eveline unaware of the priest's name despite the fact that he had 'been a school friend of her father' (*D* 30), and the 'familiar' crowd in 'Grace' misleading Mr Kernan into attending the Jesuit service. This dual sense of familiarity and estrangement instils the priest's photograph with its uncanny status and Eveline's viewing of the photographic portrait leads her to 'weigh each side of the question' as she considers leaving 'her home' (D 31). Her observation of the image initially functions at the level of its *studium*, 'an *average* affect' and 'general and [...] *polite* interest'.[19] Yet after viewing the photograph and acknowledging that the priest was in 'Melbourne', whilst also considering emigrating with Frank, she is struck by its *punctum*, the absence of the priest's name, that which 'bruises me, is poignant to me'.[20]

The 'yellowing photograph' functions as a microcosm for the text's wider concerns with hemiplegia, its association with devotion and departure mimicking Eveline's choice between her home and leaving with Frank. Duality abounds in her decision-making, as she recalls how their 'father used often to hunt them in out of the field with his blackthorn stick' but thinks 'it was not so bad then' (D 29). Alongside her viewing of the photograph, Eveline engages in 'photographic seeing', an 'aptitude for discovering beauty in what everybody sees but neglects as too ordinary'.[21] Her romantic, semi-photographic framing of Frank 'standing at the gate, his peaked cap pushed back on his head' (D 31) recalls Constantine Curran's 1904 photograph of Joyce.[22] Given his amateur photographic status and the image's exterior setting, Curran would have taken this using a handheld camera or a device mounted on a tripod. Eveline is unable to disassociate Frank from her life of familial devotion and her framing of his 'hair tumbled forward over a face of bronze' functions as an inverted version of Christ's golden halo on the 'print of promises' (D 31). Joyce's wife, Nora was able to depart with her 'sailor' in 1904 but Eveline rejects this possibility and, in choosing to remain in Dublin, the aesthetic potential in her photographic framing of Frank is lost. Her visual framing hints at her subsequent decision not to leave, with the distance involved in her proto-aesthetic contemplation encouraging 'estrangement from rather than union with nature', like the actions of those engaged in new modes of 'photographic seeing'.[23]

Eveline occupies a position outside of her usual domestic and professional settings when she accompanies Frank 'to see *The Bohemian Girl*' (D 31). Joyce describes her feeling 'elated as she sat in an unaccustomed part of the theatre with him' (D 31–32). Michael William Balfe's *The Bohemian Girl* (1843) was immensely popular during the late nineteenth and early twentieth centuries, with an 1898 review of The Gaiety Theatre's production arguing 'there is no lyric work watched with more uncompromising fondness and jealousy than the "Old Girl"'.[24] The play offers Eveline revolving, tableau images of an imagined life beyond the religious servitude embodied in the priest's photograph. The kineticism associated with the play would have been further enhanced by its

1906 showing at the Rotunda Concert Hall, Dublin, where the entertainment also featured a projection of 'sensationalist and interesting [...] living pictures' by the Irish Animated Photo Company.[25] The Round Room's 'living pictures' were animated films shown using an electric cinematograph.[26] Appropriately, given Frank's profession and the couple's anticipated departure by boat, the 1906 event included a film showing a 'scene of shipwreck and lifeboat salvage'.[27] Had Eveline accompanied Frank to a performance illustrated by similar pictures, this would have likely only enhanced her later 'maze of distress' at the portside (*D* 33).

Recalling his attendance at a performance of 'Cyrano de Bergerac' in Dublin, Stanislaus Joyce describes his fascination with the leading actress as largely being due to 'her not being Irish'.[28] In 'Eveline', rather than functioning as a source of inspiration, exoticism is presented as something to be feared, as when she remembers 'her father strutting back into the sickroom saying: Damned Italians! coming over here!' (*D* 33). Joyce coveted a photograph of the Italian actress Eleonora Duse in his youth but the most popular carte de visite portraits to be traded in Britain at this time were reportedly images of the royal family, statesmen, literary figures and clergymen.[29] Artists and singers were at the bottom of this list.[30] As in this hierarchical, visual status, Eveline aligns herself with the familiarity and servitude suggested by her household's religious objects, rather than choosing a new life with Frank. The priest's relocation to Australia posits him as an other-worldly symbol but this is complicated by the photograph's setting next to the 'print of promises made to Blessed Margaret Mary Alacoque' (*D* 30). As Katherine Mullin has noted, behind statistics on 'the rate of migration to Argentina from Ireland' lay 'Argentina's reputation in Ireland as the locus of tall tales, betrayals and disappointments'.[31] Joyce hints at the negative implications of Frank's promises to Eveline in her father's warning, 'I know these sailor chaps' (*D* 32). He expands on this theme in *Finnegans Wake*, where 'with ambitious interval band selections from *The Bo'Girl* [...] A baser meaning has been read into these characters the literal sense of which decency can scarcely hint' (*FW* 32.34–33.15). Preceding rumours of Humphrey Chimpden Earwicker's (HCE's) sexual transgression in 'having behaved with ongentilmensky immodus opposite a pair of dainty maidservants' (*FW* 34.18–19), Joyce's allusion to *'The Bo' Girl'* and its 'base meaning' (*FW* 33.14) exposes the risks associated with travelling with Frank to 'Buenos Ayres' (*D* 31).

Like the fleeting nature of the theatrical production, Frank 'had come over to the old country just for a holiday' (*D* 32), this temporality conflicting with the routine drudgery of Eveline's work and domestic duties. The claustrophobia of her home is apparent when Joyce describes her recalling how on 'the last night of her mother's illness; she was again in the close dark room at the other side of the hall and outside she heard a melancholy air of Italy' (*D* 33). Landscape photography had been used since the medium's inception but by the turn of the century, professional photographers frequently advertised their ability to capture group shots outside. In framing Eveline in 'the close dark room' as the 'melancholy air of Italy' plays, Joyce suggests the possibility of her developing and picturing a new role beyond Dublin. Eveline exists within a socially debilitating environment but Joyce suggests she is partially responsible for this stasis; she is depicted as being 'laid up for a day' (*D* 32) and is told by Miss Gavan to 'Look lively, Miss Hill, please' (*D* 30). Eveline doesn't have to be lively but just *look* lively, the performative nature of this command and her employer's desire for her to engage in movement aligning her with the stasis of the priest's image. The snapshots that Joyce presents of Eveline are at odds with the technological developments occurring around her and the move into modernity in the description of how 'a man from Belfast bought the field and built houses in it – not like their little brown houses but bright brick houses with shining roofs' (*D* 29). Eveline recognizes that 'Everything changes' (*D* 29) but in frequently returning to an imagined, idyllic past as she thinks of 'her father putting on her mother's bonnet to make the children laugh' (*D* 32), she occupies a liminal state, caught between past and future progression.

Joyce frames his protagonist in semi-photographic form when 'She sat at the window watching the evening invade the avenue' (*D* 29) and 'Her time was running out but she continued to sit by the window, leaning her head against the window curtain, inhaling the odour of dusty cretonne' (*D* 32). The first known image to be 'fixed' in a camera obscura was Nicéphore Niépce's heliograph, 'View from the Window at Le Gras' (*c.* 1826). Niépce's image shares this window framing, albeit in a heliograph looking out and showcasing the beauty of nature, rather than looking in. Joyce critiqued the photographic potential of the window setting in a 15 June 1934 letter to Lucia, sent during her stay at the Les Rives de Prangins sanatorium: 'Why do you always sit at the window? No doubt it makes a pretty picture but a girl walking in the fields also makes a pretty picture' (*LI* 342). Though 'Eveline' was first published in the *Irish Homestead* thirty years prior to his letter, in both instances he associates this setting with lethargy and emotional stasis. When Eveline is depicted as moving, her actions are frequently tinged with agitation, as when 'she had to rush out as quickly as she could' (*D* 31) and 'She stood up in a sudden impulse of terror. Escape!' (*D* 33). Despite getting as far as 'the swaying crowd in the station at the North Wall' (*D* 33), she becomes physically paralytic and stands before Frank with 'her white face to him, passive, like a helpless animal' (*D* 34). Like the image of the priest, which is devoid of obvious emotion, she gazes at Frank with 'eyes [which] gave him no sign of love or farewell or recognition' (*D* 34). With Joyce portraying her prior to this semi-photographic framing as 'moving her lips in silent fervent prayer' (*D* 34), her allegiance with her household's religious images is determined, the possibility of emigration lost to notions of duty and 'dusty cretonne' (*D* 29).

'if you wanted to succeed you had to go away'

In 'A Little Cloud', the photograph of Annie is situated in 'the room off the hall' that contains the 'pretty furniture' Little Chandler 'had bought for his house on the hire system' (*D* 77–79). The hired furniture is designed to suggest membership of a higher social class, as is the photograph, which shows Annie wearing 'the pale blue summer blouse' that she had said 'was a regular swindle to charge ten and elevenpence for that' (*D* 78). With a dozen cartes de visite costing twenty-one shillings from Lafayette's, Little Chandler and Annie would have saved to have the photograph taken, since 'To save money they kept no servant' (*D* 77).[32] The image occupies a prominent position within the 'room off the hall', where 'A little lamp with a white china shade stood upon the table and its light fell over a photograph which was enclosed in a frame of crumpled horn' (*D* 77–78). The 'little lamp' illuminates the picture, but its progressive potential is called into question by the repetition of this more limiting adjective, Little Chandler giving others the 'idea of being a little man' (*D* 65) and living in 'his little house' (*D* 79). Susan Sontag suggests that 'Nobody ever discovered ugliness through photographs', but the portrait of Annie leads Little Chandler to reflect, 'The composure of the eyes irritated him. They repelled him and defied him' (*D* 78).[33] He acknowledges that 'the eyes of the photograph […] were pretty and the face itself was pretty' (*D* 78) but whilst 'many, through photographs, have discovered beauty', he instead considers of her 'face' that 'he found something mean in it' (*D* 78).[34]

Annie's 'eyes' function as the image's *punctum*, 'that accident which pricks me (but also bruises me, is poignant to me)'.[35] After looking 'coldly' at eyes that answer him 'coldly' (*D* 78), Little Chandler experiences an epiphany and questions, 'Why had he married the eyes in the photograph?' (*D* 78). Her eyes inspire his emotional bruising and feelings of futility, as he considers, 'It was useless, useless! He was a prisoner for life' (*D* 80). Joyce was writing at a time at which the photographer's duty to their subject was 'not to portray her realistically, but idealistically' and Little Chandler's assessment of the image is more revealing of the state of his marriage than the image's subject.[36] Despite photographers' claims of enhancing beauty, Bloom similarly thinks of Molly's portrait, 'it did not do justice to her figure which came in for a lot of notice usually' (*U* 16.1445). With Joyce deeming the photograph 'not a work of art' in 1903 (*OCPW* 104), he portrays protagonists such as Little Chandler and Bloom, who consider themselves 'a bit of an artist' (*U* 16.1448–49), as questioning photography's aesthetic worth. As in the title of 'A Little Cloud' and the lamp that illuminates the photograph, Little Chandler's artistic ambitions are never wholly realized, his creativity depicted as temporal whilst remaining in Dublin.

After looking at the portrait of Annie, Little Chandler is reminded of 'what Gallaher had said about rich Jewesses. Those dark Oriental eyes [...] how full they are of passion, of voluptuous longing' (*D* 78). As with 'the eyes' in Annie's photograph, his recollection of those 'rich Jewesses' inspires his vision of life elsewhere. For Garry Leonard, 'It seems clear that he has seen these eyes, but improbable that "oriental" women in Dublin are in the habit of looking at him in this way – except through the medium of erotic photographs'.[37] This is apparent in Little Chandler's conversation with Ignatius Gallaher, in which he asks, 'is it true that Paris is so ... immoral as they say?' (*D* 72). French 'pioneers of photography often supplemented their income by producing pornographic pictures' that could be purchased via illicit trading routes or in illegally trading shops.[38] Commenting on Leonard's analysis of 'a mass-produced "erotic organization of visibility"', Deirdre Flynn concludes that 'When examined from this perspective, Chandler's route of escape into Orientalist fantasy appears to be anything but liberating'.[39] Little Chandler's fantasy situates him in relation to this commodified eroticism and exposes what he feels he is lacking. Yet the image of the 'Oriental eyes' also inspires the potential for change and leads him to consider, 'Could he not escape from his little house?' (*D* 79).

Annie's photograph is situated in 'a frame of crumpled horn' (*D* 78), evoking connotations of the nursery rhyme 'The House That Jack Built' and its lines, 'This is the Cow | With the crumpled horn | That tossed the Dog, that worried | the Cat'.[40] Joyce was familiar with this rhyme, including '*His is the House that Malt Made*' in *Finnegans Wake* (*FW* 106.27). The power struggle between Jack and the animals is apparent in 'A Little Cloud', where 'Little Chandler sustained for one moment the gaze of her eyes and his heart closed together as he met the hatred in them' (*D* 80). The destruction caused by the cow in 'This is the House that Jack Built' redeems the situation by contributing to the killing of 'the rat that ate the malt' but the rhyme's image of domestic turmoil is noticeable. That the song is designed for children is further appropriate, since the most frenetic interaction occurs in the story between Little Chandler and his son when 'The child stopped for an instant, had a spasm of fright and began to scream' (*D* 80). This contrast between stasis and kineticism adds to Little Chandler's distress and, as in Eveline's decision to avoid emigrating with Frank, he resigns himself to being 'a prisoner for life' (*D* 80). Annie also experiences this stagnation, framed within a photographic portrait and forced to wait at home whilst Little Chandler is out socialising. As Suzette A. Henke acknowledges, 'Annie, who must stay indoors, cook, clean, and tend her baby, is even more trapped and beleaguered than her timorous mate'.[41] Yet Annie has also achieved what no other character who is physically present in *Dubliners* has, in having been photographed in an image immortalizing her in print. George Eastman launched his first, Kodak handheld camera in 1888 but Annie's photograph is likely to have been taken at a studio, since Joyce does not mention them owning or operating a camera. This differs from *Ulysses*, where 'The reverend Hugh C. Love' intends to 'Bring the camera' to snapshot 'the historic council chamber of saint Mary's abbey' (*U* 10.407–37). Despite the sense of status associated with visiting a studio, Joyce portrays Annie's portrait as hemiplegic and the romantic ecstasy that Little Chandler experiences in having hunted for 'the pale blue summer blouse' is not repeated elsewhere between the couple (*D* 78).

Annie's photograph initially inspires Little Chandler's aesthetic senses. After viewing her image, he picks up 'A volume of Byron's poems [that] lay before him on the table' (*D* 79) and quotes the first stanza of Byron's poem, 'On the Death of a Young Lady, Cousin of the Author, and Very Dear to Him' (1802). He manages to read the first line and part of the second stanza before 'The wailing of the child pierced the drum of his ear' (*D* 79–80) and he is unable to reach the poem's conclusion, in which not quoted, the lines read, 'Yet fresh the memory of that beauteous face; | Still they call forth my warm affection's tear'.[42] Little Chandler may think that 'the eyes of the photograph [...] were pretty and the face itself was pretty' (*D* 78) but the image contains none of the beauty evoked in Byron's poem. Instead, the 'pretty' qualities of the photograph expose the couple's psychological stagnation and emotional sterility, as in the superficial tone Joyce attributes to the 'pretty' loaned 'furniture' (*D* 81).

Little Chandler's repeated description of the photograph as 'pretty' reveals his more limited vocabulary and the subjectivity of his visual response. After reading the poem and feeling 'the rhythm of the verse about him in the room' (*D* 79), he recalls, 'There were so many things he wanted to describe: his sensation of a few hours before on Grattan Bridge, for example' (*D* 79). His desire for creativity is thwarted by his cautious handling of the book 'with his left hand lest he should waken the child' (*D* 79) and he is unable to fully devote himself to his aesthetic contemplation. Viewing Annie's photograph leads him to wonder 'If he could only write a book and get it published, that might open the way for him' (*D* 79). Given that Joyce's mid-1906 completion of 'A Little Cloud' postdates his 1903 thesis that the 'photograph [...] [was] not a work of art' (*OPCW* 104), Little Chandler's notions of creativity are rendered questionable. Like Eveline, he is portrayed as remaining in Dublin and accepting his fate as 'useless' (*D* 79), despite earlier thinking, 'if you wanted to succeed you had to go away. You could do nothing in Dublin' (*D* 68).

Little Chandler is better able to engage his aesthetic senses outside of his household setting, as when:

> he looked down the river towards the lower quays and pitied the poor stunted houses. They seemed to him a band of tramps, huddled together along the riverbanks, their old coats covered with dust and soot, stupefied by the panorama of sunset.
>
> (*D* 68)

The 'panorama of sunset' could have been influenced by popular panoramic photographs, since technological developments in the early twentieth century changed the way in which these images were produced. In 1910, *The Quiver*, a popular Sunday magazine, praised the panoramas on display at 40 Strand, London, which had been made with 'the new Cirkut camera – a most ingenious instrument which is actuated by a motor, and will take a complete circular view'.[43] Joyce was familiar with visual, panoramic technology, including 'the whole panoromacron picture' in the *Wake* (*FW* 318.9). Panoramic displays were frequently used to showcase international locations, as in the 'panorama of the Russo-Turkish war' and Mr. Gillard's 'Great American Panorama' shown at the Rotunda, Dublin in 1875.[44] The Rotunda advertised these images as allowing viewers 'to cross the Atlantic, and to see the great natural features of the American Continent [that] may never be realized', recognizing their audience's more limited opportunities for travel.[45] Like the excitement and transformation associated with these new and continental images, Little Chandler's semi-photographic framing of the 'sunset' causes a temporary change within him, leading him 'farther from his own sober inartistic life' (*D* 68).

The transformative potential of these visual scenes is further suggested when Little Chandler looks 'out of the office window' and considers:

> The glow of a late autumn sunset covered the grass plots and walks. It cast a shower of kindly golden dust on the untidy nurses and decrepit old men who drowsed on the benches; it flickered upon all the moving figures.
>
> (*D* 65–66)

In his framing of the light that 'flickered upon all the moving figures', he fleetingly transforms the landscape into a proto-cinematic display. The 'golden dust' hints at progress and he thinks, 'A light began to tremble on the horizon of his mind' (*D* 68). His snapshot images become cinematic, as he watches 'A horde of grimy children [who] populated the streets. They stood or ran in the roadway or crawled up the steps before the gaping doors or squatted like mice upon the thresholds' (*D* 66). In early twentieth-century Dublin, 'One of the more visible signs of poverty in Dublin was the horde of ragged children trooping the streets in all weathers, barefooted and insufficiently clothed'.[46] Joyce's image of the 'grimy children' could have been inspired by photographs of these scenes, since 'Almost any street photograph of the period [...] [offered] evidence of their neglected appearance'.[47] Like the ethnographic photographer, Joyce provides a grim portrait of this over-arching poverty in attempting to enable 'the Irish people [...] [to have] one good look at themselves in my nicely polished looking-glass' (*LI* 64).

The 'poor stunted houses' and 'horde of grimy children' are reminiscent of images of the Plan of Campaign evictions captured by photographers from William Lawrence's Dublin studio in 1886–90; these featured 'scenes of evictions and of the battering rams used to break into evictees' houses' and were subsequently used as lantern slides.[48] In 1898, Maud Gonne projected images of the evictions onto a screen opposite the National Club, Rutland Square to coincide with Queen Victoria's Jubilee Day.[49] As Keith Williams has acknowledged, 'Gonne's display was widely reported and such images projected on a huge scale across Dublin's streets may have caught the attention of the fifteen year old Joyce'.[50] Irish campaigners utilized photography as a means of encouraging greater political and social awareness, but Little Chandler's panoramic-style viewing only causes him to turn inwards, as 'He felt how useless it was to struggle against fortune, this being the burden of wisdom which the ages had bequeathed to him' (*D* 66). For a character who masquerades as one seeking change and creativity, his lack of emotional consideration of others reveals a failure to see beyond his own depressive situation. At the story's ending, he stands 'back out of the lamplight' (*D* 81). The possibility of a 'pure and sensitive flash of light' conquering 'palsy' cannot yet be fully realized, with creativity and psychological transformation presented as futile whilst he is unable 'to go away' (*D* 68).[51]

'isn't the photograph wonderful when you come to think of it?'

In 'Grace', Joyce's protagonists discuss religion and photography without the presence of a photographic portrait, as they recall, 'one of Pope Leo's poems was on the invention of the photograph – in Latin, of course' (*D* 167). Though not named, this is Pope Leo XIII's 'Ars Photographica' (1867), which appeared in a bilingual collection of the Pope's poetry, *La Poesie Latine*, owned by Joyce.[52] H. T. Henry's 1902 translation, 'On Photography' reads:

> Sun-wrought with magic of the skies
> The image fair before me lies:
> Deep-vaulted brain and sparkling eyes
> And lip's fine chiselling.
> O miracle of human thought,
> O art with newest marvels fraught –
> Apelles, Nature's rival, wrought
> No fairer imagining![53]

The poem details the ability for the camera to rival nature and better capture the subject than the ancient Greek painter, Apelles. Leo XIII further attributes photographic production to God's divinity in his reference to 'the magic of the skies'. Religious figures were quick to acknowledge photography's potential. In a 1902 sermon quoted in the *British Journal of Photography*, Reverend E. Husband of Folkstone wrote, 'just as printing has taught the Bible to the masses, so photography has revealed God in nature to the people'.[54] This engagement with photography as a vehicle for God and a mirror to nature attests to the way in which religious figures sought to mitigate the threat posed by scientific progress to spirituality.

The status that Pope Leo XIII attributes to photography attests to his fascination with this topic. He was a passionate advocate of the camera and brought photography into the Vatican by 'commissioning a ceiling fresco in the Galleria dei Candelabri, which showed the new art being blessed by the Church'.[55] He experimented with cinematic display and agreed to be filmed in 1898 by the

American Mutoscope and Biograph Company. This resulted in 17,000 moving images being captured with the aid of a Biograph camera.[56] The cinematic images were recorded by Mr. William Kennedy-Laurie Dickson, who represented the English division of the company and was granted access to the Vatican due to his 'credentials from Cardinal Gibbons, Monsignor Martinelli, Archbishop Ireland, and other noted prelates'.[57] The company's images of the Pope would have been displayed using a Biograph projecting lantern, providing the viewer with access to the Vatican and the Pope in a previously unprecedented and hyperreal form.

In 'Grace', Joyce depicts Mr Kernan saying, 'I bar the candles […] I bar the magic lantern business' (D 171). In his use of the 'magic lantern', Joyce draws upon his father, John Stanislaus Joyce's prerequisite of 'I bar the candles' before a retreat with his friends (JJ 133) and the Knock apparitions of 1879, when images of the Blessed Virgin Mary, St. Joseph and St. John the Evangelist were reported to have been seen in a Roman Catholic church. The church subsequently became a site of holy pilgrimage, but concerns were raised over the veracity of these visions, with many suspecting that a magic lantern had been used to project images of the religious figures. The magic lantern was a projector device using glass slides, which by the end of the twentieth century was powered by electric light. The slides were typically illustrated or painted but photographs were also used. Theories differ as to who could have operated the projector but it is generally agreed that this was an attempt to dispel tensions between the Catholic Church and the Irish National Land League over 'local famine, high rents, intransigent landlords and mass resistance'.[58] Magic lantern slides were available to purchase in Ireland from 1862, when Horatio Yeates of Wicklow Street, Dublin sold 'stereoscope and magic lantern photographic views of Ireland'.[59] Yeates's business appears in *Ulysses*, where Bloom stands 'before the window of Yeates and Son, pricing the fieldglasses' (U 8.551–52).

Candles were used as an early light source for the magic lantern, a function suggested in 'The Sisters', where after the priest's death 'The room through the lace end of the blind was suffused with dusky golden light amid which the candles looked like pale thin flames. He had been coffined' (D 6). The image of the priest lying 'coffined' bears similarities to the photographic stereo cards produced by H. C. White Company of Pope Leo XIII lying in state. These could have been available for purchase at Yeates and Son or the Photo-Transfer Company, 18 Upper Sackville Street, since the latter store sold stereoscopic, religious slides from 1866.[60] The decision to depict the Pope in stereo card is significant, revealing both his interest in photographic and cinematic technologies and the visual potential of the stereoscopic image when viewed in three-dimensional form. The slide could have been used in a handheld or coin-operated stereoscope or as part of a projector show. Whilst only 'Grace' directly references the magic lantern, the phantasmagoria associated with the device is also apparent in 'The Sisters', where the 'heavy grey face of the paralytic' priest initially appears in the dreams of the young narrator (*D* 3). The priest is visually 'paralytic' but the child near-replicates this state, when he remembers 'that it had died of paralysis, and I felt that I too was smiling feebly' (*D* 3). Like the black cloth draped over the tripod in early photography, enabling the photographer to better focus their lens, the child's position under 'the blankets' enables him to conjure up his image of the priest.

As in Tristan Tzara's comments on May Ray's rayographs, the magic lantern was deeply reliant on 'the thousand-candle-power lamp' and 'a pure and sensitive flash of light'.[61] Joyce's allusion to this device also hints at the medium's more regressive elements, as when he depicts 'The Sisters' opening in a scene of darkness:

> There was no hope for him this time: it was the third stroke. Night after night I had passed the house (it was vacation time) and studied the lighted square of window: and night after night I had found it lighted in the same way, faintly and evenly.
>
> (*D* 1)

The 'lighted square' of the priest's window is reminiscent of Joyce's early sketch *Silhouettes* (*c.* 1897), where the exterior view through the 'lowered window-blind' is similarly 'illuminated dimly, by a candle no doubt'.[62] Whereas for Tzara light aids illumination, for Joyce's narrator in 'The Sisters', the 'lighted square of [the] window' reinforces the idea of stasis, as he considers, 'Every night as I gazed up at the window I said softly to myself the word *paralysis*. It had always sounded strangely in my ears, like the word *gnomon* in the Euclid and the word *simony* in the Catechism' (*D* 1). With 'simony' being the practice of 'selling or giving in exchange of a temporal thing for a spiritual thing' in an act that infringed Roman Catholic teachings, Joyce's allusion to potential religious falsity demonstrates the importance of religious and visual coercion to his work.[63] Like the confinement of the window in 'Eveline', the narrator in 'The Sisters' is able to temporarily elude his domestic sterility whilst enjoying a 'sensation of freedom' elsewhere (*D* 4). His youth grants him a level of freedom not afforded in *Dubliners* to mature and public life, suggesting that he may yet evade Joyce's protagonists' later experiences of more sustained stagnation.

Joyce's reference to Pope Leo XIII in 'Grace', amidst the men's declarations 'isn't the photograph wonderful', initially appears to function as praise for the medium. His playful mocking is apparent when Mr Fogarty misquotes John Dryden (*D* 167–68). As with Little Chandler's use of Annie's photograph to project an enhanced social status, the men use their discussion of photography to evoke a state of heightened intellectualism. Their intellectual pretensions are rendered questionable by their misquotation of Dryden and inability to remember the 'two men' who voted against 'the promulgation of the doctrine of Infallibility' (*D* 169). However, as Keith Williams has noted, their reference to the Pope's poem 'is one of the few facts that Joyce allows [...] Martin Cunningham to get right'.[64] Mr M'Coy's claim that photography is 'wonderful' causes Mr Kernan to doubt the veracity of their conversation and he wonders, 'Weren't some of the Popes – of course, not our present man, or his predecessor, but some of the old Popes – not exactly... you know... up to the knocker?' (*D* 168). An air of superstition runs throughout 'Grace', the constable moving 'his head slowly to right and left and from the manager to the person on the floor, as if he feared to be the victim of some delusion' (*D* 150) and Mrs Kernan believing 'in the banshee and in the Holy Ghost' (*D* 157). Similarly, Mr Kernan is 'quite unconscious that he was the victim of a plot' (*D* 156), despite Mr Power's actions in striking 'a match and, sheltering it in the shell of his hands' (*D* 152) hinting at the same magic lantern he seeks to avoid.

When Mr Kernan attends the religious retreat, he finds himself experiencing a sensation similar to that of the magic lantern audience member, as 'The gentlemen [...] sat well back and gazed formally at the distant speck of red light which was suspended before the high altar' (*D* 172). This spectacle has a tangible and coercive effect on him, and despite his initial reservations, he becomes 'sensible of the decorous atmosphere and even he began to respond to the religious stimulus' (*D* 172). As Williams has acknowledged, Joyce may have been inspired by magic lantern shows by 'campaigning organisations such as the Temperance Movement', who by the mid-nineteenth century were capitalizing on the '"fear of God"-inducing effects from [...] phantasmagoria'.[65] Despite Mr Kernan's drinking and decline into alcoholism, the hardships that typically befall Joyce's protagonists do not wholly affect his character. Unlike Mr Doran, whose marital regret only increases between *Dubliners* and *Ulysses*, Mr Kernan maintains the same largely care-free manner in 'Grace' as Joyce's later work, where he thinks 'Saw him looking at my frockcoat. Dress does it. Nothing like a dressy appearance. Bowls them over' (*U* 10.738–39).

The Kernans are one of the few married couples in *Dubliners* to appear relatively content, as Mrs Kernan 'hurried to the chapel door whenever a wedding was reported and, seeing the bridal pair, recalled with vivid pleasure how she had passed out of the Star of the Sea Church in Sandymount' (*D* 155). Wedding photographs were initially taken at photographers' studios, before the gelatin dry plate process reduced lengthy exposure times. Photographers were subsequently able to pre-prepare photographic plates for use outside of a studio setting but this was still a time-consuming process. It was not until the post-Second World War 'wedding boom' that photographing a wedding became common. Images such as Mrs Kernan's view of the 'bridal pair' could still be captured outside, with groups required to remain still for the duration of the exposure time.

Mrs Kernan recalls her wedding day with fond nostalgia and the framing of 'the chapel door' offers her a momentary snapshot of wedded bliss (*D* 155). In viewing the wedding party, she is able to temporarily escape the monotony of a life where 'Her faith was bounded by her kitchen' (*D* 157) and instead remember how she had leant 'on the arm of a jovial well-fed man who was dressed smartly in a frockcoat and lavender trousers' (*D* 155). The wedding scene and its associated memories grant her respite from familial duty, which she acknowledges had at times become 'irksome' and 'unbearable' (*D* 155). In the late nineteenth century, female photographers were increasingly sought after, and although Milly pursues a role as a photographer's assistant in *Ulysses*, this is not an avenue available to Mrs Kernan. Instead, she is confined to keeping 'house shrewdly for her husband' and making sure that 'Her two eldest sons were launched' (*D* 155). Her 'photographic seeing' enables her to escape routine drudgery and encourages 'union with' rather than 'estrangement from [...] nature'.[66] Limited progress is suggested in Mrs Kernan's thought that 'Religion for her was a habit' (*D* 156) but the 'pleasure' that she associates with her visual, marital recall suggests a hint of light amidst more limiting domestic 'palsy' (*D* 155).

Photographic haunting in 'The Dead'

In 'The Dead', the Conroy family photograph stands 'before the pierglass' and shows Gabriel's mother and brother posing as 'She held an open book on her knees and was pointing out something in it to Constantine who, dressed in a man-o'-war suit, lay at her feet' (*D* 187). Joyce based the image on an 1888 photograph taken during his studio visit to Lafayette's with his mother, father and maternal grandfather. Joyce was also photographed by himself in his 'man-o'war suit' at the photographic session, achieving a visual status that he denies to his childhood protagonists. In Figure 1.2, the image by either Lafayette or one of the studio's other photographers reveals the multiple prints produced, as it is a close-up or a cut-out of a wider image. At the studio session, Joyce would have been looking at a large print containing multiple photographs of priests, since Lafayette's produced these for religious

Figure 1.2 Lafayette Photography, James Joyce at Age 6 ½, with his Parents John and Mary Jane, and his Maternal Grandfather, John Murray, 1888. Courtesy of Lafayette Photography, Dublin.

institutions and colleges.⁶⁷ The studio visit was arranged to commemorate Joyce's departure to boarding school at Clongowes Wood College, County Kildare, hence the image's focus on Joyce rather than his siblings. Gabriel's absence from the photograph in 'The Dead' initially appears to enhance the resentment that he feels towards his mother. Yet the original image's focus on Joyce suggests that the Conroy photograph may have also been intended to mark Constantine's move into education, hence his absence and Gabriel's possible jealousy.

Like Little Chandler, Gabriel's engagement with his family portrait is underscored by social pretensions and his awareness of 'the dignity of family life' (*D* 187). His viewing of the photograph leads him to recall that 'Constantine was now senior curate in Balbriggan and, thanks to her, Gabriel himself had taken his degree in the Royal University' (*D* 187). Little Chandler thinks of Annie's image, 'Why had he married the eyes in the photograph?' (*D* 78). Gabriel's viewing of his wife's photograph initially enhances his affection for her in opposition to his mother, as 'A shadow passed over his face as he remembered her sullen opposition to his marriage. [...] It was Gretta who had nursed her during all her last long illness' (*D* 187). In 'Eveline' and 'The Dead', Joyce refers to deceased mothers, but it is only in the later story that Mrs Conroy is immortalized in photography. Unlike Annie and Little Chandler, there is no mention of the Conroys having saved to have this image taken, enhancing the social and economic disparities between the two families. The image of Constantine and his mother encapsulates the story's wider concerns; Gabriel's memory of the 'slighting phrases' (*D* 187) used by his mother causes him to recall the earlier 'bitterness' with which Lily had spoken to him (*D* 128) and prefigures the later 'agitation' caused by his conversation with Miss Ivors (*D* 190).

Gabriel's European pretensions are posited against the rural nationalism invoked by Miss Ivors. Joyce's description of her outfit reveals her nationalistic tendencies. Her 'large brooch which was fixed in the front of her collar' demonstrates support for the Celtic revival, which encouraged 'the self-conscious adoption of Celtic design in fashions and costume jewellery' (*D* 187).⁶⁸ In the late nineteenth century, photography was a keen interest of the Celtic Revival, with supporters utilizing photographic images to 'express similar cultural interests in how Ireland's Celtic heritage shaped contemporary cultural identity'.⁶⁹ Miss Ivors's choice of 'the Aran Isles' for her impending summer excursion performs a similar function, since the three islands were 'the focus of much nationalist mythologizing' (*D* 189).⁷⁰ After the riots caused by the production of John Millington Synge's *The Playboy of the Western World* at the

Abbey Theatre in February 1907, Joyce wrote to Stanislaus from Rome, 'This whole affair has upset me [...] It has put me off the story I was "going to write" – to wit: *The Dead*' (*JJ* 239). Synge's production initially disrupted Joyce's literary progress but the presence of the 'Aran Isles' in 'The Dead' (*D* 189), in a story deeply concerned with haunting, hints at the same rural primitivism captured by Synge in his island photography between 1898 and 1902.

During his early twentieth-century stay in Paris, Joyce's 'main literary association' was 'John Synge, who arrived at the Hôtel Corneille on 6 March 1903' (*JJ* 124). Anne Fogarty has acknowledged their literary connections, arguing that 'The recurrent presence of Synge in Joyce's work and the ghostly traces by which he may be tracked are not simply an instance of the anxiety of influence'.[71] For Fogarty, Synge exposes Joyce to 'the besetting problems of the Irish modernist artist who attempted to forge a new aesthetic and to articulate a culture torn between the forces of tradition and modernity'.[72] This paradox is visible in Synge's photographs of rural communities in the West of Ireland. Using Eastern references, he fuses West and East and Anglo-Irish culture and modernity in images that juxtapose the primitivism of the scenes captured with the photographic technology used.[73] As Justin Carville has noted, 'Synge turned to the rural communities of the west of Ireland as if turning to a past that had yet to be corrupted by Anglocentric modernity'.[74] In similarly turning to the 'Aran Isles' in 'The Dead' (*D* 189), Joyce engages Gabriel in a conflict between tradition and modernity also captured by Synge with his camera.

Joyce travelled to the Aran Isles in 1912 and depicted the islands in a series of articles for the Italian newspaper, *Il Piccolo della Sera* 'with the affection of a tourist who has read Synge, noted the peculiarities in the islanders' dialect, and described curious local customs and history' (*JJ* 325). Gabriel initially declines Miss Ivors's invitation to the islands but by the end of the story has begun to consider 'his journey westward' (*D* 225). As he observes the snow 'on the treeless hills, falling softly upon the Bog of Allen and, farther westward, softly falling into the dark mutinous Shannon waves' (*D* 225), his proto-cinematic viewing evokes the mutiny of Synge's photograph, 'Currach collecting turf from a Galway hooker' (*c*.1900), in which rough waves are accompanied by glimmers of sunlight (*D* 225).[75] In *The Aran Islands* (1907), Synge wrote, 'This year I see a darker side of life in the islands. [...] The sun seldom shines, and day after day a cold south-western wind blows over the cliffs, bringing up showers of hail and dense masses of cloud'.[76] Just as Synge's images capture the duality of the islands' beauty and darkness, Gabriel's vision of the 'snow falling faintly through the universe' contains the hemiplegic possibility of regrowth (*D* 225). In recognizing the influence of 'the lonely churchyard on the hill where Michael Furey lay buried' on his relationship with Gretta (*D* 225), Gabriel accepts that rather than being 'sick' of his 'own country', he must fuse past and present (*D* 190). Change will only be possible through him participating in 'another person's (or thing's) mortality, vulnerability, mutability'.[77]

In his film adaptation of *The Dead* (1987), John Huston divides the Conroy photograph into multiple, faded images.[78] These include a photograph of a man in military uniform, a snapshot of Gabriel's two aunts with what appears to be Mrs Conroy and a final photographic portrait of father, mother and baby. By splitting the original picture into multiple photographs, including images of those now deceased, Huston hints at their fractured family relations and the way in which those present within the story are haunted by the past. In both versions, the photographs perform a memorializing and memento mori function, Latin for 'remember that you [must] die'. These are not photographs to be carried around and displayed to others, like Bloom's photograph of Molly in *Ulysses*, but are instead images imbued with a sense of death, as in Sontag's suggestion that 'All photographs are memento mori'.[79] R. Brandon Kershner has addressed the importance of the apparition of the Blooms' deceased son, Rudy in *Ulysses*'s 'Circe' episode and argues that Leopold Bloom participates in his son's appearance 'out of a context of practices and conventions that surrounded the popular art form of photography and its iconography'.[80] As Kershner has acknowledged, this image is not memento mori, since Rudy was not photographed dead or alive. Instead, the apparition shares the 'embalming' quality and importance of the 'gaze of the observer' present in memorial photography.[81]

The Conroy photograph is equally not explicitly memento mori but in its association with haunting and the deceased attests to a particular societal culture of commemorating the dead. Memento mori or post-mortem photographs were more common in America than Britain or Ireland, but they were still socially accepted and acknowledged during the late nineteenth century, fuelled in part by Queen Victoria's elaborate displays of mourning.[82] Infant subjects were often posed with their mothers or other family members. Deceased adults were usually coffined, forcing the photographer to attempt to capture their image whilst hiding the coffin from view. These photographs were typically taken by assistant photographers, with principal photographers refusing on account of it not being 'the pleasantest description'.[83] That the work was relegated to lesser-paid studio employees prompted ethical issues, as assistants were forced to choose between declining a request and risking losing their job or bringing infection home to their families.

Memento mori images may appear macabre today but before the invention of the gelatin dry plate process and a subsequent reduction in photographic costs, they were often the only photograph that a family could afford to have taken of their relatives. By the early twentieth century, the availability of handheld cameras rendered the need for professional post-mortem photographs largely negligible and 'by the 1930s and 1940s new funerary rites and customs had supplanted the high Victorian funerary practices'.[84] Memento mori photographs were rarely capable of realism. The *British Journal of Photography* satirically wrote in 1887 that, despite the dead possessing 'the inestimable virtues of keeping still and wearing a natural expression', these images depicted 'glorified untruthfulness'.[85]

A sense of mortality runs throughout Joyce's final short story, as Gabriel imagines after remembering the 'haggard look upon her [Aunt Julia's] face' that 'One by one they were all becoming shades' (*D* 224). This premonition of death is nearly realized by *Ulysses*, where Stephen thinks of 'his godmother Miss Kate Morkan in the house of her dying sister Miss Julia Morkan at 15 Usher's Island' (*U* 17.139–41). The aunts appear in a photographic portrait in Huston's adaptation but in Joyce's short story they are not captured directly in visual media. Instead, in 'The Dead', the lingering presence of death is suggested through the image of Gabriel's mother and its position close to the 'picture of the balcony scene in Romeo and Juliet' and the 'picture of the two murdered princes in the Tower' (*D* 186–87). The aunts' servant Lily is similarly associated with the photograph's 'imperious sign of [...] future death', as Gabriel observes, 'She was a slim, growing girl, pale in complexion and with hay-coloured hair. The gas in the pantry made her look still paler' (*D* 177).[86] The vision of Lily amidst 'The gas in the pantry' pre-empts the later intrusion of the deceased Michael Furey who had worked 'in the gasworks' (*D* 221), this earlier 'gas' functioning as what Fritz Senn terms 'delayed identification'.[87]

Lily's presence beneath 'the pantry ceiling' (*D* 177) evokes a sense of liminality between life and death also apparent in 'The Sisters', where the priest has been 'coffined' in a room containing 'candles [which] looked like pale thin flames' (*D* 6). Gretta too is associated with this haunted, spectral imagery, as Gabriel observes her 'standing right under the dusty fanlight and the flame of the gas lit up the rich bronze of her hair' (*D* 213) and walking 'along the shaft of light towards him' (*D* 217–18). He considers Gretta to be in the 'same attitude' (*D* 213) as that in which he had previously wondered 'if she were a symbol of something' and he had thought, 'If he were a painter he would paint her in that attitude' (*D* 211). Joyce suggests Gabriel's creative tendencies when he depicts him deciding, '*Distant Music* he would call the picture if he were a painter' (*D* 213). Yet in portraying him as able to name the picture only *if* 'he were a painter', he imbues his protagonist with the same aesthetic uncertainty experienced by Little Chandler and Bloom, the latter figure who is described as a 'bit of an artist' in *Ulysses* (*U* 16.1448–49). Joyce presents creative ambitions as fated to failure in those lacking confidence in their aesthetic abilities and inhabiting environments that fail to nurture their skills. Gabriel recognizes the limitations of his semi-artistic framing of Gretta and later reflects, 'He did not like to say even to himself that her face was no longer beautiful but he knew that it was no longer the face for which Michael Furey had braved death' (*D* 223). In acknowledging the passing of time and its impact on his wife, Gabriel moves from a show of solidarity with Gretta encouraged by his earlier viewing of the Conroy photograph to increasing, romantic estrangement.

With gaslight predating electric lighting, Joyce uses the failure of 'electric-light' at the story's ending to emphasize its concerns with tradition and modernity. Gretta and Gabriel are instead lit by 'A ghostly light from the street lamp', whilst he '[longed] to cry to her from his soul, to crush her body against his, to overmaster her' (*D* 218). Gabriel may suggest 'We have light enough from the street' (*D* 217) but this light is tinged with mortality, as when 'A ghostly light from the street lamp lay in a long shaft from one window to the door' (*D* 217). The invention of electric light heralded technological change but in turning 'his back more to the light' (*D* 221), Gabriel rejects this innovation and risks his 'identity […] fading out into a grey impalpable world' (*D* 225). The photograph of Gabriel's mother is situated before the large 'pierglass' mirror (*D* 187). Joyce posits his protagonist as an embodiment of this image as he passes before 'the cheval-glass […] [and] caught sight of himself in full length […] the face whose expression always puzzled him when he saw it in a mirror' (*D* 219). In positioning Gabriel first as an observer of the photograph and then as its near-replica, Joyce associates this visual image with a sense of mortality and the ability to capture 'Death in person'.[88]

In *Dubliners*, Joyce uses photography to enable the 'Irish people' to have 'one good look at themselves in my nicely polished looking-glass' (*LI* 64). In his portrayal of photographic portraits and allusions to this visual medium, he situates his protagonists in a hemiplegic conflict between creativity and their social, religious and domestic demands. For Roland Barthes, 'the photograph itself is in no way animated (I do not believe in "lifelike" photographs), but it animates me: this is what creates every adventure'.[89] Joyce depicts his Dublin citizens experiencing moments of epiphanic contemplation inspired by photography, but these are always tinged with stagnation and a dual sense of paralysis. In a letter to Stanislaus Joyce on 25 September 1906, prior to his composition of 'The Dead', he acknowledged:

> Sometimes thinking of Ireland it seems to me that I have been unnecessarily harsh. I have produced (in *Dubliners* at least) none of the attraction of the city.... I have not been just to its beauty.
>
> (*LII* 166)

In closing the collection with Gabriel's vision of the snow 'falling, like the descent of their last end, upon all the living and the dead', as he considers, 'The time had come for him to set out on his journey westward' (*D* 225), Joyce hints at the potential for self-exile denied to Eveline and Little Chandler. Gabriel's final thought of journeying 'westward', here suggesting 'Connacht' or 'the Aran Isles', encapsulates the hemiplegic nature of his literary engagement with photography, where the potential for a visually innovative 'pure and sensitive flash of light' to combat 'palsy' is rendered questionable for those remaining in Dublin.[90]

2

That 'spoof of visibility': stereoscopic 'realism' in *Stephen Hero* to *Finnegans Wake*

In the 'Proteus' episode of *Ulysses* (1922), James Joyce portrays Stephen Dedalus contemplating:

> Flat I see, then think distance, near, far, flat I see, east, back. Ah, see now! Falls back suddenly, frozen in stereoscope. Click does the trick.
>
> (*U* 3.418–20)

In his depiction of Stephen's concerns with stereoscopic vision, and his use of erotic and phantasmagoric imagery in *Stephen Hero* (1944), roughly composed between 1904 and 1906 and published posthumously, to *Finnegans Wake* (1939), Joyce was writing during a century in which photographic stereo cards had fallen in and out of favour. In the 1870s–80s, demand declined in Europe, only to be reinvigorated by the import of American stereo card sets.[1] Joyce would have struggled to use Scottish physicist, Sir David Brewster's early stereoscope, as the device had 'fixed lenses with no provision for focusing' and caused difficulties for 'people with long or short sight'.[2] In his 1856 publication, *The Stereoscope: Its History, Theory, and Construction, with Its Application to the Fine and Useful Arts and to Education,* Brewster revealed its 'remarkable effects cannot be properly appreciated by those whose eyes are not equally good'.[3] He later added focusing adjustments but, prior to his failing eyesight, Joyce would have been unable to view stereo cards without wearing his glasses.

Joyce denies this option to Stephen in *A Portrait of the Artist as a Young Man* (1914), where 'his spectacles had been broken in three pieces' (*P* 34) and in *Ulysses*, 'Must get glasses. Broke them yesterday. Sixteen years. Distance. The eye sees all flat' (*U* 15.3628–29). Later innovations in stereoscopic technology included the penny-in-the-slot stereoscope, through which sets of stereo cards could be viewed at photographic studios, fairs and seaside resorts. Through manipulation of exposure times, photographers produced mock-supernatural images for use with handheld stereoscopes or projectors, such as the stereopticon. By the 1920s, colour anaglyph stereo cards were regularly featured in *The Illustrated London News* and could be viewed with an 'Anaglyph Viewing-Mask'.[4] Concerns about stereoscopic hyperreality, eroticism and the supernatural abound in Joyce's literature and attest to a cultural moment in which the 'introduction of the Stereoscope' promised the public 'the aspect of almost life-like reality'.[5]

Sir Charles Wheatstone is credited with having invented the practical apparatus of the stereoscope in 1832, after designing a wooden device using mirrors and two near-identical drawings to replicate the fields of vision in the left and right eyes. Wheatstone published his findings in *Philosophical Transactions of the Royal Society* (1838), where he described how:

> The observer must place his eyes as near as possible to the mirrors, the right eye before the right hand mirror, and the left eye before the left hand mirror, and he must move the sliding panels [...] to or from him until the two reflected images coincide at the intersection of the optic axes, and form an image of the same apparent magnitude as each of the component pictures.[6]

Following William Henry Fox Talbot and Louis-Jacques-Mandé Daguerre's photographic discoveries, Brewster spotted the potential for photography to be applied to the stereoscope. Assisted by the Parisian optician, François Soleil and his son-in-law Jules Duboscq, Brewster invented a rudimentary device.[7] After developing his designs, he showcased his improved Brewster stereoscope at London's 1851 Crystal Palace Exhibition.[8] Commenting on its popularity only four years later, Brewster estimated 'that upwards of half a million of these instruments have been sold'.[9]

Photographic stereo cards were available in Ireland from the device's inception. Their popularity was such that photographic studios were 'converted or even newly created in response to the growing demand for such views'.[10] Photography's invention provided the public with previously unprecedented levels of realism, but the stereoscope now offered them the chance to engage with this 'almost life-like reality' in heightened, three-dimensional form. Stereo cards could be viewed using coin-operated devices, at projector shows or at home in handheld stereoscopes. Multiple types of stereo cards were sold in Dublin, including views of Irish landscapes and images of celebrated figures.[11] In an 1858 advertisement, 'Photographers, Artists, Manufacturers and Importers', Simonton and Millard, Dublin announced the availability of their 'splendid photographic portraits' of Charles Dickens, 'standing out in life-like reality, as he appears nightly at the Rotundo, price 2s. 6d. each'.[12] Recognizing the additional value of personal stereoscopic portraits, they further advertised 'Group and Portraits taken daily for the Stereoscope in the largest Gallery in the world'.[13]

In 1858, English publisher Lovell Reeve began producing *The Stereoscopic Magazine*, a publication costing two shillings and six pence and featuring stereo cards with each edition for 'visual consumption and tactile delight'.[14] *The Stereoscopic Magazine* was published for seven years and reveals the importance of stereoscopic photography in Ireland. Irish stereo cards frequently appear, with titles such as 'Sackville Street, Dublin', 'The Wicklow Railway at Bray Head' and 'On the Banks of the Liffey', the latter as shown in Figure 2.1.[15] In order to view these stereo cards as intended, the reader had to purchase a 'portable stereoscope, adapted for use in books', which was 'manufactured by instrument makers Negretti & Zambra and sold with the magazine'.[16] The magazine also printed stereo cards of museum interiors, including 1850s images captured by Roger Fenton of Greek and Roman sculptures.[17] The stereoscope's illusory potential was part of its appeal and Oliver Wendell Holmes revealed of his more affordable Holmes device in 1861, 'by this instrument that effect is so heightened as to produce an appearance of reality which cheats the senses with its seeming truth'.[18]

The popularity of the handheld stereoscope was founded on its unique fusion of vision and touch and the near-tangibility of the three-dimensional image.

Figure 2.1 Unknown Photographer, On the Banks of the Liffey, Dublin, Ireland, *c.* 1859–64. Digital image courtesy of the Getty's Open Content Program.

The corporeal sensations inspired by the device were at their most alluring in nude and erotically charged stereo cards. Debates surrounding these images were well-reported long before Joyce's composition of *Stephen Hero* and his beginning *Ulysses*'s 'Circe' episode on 16 August 1920.[19] Responding to public interest in the stereoscope in 1859, Charles Baudelaire described how 'It was not long before thousands of pairs of greedy eyes were glued to the peepholes of the stereoscope'.[20] This 'love of pornography' was not confined to 'children on their way back from school' and Baudelaire recalled an incident in which 'a woman of high society' had requested to see 'such pictures'.[21] Photographers typically left erotic stereoscopic slides unsigned due to the threat of prosecution and police harassment.[22] These images were often produced in France but could still be purchased in Dublin, despite store owners facing prosecution if they were found to be selling images that met the wide-ranging legal definition of obscenity as 'anything that tended to corrupt and demoralise youth'.[23] Pornographic photographs were transported via covert trading routes and entered Great Britain and Ireland through 'dummy corporations and false fronts'.[24]

In a draft of I.5 of *Finnegans Wake* written in December 1923, Joyce includes 'stereoptican relief'.[25] Using the American spelling, he invokes the stereopticon. This could refer to a standard magic lantern using single pictures or photographs or a projector using two near-identical stereo cards, which when projected onto a background wall appeared 'to approach the audience' as one.[26] The device was frequently used for religious showings and a 1910 article in *The Kerry Sentinel* details 'An interesting and instructive stereopticon lecture on the Passion Play [that] was given on Sunday evening at the Parish Church, Ballyheigue'.[27] This lecture was one of 'a series of entertainments which the esteemed pastor, Rev. M. D. Allman, has provided for his people [...] which, while affording the audience ample enjoyment, have also their spiritual and patriotic features'.[28] In 1903, Mr Theodore Brown of Salisbury applied the principles of stereoscopy to the cinematograph camera projector and patented his invention through which moving figures on screen could be provided with a 'depth and fulness that invest[s] them with a wonderful realism'.[29] Experiments with anaglyph technology in the 1920s aided developments in colour cinematic technology but photographic anaglyph stereo cards still enjoyed popularity.

In 'Stephen Dedalus: Rimbaud or Baudelaire?' (1980), David Weir compares Stephen to Baudelaire, arguing that 'It is largely because of this romantic dualism that Stephen more closely resembles Baudelaire than he does Rimbaud'.[30] Weir suggests that a 'Baudelairean reading' of Stephen ultimately 'points out more clearly the doomed nature of the out-of-place romantic hero'.[31] Joyce depicts

Stephen as sharing a similar vision of art and progress to that expressed by Baudelaire in 'The Salon of 1859', where he critiques the view that 'art is photography'.³² Joyce transfers his thesis on photography's aesthetic value to Leopold Bloom in *Ulysses*, who considers, 'Marble could give the original, shoulders, back, all the symmetry, all the rest. [...] Whereas no photo could because it simply wasn't art in a word' (*U* 16.1451–55). In *Stephen Hero*, Joyce portrays Stephen also thinking that art is 'neither a copy nor an imitation of nature' (*SH* 154). Joyce believed that the photograph was intrinsically 'not a work of art' (*OCPW* 104) but he makes use of photographic principles in his literary engagement with stereoscopy and visual veracity.

Critics have devoted attention to Joyce's interaction with the stereoscope and stereoscopic theories. In *Structure and Motif in 'Finnegans Wake'* (1962), Clive Hart acknowledges the presence of stereoscopy in the *Wake* and comments of II.3:

> The pictures of Butt and Taff are made to converge like a pair of flat photographs in a stereoscope to produce a fully rounded and comprehensible figure. (In this episode Joyce evidently predicted 3-D television along with the atom bomb (353.22) and the destruction of the world.)³³

In 'Stereoscopy, modernism and the "haptic"' (2004), David Trotter argues that Stephen's interest is primarily in the 'tableau-effect' of the stereoscope, as opposed to Bloom's interest in its 'tangibility-effect'.³⁴ Stephen responds to this 'tableau-effect' in his contemplation of the body's 'apprehensive faculty' (*SH* 189) but is able to replicate the 'tangibility-effect' in his observation of Emma Clery.³⁵ In *James Joyce and the Phenomenology of Film* (2017), Cleo Hanaway-Oakley argues that in *Ulysses*, stereoscopy enables Stephen to think through 'Bishop Berkeley's early eighteenth-century philosophy of depth perception', providing the 'illusion of touch' and the 'illusion of three-dimensionality'.³⁶ Hanaway-Oakley's cinematic approach to Stephen and Bloom's stereoscopic tangibility is underscored by an acknowledgement that 'tactility, tangibility, and the closeness of seeing and touching were key to the stereoscope's commercial success'.³⁷ Joseph Duncan and Fritz Senn have variously posited Stephen's visual theories in 'Proteus' as influenced by Aristotle, Jacob Boehme and Gotthold Ephraim Lessing.³⁸ This engagement with critical thinking substantially aids understanding of the 'Proteus' episode but does not approach stereoscopy principally via photography'.

In *'Ulysses,' Film and Visual Culture* (2018), Philip Sicker conclusively demonstrates that 'The optical invention that explicitly frames Stephen's experiment with Berkeleyan epistemology is the "stereoscope"'.³⁹ He further suggests that the stereoscope allows Stephen to 'imagine himself the artist-god of his own creation, transforming and dissolving the world with the same capricious freedom he uses to change the shape and position of his shadow'.[40] In *James Joyce and Cinematicity: Before and After Film* (2020), Keith Williams notes the popularity of French *diableries* from the 1850s–90s, miniature clay infernos that were 'converted into colour stereoscopic images'.[41] Though not necessarily shown in Ireland, Williams reveals how *A Portrait* and 'Circe' share their 'uncannily vivid sense of movement and immersion, just as film remediated lantern and moving panorama techniques'.[42] Stephen's explicit view of photography as 'not a work of art' is never stated (*OCWP* 104) but Joyce imbues him with the ability to engage with visual culture from a position of aesthetic and critical detachment, encouraged by his interest in optical principles. Stephen's isolated, artistic endeavours are best suited to the handheld or penny-in-the-slot stereoscope, given that these were operated by a sole viewer and enabled the transgression of private boundaries. Stereoscopes were often used in settings in which multiple members of a family were present, such as in households or at fairs but the viewer–machine interaction was still an intimate relationship in which images were viewed via a device rather than a projector.

In *Stephen Hero* and *A Portrait*, Stephen's frequent focus on Emma Clery's body in near-fragmented form attests to a culture in which erotic stereo card series frequently depicted the gradual undressing of women. The stereoscope's tangibility effect enabled the viewer to visually invade domestic scenes in heightened, hyperreal forms. This was apparent in coin-operated stereoscopes, where images were progressed by pressing a button on the front of the machine or using a handheld lever at its side. The mechanics of the penny-in-the-slot stereoscope are suggested in Stephen's early engagement with women and in *Ulysses*'s 'Circe' episode, in his fragmented and visually distorted interactions with prostitutes. In *Ulysses*, Joyce invokes supernatural trickery and uses phantasmagoric resurrections of the dead to interrogate the 'reality' of Stephen's experience. Stereoscopy allows him to explore photography's tangible and illusory potential, often in the medium's more playful forms. In *Finnegans Wake*, stereoscopic technology is integral to Joyce's portrayal of rumour and transgression, where 'we need the loan of a lens to see as much as the hen saw' (*FW* 112.1–2). Examining allusions to the stereopticon projector and anaglyph technology in I.5 and III.1, with brief reference to 'How Burghley shuck the rackushant Germanon' (*FW* 338.2–3) and the Crimean War (1853–6) in II.3, reveals his continued interest in stereoscopy throughout his literary works, and his use of the device's 'tantalising purchase on the real' to interrogate visual veracity.[43]

'The mind feels its way to the very depths of the picture'

Stephen occupies a critically estranged position from photography in *Stephen Hero* and *A Portrait* where, bar his 'sootcoated packet of pictures' (*P* 97), he is predominantly concerned with scientific and philosophical theories of vision, rather than explicit images. As in *Dubliners*, where photographic seeing frequently encourages 'estrangement from, rather than union with, nature', Stephen experiences a similar level of detachment in his observatory, street scenes, as Joyce describes how he 'felt very solitary and purposeless as he traversed empty street after empty street' (*SH* 109).[44] Stephen's pursuit of a personal, artistic doctrine sees him expound at length theories that are 'in the main applied [Thomas] Aquinas' and are influenced by his concept of art as 'the human disposition of intelligible or sensible matter' (*SH* 72). Reminding Cranly of 'what Aquinas says' about beauty, he explains that 'the mind receives the impression of the symmetry of the object. The mind recognizes that the object is in the strict sense of the word, a *thing*, a definitely constituted entity' (*SH* 190). His merging of aesthetic and visual concepts allows him to recognize the active role of the body in perceiving an object and to reject pre-stereoscopic optical ideas based on a 'single, ideal eye'.[45]

As Stephen walks through Dublin with 'his ears and eyes ever prompt to receive impressions', he begins to view his surroundings with innate, photographic realism (*SH* 33), in an experience similar to that of using a stereoscope. Describing the minutia of his observations, Joyce writes:

> Stephen halted at the end of a narrow path beside a few laurel bushes, watching at the end of a leaf a tiny point of rain form and twinkle and hesitate and finally take the plunge into the sodden clay beneath.
>
> (*SH* 70)

The level of detail as Stephen watches the 'tiny point of rain' is reminiscent of comments by Holmes, who noted of his stereoscope in 1859, 'The mind feels its way to the very depths of the picture. The scraggy branches of a tree in the foreground run out at us as if they would scratch our eyes out.'[46] Holmes's integration of mind and image and his personification of the trees attest to the way in which the invention of photography and its use in stereoscopy changed not only '*the overall mode of being of the human collective*' but altered '*the manner of its sense perception*'.[47]

Like the three-dimensional image of the 'scraggy branches of a tree', the 'tiny point of rain' that Stephen watches exists for only a moment, offering a paradoxical fusion of enhanced realism and temporary pleasure (*SH* 70). For Juliana Bruno, the haptic shapes 'the texture of habitable space and, ultimately [...] [maps] our ways of being in touch with the environment'.[48] Stephen's actions as he walks through the streets of Dublin are informed by this tactile engagement with the 'texture of the habitable space', as 'His morning walks were critical, his evening walks imaginative and whatever had seemed plausible in the evening was always rigorously examined in the light of day' (*SH* 66). Stephen's bodily demands are crucial to his aesthetic contemplation, as he acknowledges, 'His body disturbed him and he adapted the expedient of appeasing it by gentle promenading' (*SH* 66). In *A Portrait*, he attempts to 'mortify the sense of sight' by making 'it his rule to walk in the street with downcast eyes, glancing neither to right nor left and never behind him' (*P* 127) but recognizes the dual necessity of the mind and body in 'analysis of apprehension' (*P* 178).

Stephen and the penny-in-the-slot stereoscope

In *James Joyce, Sexuality and Social Purity* (2003), Katherine Mullin argues that Leopold Bloom's erotic enjoyment is intrinsically connected with the mutoscope, a 'contemporary motion picture device containing a sequential series of photographs'.[49] Joyce refers to this specific proto-cinematic device in *Ulysses* but it is possible to also detect the scopophilia that Mullin attributes to the mutoscope in Stephen's engagement with stereoscopy given the popularity of the penny-in-the-slot 'automatic' stereoscope. The cultural significance of coin-operated stereoscopes has been generally overlooked in contemporary criticism, despite the device provoking 'at least as much anxiety as the mutoscope concerning the corruption of juveniles'.[50] This device is often confused with the mutoscope but differs in that it contained 'ten to twelve' stereo cards, rather than the mutoscope's flip-photographs which were rotated in a coin-operated reel.[51] Penny-in-the-slot stereoscopes could be found in photographic studios, as well as at 'penny gaffs, pleasure gardens, fairs, and seaside resorts'.[52]

Tim Conley has acknowledged Joyce's interest in Irish businessman, Charles Augustus James and his Dublin 'World's Fair Stores', run from the 1890s.[53] James's 'world's fancy fair and waxwork exhibition' was located at '30 Henry street' (*U* 17.579–80). In 'Ithaca', Joyce refers to their admission price as '2d, children 1d' (*U* 17.580). Had he gained this knowledge from the popular press, he may have been aware that thirty shillings was stolen from their 'two penny-in-the-slot machines' on 11 July 1899, as reported in the *Freeman's Journal*.⁵⁴ James's collection of machines included an animatograph, a motion-picture projector that he lent to Dublin's Cyclopia Bazaar in 1896.⁵⁵ He also lent out a phantasmascope, more commonly referred to as a phenakistoscope, which required the viewer to rotate a cardboard disk of illustrated pictures which provided the illusion of movement.⁵⁶ His collection may have also included coin-operated stereoscopes. At the turn of the century, James advertised for entertainers in *The Era*, a British weekly newspaper.⁵⁷ During the same period, the paper includes frequent requests from entertainers looking to purchase a kalloscope, a penny-in-the-slot stereo viewer. In 1888, the German inventor C. Bach patented this device, but similar machines had been in use for several years.⁵⁸ The kalloscope was a wooden machine with binocular-style eyeholes and space for sets of stereo cards, which were advanced by pressing a button on the front of the machine.

Societal fears were rife regarding coin-operated stereoscopes. In 1908, a London Joint Select Committee report on 'Lotteries and Indecent Advertisements' revealed 'the widespread installation of stereoscopic machines in penny arcades'.⁵⁹ Responding to their findings, *The Spectator* newspaper commented:

> The category of punishable offences seems complete; and the Committee report that the police are active, and have done much to suppress the traffic through the post, and the accumulation of stocks of offensive literature. But [...] the photographs exhibited in "penny-in-the-slot" stereoscopic machines are too often of a foul and polluting nature.⁶⁰

Store owners found to be making available erotic stereo cards were at risk of prosecution, as two proprietors of a 'cheap shop-front show in Parliament Street, Dublin' found in 1899, after being caught displaying indecent pictures in their 'stereoscopic machine'.⁶¹ The judge initially decided that their photographs were indecent, rather than obscene, but later felt compelled to 'declare the offending stereographs obscene and order them to be destroyed'.⁶² Joyce hints at the 'foul and polluting nature' of these machines in *Finnegans Wake*, where he writes 'Plunk! said he. [...] a handsome sovereign was freely pledged in their pennis in the sluts maschine' (*FW* 495.20–23). Just as in the penny-in-the-slot stereoscope, the depositing of money into the 'sluts maschine' in the *Wake* enables the rotation of these images of women, showing 'the legitimate lady performers of display unquestionable, Elsebett and Marryetta Gunning' (*FW* 495.25–26).

With Stephen engaging in 'corporealized observation' throughout Joyce's literature, the erotic potential of the kalloscope is likely to have held an appeal.[63] Williams suggests that Stephen's 'hypothetical mental snapshot' may possibly refer 'as much to the sound of the photographic mechanism as to patent stereoscopes, as their double images "click" into the right focal position'.[64] In *Stephen Hero*, Joyce hints at this 'photographic mechanism[s]', as Stephen tells Madden, 'I fully recognize that my countrymen have not yet advanced [to] as far as the machinery of Parisian harlotry because [...] they can do it by hand, that's why!' (*SH* 54). Critics have noted the potential references to masturbation but Joyce's description of doing 'it by hand' also hints at the actions of the viewer progressing coin-operated stereo cards.[65] Stephen's 'little ejaculations' are inspired by his 'glances in the wake of a hospital nurse who wore brown stockings and pink petticoats', who he had 'been quietly observing for a long time' after being 'not at all displeased by the spectacle' (*SH* 135–36). Stephen is disturbed by Moynihan's encroaching presence and his fellow student's 'desirous ejaculations' remind him of 'the clicking of a type-writing machine' (*SH* 136). In this association, Stephen fuses Moynihan into a near-hybrid of man and machine, attesting to the mechanized nature of his scopophilia and his visually inspired 'ejaculations'.

Stereoscopic slides of women 'served to heighten the spectator's fantasy through a titillating display of what could be penetrated only in the imagination'.[66] Professional photographers critiqued these images and in 1894, the *British Journal of Photography* revealed that 'the market was all at once flooded with indifferent, if not rubbishing, stereoscopes and so-called pictures [...] [of] the most extravagant and eccentric subjects, but also the most suggestively indecent'.[67] Only a year later, they described the introduction of 'vulgar or indecent' American stereoscopic slides' as a 'lamentable thing', threatening the 'popularity of stereo-photography'.[68] If using a penny-in-the-slot stereoscope, Stephen would have been able to move between multiple stereo cards. As when he imagines of the 'Mouth to her kiss' in *Ulysses* that there 'Must be two of em', two near-identical images were required with a stereo card for this to be transformed into one, three-dimensional image (*U* 3.400). Women often appeared nude or semi-draped in 'pairs of provocatives' (*FW* 52.2). In *Stephen Hero*, Joyce depicts Stephen observing Emma Clery and the 'rise and fall of her bosom' (*SH* 141). His interaction with Emma reveals his desire for corporeality, as he tells her, 'I felt that I longed to hold you in my arms – your body. I longed for you to take me in your arms' (*SH* 177) and requests that they 'live one night together' (*SH* 178). Joyce renders the idea that Emma would want to give her 'body' to Stephen questionable but in nude stereo cards circulated at the turn of the century, women can be seen aiming their 'gleaming jewel eyes' at the camera (*P* 97) whilst inviting the possibility of 'one night together' (*SH* 177). In *c.* 1900 stereo cards produced by E. Angelou, the female model is deliberately positioned to invite the viewer to return the gaze of her 'incorrigible eyes' (*SH* 168).[69] The awkward folding of the subject's body reveals the erotic fragmentation typically found in these images. The partial draping of the model further hints at the mock classical displays used in fine art, pornographic photography, as explored in Chapter 3 of this project.

In George du Maurier's *Trilby* (1895), referenced by Joyce in *Stephen Hero*, *Ulysses* and *Finnegans Wake*, half-Irish, artist's model Trilby O'Farrall is renowned for having 'the handsomest foot in all Paris'.[70] Trilby is subject to an erotic and fragmentary focus on her body, as Du Maurier describes Little Billee being 'quite bewildered to find that a real, bare, live human foot could be such a charming object to look at'.[71] Stephen similarly struggles between viewing Emma as a sum of her bodily parts and responding to her 'body [that] seemed so compact of pleasure' in its entirety (*SH* 64). In utilizing the movement of her 'hips' as a means of voyeuristic pleasure, he attempts to transcend his erotic fantasies into 'reality' but misreads this suggestion, leaving Emma to respond, 'You are mad, Stephen' (*SH* 177).[72] Just as Bloom observes the 'vigorous hips' of 'the nextdoor girl at the counter' in *Ulysses* (*U* 4.146–48), the sight of Emma's 'hips moving inside [...] [her] waterproof' initially inspires Stephen's voyeurism (*SH* 177). He becomes embroiled in the hyperreality of his encounters, where a 'certain ingenuous disattachment [was] guiding his excited passion' (*SH* 177). The appeal of the Victorian nude rested on 'the constant renegotiation of the boundaries separating real from ideal; natural from artificial; pure from impure; public from private'.[73] As he propositions Emma, Stephen fails to distinguish the 'real from ideal', only later recognizing that he had 'acted like a lunatic' (*SH* 179).

Had Joyce anticipated Stephen viewing stereo cards, as is possible given his later engagement with the principles of stereoscopy and his 'sootcoated packet of pictures' in *A Portrait* (*P* 97), he could have easily misinterpreted the device's transgression of private boundaries, conflating 'the world of his experience and the world of his dreams' (*SH* 73). In *A Portrait,* Stephen initially detaches himself from the fervour surrounding the 'picture' of the 'demurely taunting eyes' of Mabel Hunter (*P* 56). His description of himself at the party as 'hiding from other eyes the feverish agitation of his blood' reveals the photograph's corporeal impact (*P* 57). In considering how Emma's 'glance travelled to his corner, flattering, taunting, searching, exciting his heart' (*P* 57), Stephen attempts to transmute Mabel Hunter's 'taunting eyes' into reality, creating 'a representational system that […] [possesses] a tantalising purchase on the real'.⁷⁴ Photography initially acts as a substitute for tangible encounters for Stephen, as his 'sootcoated packet of pictures' allow him to lie 'for hours sinning in thought and deed' *(P* 97). Yet these are not enough to sustain his interest, as Joyce writes, 'He bore cynically with the shameful details of his secret riots in which he exulted to defile with patience whatever image had attracted his eyes' (*P* 83). Stephen describes the prostitutes that he encounters as 'image[s]' and renders them as static forms subsequently transformed into hyperreal faces of 'lecherous cunning […] [and] eyes bright with brutish joy' (*P* 83).

The stereoscope enabled the viewer to feel that they could 'reach out and touch' objects and be touched by them in return.⁷⁵ Stephen's decision to sleep with prostitutes sees him transform his 'distorted images of the outer world' into an experience of 'touch' as he attempts to fulfil 'the savage desire within him' (*P* 83). In one of his encounters:

> Her room was warm and lightsome. A huge doll sat with her legs apart in the copious easychair beside the bed. He tried to bid his tongue speak that he might seem at ease, watching her as she undid her gown, noting the proud conscious movements of her perfumed head.
>
> (*P* 84)

Like Stephen's experience of the room and the woman's gradual undressing, erotically charged stereo cards also enabled this boundary transgression, as in the London Stereoscopic Company's *c.* 1865 image shown in Figure 2.2.

Figure 2.2 London Stereoscopic Company, Woman Seated, Pulling on Her Stocking, *c.* 1865. Digital image courtesy of the Getty's Open Content Program.

Stephen's interactions with prostitutes initially enhance his confidence, as Joyce describes how 'he had suddenly become strong and fearless and sure of himself' (*P* 85). This is subsequently threatened by the intrusion of politics and religiously inspired shame, as when:

> He would pass by them calmly waiting for a sudden movement of his own will or a sudden call to his sinloving soul from their soft perfumed flesh. Yet as he prowled in quest of that call, his senses, stultified only by his desire, would note keenly all that wounded or shamed them; his eyes, a ring of porter froth on a clothless table or a photograph of two soldiers standing to attention or a gaudy playbill.
>
> (*P* 86)

In Joyce's sexual innuendo in his reference to the soldiers 'standing to attention', he playfully mocks Stephen's 'sudden call to his sinloving soul'. Yet the photographic appearance of the 'two soldiers' also suggests the presence of policing and outside influences, as in societal attempts at suppressing the 'foul and polluting' stereo card.[76]

The photograph of the 'two soldiers' is likely to have shown British soldiers stationed in Ireland or Irish soldiers serving in the Boer War (1899–1902). Richard Ellman describes how during a May 1900 visit to London, Joyce's father picked 'quarrels about the Boer War with Stolid Englishmen' (*JJ* 77). He further highlights the influence of Dublin's 'Monto' brothel area on Joyce's depiction of 'Circe' (*JJ* 77). The Monto area enjoyed heightened business from Irish Battalion of Yeomanry Boer War soldiers returning from South Africa (*JJ* 367). The Boer War was photographed and Joyce could have seen these images, with *The Irish Times* revealing in 1900, 'A photographer displayed in his windows a Boer photograph of the British dead on Spion Kop, but […] no photographer was ever allowed to make a picture of the Boer dead'.[77] In *A Portrait*, Stephen refuses to sign MacCann's petition supporting Czar Nicholas's pursuit of 'universal peace' and critically disengages from his photograph (*P* 166). He cannot escape the interruption of politics and religion in his sexual encounters, with his awareness of his 'mortal sin' feeding into the hallucinatory 'Circe' (*P* 117).

In *Ulysses*, Stephen's engagement with prostitutes does not include the same 'surrendering himself to her, body and mind, conscious of nothing in the world' as *A Portrait* (*P* 85), and instead he experiences a sense of phantasmagoric bewilderment. In 'Circe', Bella tells the assembled crowd,

'This isn't a musical peepshow' (*U* 15.3528) but the scenes that preclude her statement suggest otherwise, given their erotically charged nature. Stephen actively pays for his viewing experience, as he '*fumbles in his pocket and, taking out a banknote by its corner, hands it to her* [Bella]' (*U* 15.3530–31) and provides '*two crowns*' for '*Zoe, Florry and Kitty*' (*U* 15.3542–46). With no noticeable intimacy occurring between Stephen and the women, his money provides him with the allure of tangibility and enhanced visuality, rather than an actual sexual encounter.

The image of Zoe, Florry and Kitty grouped together recalls the erotic stereo cards of Joyce's time, which often featured multiple women on one slide, in series in which they would 'arrive full of modesty and then disrobe' (*U* 15.3891–92). In his engagement with the women:

> *(Bella goes to the table to count the money while Stephen talks to himself in monosyllables. Zoe bends over the table. Kitty leans over Zoe's neck. Lynch gets up, rights his cap and, clasping Kitty's waist, adds his head to the group.)*
>
> (*U* 15.3548–51)

Like the mechanics of the coin-operated stereoscope, Joyce depicts the scene in fragmentary, mechanized images enhancing Stephen's hallucinatory turmoil. The short, condensed sentences in the parentheses lend themselves to the mechanistic nature of the coin-operated stereoscope, with the movement from the table to the neck to the waist enhancing this visual performance. Stephen's observation in 'Circe' occasionally veers towards the corporeality of *A Portrait*, as when he '*murmurs*' to Zoe as she touches his hand, 'Continue. Lie. Hold me. Caress' (*U* 15.3680). With Stephen ending the episode with Private Carr striking '*him in the face*' (*U* 15.4747–48), his actions are once again policed by political intruders, serving to enhance the text's suggestion of his potential re-departure from Dublin, 'the farthest remove from the centre of European culture' (*SH* 174).

Supernatural stereoscopy in 'Circe'

In *A Portrait*, Joyce describes Stephen 'listening to the words' of the 'old woman' at the fire, before he 'Suddenly [...] became aware of something in the doorway. A skull appeared suspended in the gloom of the doorway' (*P* 56–57). His image of Ellen's 'skull' as it 'appeared suspended in the gloom' hints at the phantasmagoria associated with supernatural stereoscopy and its illusory techniques. Stephen identifies with 'the gloom of the doorway', imagining himself as a 'gloomy figure' at the 'children's party at Harold's Cross' (*P* 57). In self-identifying with the original image, Stephen occupies a position of estrangement, as he realizes that he had begun 'to taste the joy of loneliness' (*P* 57). This use of visual imagery is made explicit with reference to photography in *Ulysses*, where Leopold Bloom's having been 'soiled by the dust of travel' (*U* 14.1218) foreshadows the 'slight soiling' of Molly's photograph (*U* 16.1468). In each instance, Joyce provides linguistic clues to the reader of the significance of images and phantasmagoric techniques to his protagonists' engagement with their surroundings.

Keith Williams has acknowledged the popularity of French *diableries* from the mid-nineteenth century to the 1890s, miniature clay infernos that were 'converted into colour stereoscopic images'.[78] These were constructed as sets of slides in paper form, as in a series entitled 'Satanic Slides', which shows scenes such as 'a railway train [...] filled with skeletons' and 'a ghastly band in skeleton-suits playing an accompaniment to the dancers'.[79] Mock-supernatural stereo cards were produced as photographs. By combining multiple photographic exposures or having the subject move part-way through the exposure, the photographer could render the resulting image blurred or appearing to show a ghostly character. In *The Stereoscope, Its History, Theory, and Construction* (1856), Brewster describes how a stereo card could be transformed into the 'regions of the supernatural':

> When the party have nearly sat the proper length of time, the female figure, suitably attired, walks quickly into the place assigned her, and after standing a few seconds in the proper attitudes, retires quickly, or takes as quickly, a second or even a third place in the picture if is required.[80]

By manipulating the exposure process, the subject could appear transparent, as in the hand-coloured albumen silver stereo card shown in Figure 2.3. This image would have been hand coloured after production, as the Lumière brothers only launched their autochrome plate process capable of producing full colour images in 1907 and even then, this proved expensive and complex. Commenting on photography's illusory potential, Brewster explained, 'This experiment may be varied in many ways. One body may be placed within another, a chicken for example, within an egg.'[81]

Following these innovations in visual experimentation, photographers were quick to capitalize on the public's desire for 'ghost' photographs. These were frequently sold as stereoscopic slides and were marketed as 'novelties and

Figure 2.3 London Stereoscopic Company, A Ghost, *c.* 1865. Digital image courtesy of the Getty's Open Content Program.

amusements'.[82] Jocular spirit photographs were popular in Dublin and included mock-comic photographs of Irish ghosts or funeral scenes in a 'spoof of visibility', with figures comically 'haunted always' (*FW* 48.1–49.22). Supernatural stereoscopy has its origins in phantasmagoric techniques developed by Henry Dirck, who in 1858 invented the 'Pepper's Ghost' illusion, which was marketed under this name by Professor John Henry Pepper.[83] This process involved use of concealed lanterns to project 'moving images of actors or skeletons' to audience members.[84] An 1874 advertisement in the *Freeman's Journal* for the 'Original Pepper's Ghost' at the Rotunda Concert Hall, Dublin praises the 'Appropriate Scenery by First-class Artists' and 'Costumes carefully studied from German authorities', with tickets priced at 'Reserved Seats (Numbered) 3s; Front Seats, 2s; Second Seats, 1s; Back Seats, 6d. Juveniles Half-price'.[85] One of the first plays to use Pepper's Ghost was *Hamlet*, that of Stephen's fervent interest.

Describing the process of using this illusion in 1904, lanternist Edmund H. Wilkie noted, 'light was allowed to gradually diffuse itself over the apparition from the side, the door melted away and the figure was seen in relief'.[86] Joyce was familiar with this trick, portraying Leopold Bloom as thinking in *Ulysses*, 'Our Saviour. Wake up in the dead of night and see him on the wall, hanging. Pepper's ghost idea' (*U* 8.19–20). He refers to this visual spectacle again in the *Wake*, where Shem invokes the 'rotten little ghost of a Peppybeg' (*FW* 173.26). Joyce had an early interest in the potential for supernatural imagery and Richard Ellmann notes his delight at rumours at Clongowes Wood College that the ghost of Maximillian Ulysses Browne wore 'a bloodstained white uniform, ascended the stairs of the castle to a gallery, then walked along it to a room at the end' (*JJ* 29). Joyce returns to General Browne in *Ulysses*, where he describes John Wyse recalling fighting alongside 'Sarsfield and O'Donnell, duke of Tetuan in Spain, and Ulysses Browne of Camus that was fieldmarshal to Maria Teresa' (*U* 12.1382–83). The same episode features the haunting appearance of Mr Dignam, when 'a faint but increasing luminosity of ruby light became gradually visible, the apparition of the etheric double being particularly lifelike' (*U* 12.339– 41). Critics have long recognized the cinematic elements of the 'Circe' episode, but supernatural stereo cards could have also contributed to Joyce's portrayal of this invocation of the dead, particularly given that Stephen observes these images in hyperreal and phantasmagoric form.

Writing on cinematography in 'Circe', Maria DiBattista argues that many of the episode's ghost effects 'were learned from the stage magic of the theatre and from the haunted pages of Gothic literature and folklores [...] and inventions of early cinema'.[87] The three-dimensionality of the supernatural stereo card contains resonances of 'early cinema' but these hallucinatory images largely function in *Ulysses* to remind Stephen of the futility of his 'solitary and purposeless' existence (*SH* 109). When the scenes around him do take on a non-jocular quality, as in the appearance of his mother, they further inspire his rejection of tradition and fuel his desire to 'live his own life according to what he recognized as the voice of a new humanity' (*SH* 174). The popularity of trick photographs in Dublin in the early twentieth century was such that Robinson's studio enlarged their 'Magical Department' whilst Professor James Nutman of 24 Upper Temple Street successfully marketed 'the Decapitated Head' and other optical illusions'.[88] In 'Circe', Stephen is subject to an array of optical illusions, as in *'the head of Don John Connee'* that rises *'from the pianola coffin'* (*U* 15.3673–74) and *'The face of Martin Cunningham,* [that] *bearded, refeatures Shakespeare's beardless face'* (*U* 15.3854–55). Early-twentieth-century stereo cards include titles such as 'And in trying to please both, this is the result', in which the face of a man sitting between two women is deliberately blurred to allow him to look at both of them.[89] Joyce's fusion of Martin Cunningham with William Shakespeare suggests the influence of this optical trickery and the phantasmagoria involved.

In 'Circe', Stephen experiences a sense of emotional estrangement in his response to his surroundings, as Joyce describes how *'he stands with shrugged shoulders, finny hands outspread, a painted smile on his face'* (*U* 15.3877–78). Stephen's *'painted smile'* posits him as an embodiment of the stereo card, mocked up for display for others in initially static form (*U* 15.3878). He goes on to seize *'Zoe around the waist'* (*U* 15.4029) and *'seizes Florry and turns with her'* (*U* 15.4095–96), but his reference to their movements as a 'Dance of death' merges the boundaries between reality and supernaturality (*U* 15.4139). Within this phantasmagoric setting, Stephen's intellectual capacity begins to degenerate, and he struggles to articulate his thoughts, telling The Cap '*(with an effort)* Interval which. Is the greatest possible ellipse. Consistent with. The ultimate return' (*U* 15.2111–12). Just as the stereoscope provided a 'tantalising purchase on the real', the brothel functions as a claustrophobic, mid-point between reality and fantasy, in which Stephen risks succumbing to the illusion of '*the lamp image*' (*U* 15.99).

Humour was a key part of the stereo card's appeal. If one stereoscopic slide did not suffice, photographers could instead present the 'appreciative public' with slides containing a comic 'beginning, middle, and end'.[90] Stereo card sets frequently mocked supposedly serious occasions. In an 1894 series by Strohmeyer & Wyman, New York entitled '"Be the Howly St. Patrick! – there's Mickie's Ghost"', Mickie O'Hoolihan's mourners are confronted with the sudden, surprise appearance of his ghost.[91] The first two stereo cards are near-identical, bar the addition of the woman's shawl, with the third set designed to demonstrate the passing of time. The relatives' carnivalesque horror is typical of supernatural stereoscopy, as suggested in 'Circe' when the group respond to the appearance of 'saint Patrick': the '*women's heads coalesce*' and '*Old Gummy Granny in sugarloaf hat appears*' (*U* 15.4578–79).

This visual spectacle becomes gradually more debased when:

(Reuben J. Antichrist, wandering jew, a clutching hand open on his spine, stumps forward. [...] Aloft over his shoulder he bears a long boatpole from the hook of which the sodden huddled mass of his only son, saved from Liffey waters, hangs from the slack of its breeches. A hobgoblin in the image of Punch Costello, hipshot, crookbacked, hydrocephalic, prognathic with receding forehead and Ally Sloper nose, tumbles in somersaults through the gathering darkness.)

(*U* 15.2145–53)

The comically exaggerated movement of 'Reuben J. Antichrist' as he 'tumbles in somersaults through the gathering darkness' is designed to amuse as well as shock, yet the reaction of Joyce's protagonists is one of dazed, near-paralytic indifference, as they answer as one with 'What?' (*U* 15.2155). The appearance of the hobgoblin with '*jaws chattering* [...] *kangaroohopping with outstretched clutching arms*' (*U* 15.2157–58) enhances the absurdity of the scene and disturbs the liminality between living and dead. Stephen's description of the brothel adds to the episode's optical trickery, as he explains how 'gentlemen' enter 'to see in mirrors every positions trapezes all that machine' (*U* 15.3907–08). The 'mirror' and 'machine' recall Sir Charles Wheatstone's original mirror stereoscope, where the viewing of two dissimilar pictures reflected in the device's mirrors provided the scene with the appearance of depth. In fusing 'mirror' and 'machine' in 'Circe', Joyce posits stereoscopy's more archaic elements against the three-dimensionality of mock-supernaturality, veering into cinematic form. Stephen further descends into chaos as he departs the brothel, as he '*totters, collapses, falls, stunned*' (*U* 15.4748). His words before leaving confirm the dangers of visual overconsumption, as Joyce portrays him saying, after laughing '*emptily*', 'My centre of gravity is displaced. I have forgotten the trick' (*U* 15.4433–34).

The haunting nature of Joyce's supernatural invocations are at their most grotesque in the appearance of Stephen's deceased mother, with this exacerbating his fear of being held partially accountable for her death. He first encounters his mother's ghost in the 'Telemachus' episode, where he thinks, 'Silently, in a dream she had come to him after her death, her wasted body within its loose brown graveclothes giving off an odour of wax and rosewood' (*U* 1.102–04). In a later repetition of 'her wasted body within its loose graveclothes', he imagines:

> Her glazing eyes, staring out of death, to shake and bend my soul. On me alone. The ghostcandle to light her agony. Ghostly light on the tortured face. Her hoarse loud breath rattling in horror, while all prayed on their knees. Her eyes on me to strike me down.
>
> (*U* 1.273–76)

The 'odour' of his mother's body adds to the pervading horror of the image and her 'hoarse loud breath' reminds him of his failure to have prayed for her as others did 'on their knees' (*U* 1.275–76). The 'ghostcandle' and 'Ghostly light' suggest the dissolves and fades of the Pepper's Ghost show and the candles used in the magic lantern projector. Yet the shared gaze between Stephen and his mother also hints at a more intimate encounter, as in that of the relationship between viewer and image in the hand-held or coin-operated stereoscope.

Responding to his mother's appearance, Stephen works himself into a frenzy, exclaiming 'Ghoul! Chewer of corpses! No, mother! Let me be and let me live' (*U* 1.278–79). Mrs Dedalus reappears in 'Circe', where '*Stephen's mother, emaciated, rises stark through the floor, in leper grey with a wreath of faded orangeblossoms and a torn bridal veil, her face worn and noseless, green with gravemould*' (*U* 15.4158–59). Stephen initially challenges the veracity of this scene, asking 'What bogeyman's trick is this?' (*U* 15.4176). He acknowledges its falsity and attributes her appearance to the 'The intellectual imagination!' (*U* 15.4227). Despite being aware of this deception, he continues to punish himself by conjuring up her ghost, as he imagines her crying, '(*in the agony of her deathrattle*) Have mercy on Stephen, Lord, for my sake!' (*U* 15.4238–39). He confronts the scene's visual distortion and exclaims, 'With me all or not at all. *Non serviam!*' (*U* 15.4227–28). Stephen's insistence that he 'will not serve' sees him ultimately reject this phantasmagoria and he commands, 'Break my spirit, all of you, if you can! I'll bring you all to heel!' (*U* 15.4235–36). His turn away from this mock-supernaturality allows him to relinquish what Mary Lowe-Evans describes as that Catholic nostalgia, 'the obsessive urge to return to a, paradoxically, dead but mysteriously vital and intellectually challenging body of Catholic dogma and ritual'.[92] The image of Stephen's mother may continue to haunt him but in bringing these fantasies to 'heel', he moves towards an acceptance of his refusal to 'have knelt down' before his 'dying mother' (*U* 1.91–92) and a recognition of the visual absurdity of this hallucinatory encounter.

Visual veracity and the stereopticon (I.5)

Following its initial popularity in the 1850s–60s, and its revival in the late nineteenth to early twentieth century, by *Finnegans Wake* (1939), the stereoscope was largely obsolete. Despite waning public interest, Joyce continues to engage with stereoscopy in his final work. He uses the stereopticon and anaglyph technology to support the *Wake*'s interrogation of rumour and duality, where there could be 'two sights for ever[y] [...] picture' (*FW* 11.36). In I.5, Joyce frequently invokes more outdated photographic processes, such as the 'capecloaked hoodoodman' of the early photographer (*FW* 339.29–30), before turning to the 'Tulloch-Turnbull girl with her coldblood kodak' in I.7, as explored in Chapter 4 of this project (*FW* 171.31–32). With Joyce increasingly interested in cinema throughout his literary career, his Wakean allusions to the stereopticon and anaglyptics suggest a marrying of these visual interests, as he draws upon proto-cinematic techniques and the malleability of the stereoscope to enhance the text's concerns with visual veracity.

In I.5, the list of names given to ALP's letter include '*My Skin Appeals to Three Senses and My Curly Lips Demand Columbkisses*' and '*In My Lord's Bed by One Whore Went Through It*' (*FW* 105.31–32). The idea of the '*Skin*' appealing to the '*Three senses*' hints at the corporeality and heightened sensations associated with the coin-operated stereoscope, as do the titles' implied pornography

(*FW* 105.31–32). Photography's influence is further suggested when Joyce writes, 'it has shown a very sexmosaic of nymphosis in which the eternal chimerahunter Oriolopos, [...] the sensory crowd in his belly coupled with an eye for the goods' (*FW* 107.13–16). For Roland McHugh, this description can be taken to be a 'sexual mosaic or chimaera: [an] organism with some male parts, some female' and 'Orion, [the] hunter'.[93] Yet the 'chimerahunter' may also refer to the camera hunter or photographer, particularly given that Joyce later invokes the 'photoist' (*FW* 111.26) and Aran photographer, John Millington Synge in '*the Aranman ingperwhis through the hole of his hat*' (*FW* 121.12), whose work is explored in Chapter 1 of this project.

In an episode centred on the contents of the *Wake*'s letter, the short, potential titles that Joyce ascribes to it reveal the 'multiplicity of personalities inflicted on the documents or document' (*FW* 107.24–25). In a draft of I.5 written in December 1923, Joyce referred to the duality of 'this gryphonic script' in association with the 'stereoptican':

> Wonderfully well this explains the double nature of this gryphonic script and while its ingredients stand out with stereoptican relief we can ~~see peep~~ tour beyond the figure of the scriptor into the subconscious writer's mind.[94]

In a second draft written in the same month, he removed the 'stereoptican relief' but its implications on the chapter's concerns with visual comprehension remain. The stereopticon is a double lantern using two, near-identical pictures, which when projected through the device appear as one, three-dimensional image. The term was in use as a 'common American synonym for the [magic] lantern itself from the 1860s' and could allude 'to the stereoscope and the effect of almost palpable prominence and depth in large-scale projections'.[95] Joyce is likely to have had this phantasmagoric spectacle in mind when writing of the 'stereoptican', given his reference to the device's 'double nature' and his use of the projector's American spelling.[96]

The stereopticon was used at lectures and religious sermons in Ireland, with common titles of slides including 'The Ten Commandments', 'The Lord's Prayer' and 'The Drunkard's Career and End'.[97] These slides were often photographic and in a stereopticon showing at the Rotunda, Dublin in April 1892, the visiting Major-General St. Clair A. Mulholland presented 'A tour through the United States, the Great American Civil War, Ireland, London, and Paris, All graphically described and beautifully illustrated by a new and improved stereopticon'.[98] Describing the impact of a similar show in 1862, the

Philadelphia Press praised the ability for the audience member 'to be a child again; to re-enact the scenes of youth and manhood; to be transported to far distant lands; to see strange cities, palaces, and people'.[99] In 1864, Robinsons of Grafton Street, Dublin lent their stereopticons to 'schools and private parties' to display 'transformations', 'ghosts' and 'spectral appearances' to their respective audiences.[100] Joyce's invocation of a device capable of projecting multiple 'unreal' and potentially 'spectral appearances' is particularly appropriate in I.5, in an episode in which 'we need the loan of a lens to see as much as the hen saw' (*FW* 112.1–2).

Just as the contents of the *Wake*'s 'everydaylooking stamped addressed envelope' are capable of being falsely 'stretched, filled out, if need or wish were', so too could the stereopticon heighten and distort a viewing experience (*FW* 109.7–28). As in his reference to the 'magic lantern' in *Dubliners* in 'Grace' (*D* 171), Joyce uses lantern technology in the *Wake* to interrogate concerns with visual veracity, where 'the eyes' may 'find it devilish hard now and again even to believe itself' (*FW* 113.29). Joyce reveals the letter's 'transhipt from Boston (Mass.)' and its inclusion of 'the first to Dear whom it proceded to mention Maggy' (*FW* 111.9–11) but its contents are still frequently reconfigured and subject to reinterpretation. Writing on the original appearance of ALP's letter in I.4, David Hayman argues:

> The reference to the 'subconscious editor,' written in a different Joycean hand and probably not designed for inclusion in the text, was most certainly an afterthought, an elaboration upon the "stereopticon" presentation of the letter writer, who became far more than an "editor" in what followed.[101]

Hayman further describes how the '"original" foraging hen [...] was brought to mind by the allusion to the "stereopticon," a device that simulates two-eyed vision and hence depth perception, the sort of vision most marked in birds'.[102] With the stereopticon enjoying the height of its popularity in the mid-nineteenth century, Joyce's increasing interest in cinema may have led him to discard this sentence in favour of new and emerging cinematic technologies. Yet whilst Hayman attributes this reference to an 'afterthought', in choosing a device centred on visual spectacle, Joyce underscores the importance of stereoscopy on his depiction of the *Wake*'s letter and rumours of Humphrey Chimpden Earwicker's (HCE's) impropriety.

Had the 'stereoptican relief' appeared in the final edition of I.5, it would have immediately precluded Joyce's reference to photography, when the letter uncovered by Biddy Doran is compared to the image produced by the 'photoist worth his chemicots' (*FW* 111.26):

> Well, almost any photoist worth his chemicots will tip anyone asking him the teaser that if a negative of a horse happens to melt enough while drying, well, what you do get is, well, a positively grotesquely distorted macromass of all sorts of horsehappy values and masses of meltwhile horse. Tip.
>
> (*FW* 111.26–30)

The use of 'purely negatively from the positive absence' suggests the negative-positive, calotype photographic process invented by William Henry Fox Talbot in the 1830s where, by bringing the calotype negative into contact with sheets of paper sensitized in silver chloride, the photographer could produce multiple photographic positives. As with the text's spread of rumours regarding HCE's actions in Phoenix Park, this photographic 'positive' effectively functions as a 'positive absence', with each print distorted and further removed from the original scene (*FW* 108.30).

In I.4, in his references to guns and prior allusion to 'The pair' (here the Cad and HCE) as 'Nippoluono [...] the general Boukeleff' (*FW* 81.33–35), it is impossible to verify whether the 'pair' are who they claim to be, 'man may not say' (*FW* 81.35). HCE's actions in 'having behaved with ongentilmensky immodus opposite a pair of dainty maidservants' continue to be repurposed and retold (*FW* 34.18–19). The impossibility of ascertaining the exact nature of HCE's interaction with the 'maidservants' is further apparent when he goes on trial for having reportedly 'expose[d] his person' (*FW* 89.6). The use of 'Remarkable evidence [...] given, anon, by an eye, ear, nose and throat witness' (*FW* 86.32–33) descends into a farce in which Butt and Taff appear in near-stereoscopic form as a 'hilariohoot of Pegger's Windup cumjustled [...] equals of opposites' (*FW* 92.6–8). Stammering is used to indicate guilt, with HCE's suggestion 'Woowoo would you be grossly surprised [...] but I believe I can see my way' (*FW* 82.31–35) revealing the additional difficulties he faces in defending his actions.

In Joyce's 'horsehappy values' in the 'negative of a horse', he invokes photographer, Eadweard Muybridge's late-nineteenth-century, proto-cinematic experimentation with motion images of horses. Muybridge produced a series of images titled 'The Horse in Motion' in response to the question, 'When a horse trots or gallops, does it ever become fully airborne?' In I.5, possibly blurred by the movement of Muybridge's horse in flight or its appearance in the 'Dirtdump', the 'horsehappy values and [...] meltwhile horse' become graphically distorted. The fact that the 'negative' was 'partly obliterated [...] to start with' (*FW* 111.34–35) destabilizes the possibility of comprehending image or text. For Eric McLuhan, Joyce presents the 'negative of a horse' as 'a subplot in order to "tip" off the reader to what is going on'.[103] Elaborating on the connections between the 'photoist' and Anna Livia Plurabelle's (ALP's) letter, McLuhan argues that 'Both photo and Letter are litter [...] Both inject a new aesthetic into reproduction and re-presentation, and both intensify the visual and literal, "sterilized" of the other senses'.[104] In this visual spectacle, the melting of the photographic negative renders it 'grotesquely distorted' (*FW* 111.29). That Joyce ultimately removes the stereopticon and leaves in the reference to the 'negative of a horse' suggests his potential conflict between stereoscopy in its more archaic forms and the kinesis and 'wiggle' of film (*FW* 112.1). He later writes, 'did we care to sell our feebought silence *in camera*' (*FW* 115.25), with '*in camera*' a play on photography and the Latin legal terminology for a private jury session in which press and public are absent (*FW* 115.22–23). In doing so, he hints that photography in its non-distorted forms could offer HCE the possibility of corroborating the multiple 'contexts' of his actions (*FW* 115.25–26).

In *Ulysses*, Joyce recognizes the stereoscopes 'click' (*U* 3.420). In I.4 the 'Tip' in the 'positively grotesquely distorted macromass' also suggests the mechanics of the stereoscopic device. In 1859, Oliver Wendell Holmes wrote of his production of stereoscopic images, 'Just as we must have a mould before we can make a cast, we must get a negative or reversed picture on glass before we can get our positive or natural picture.'[105] In invoking the 'negative' and 'positive' photographic process alongside reference to the 'grotesquely distorted macromass', Joyce applies a shared incomprehension to letter and photograph, when 'We cannot say aye to aye' (*FW* 114.1–2). He further attests to the challenges faced in determining the letter's contents, writing:

> To conclude purely negatively from the positive absence of political odia and monetary requests that its page cannot ever have been a penproduct of a man or woman of that period or those parts is only one more unlookedfor conclusion leaped at.
>
> (*FW* 108.29–33)

The idea of formulating an opinion 'purely negatively from the positive absence' recalls the first photographic experiments, where the exposure of the photographic negative to light destroyed the image and thus, by way of oppositions, rendered the negative a 'positive absence' (*FW* 108.30). Photography proves incapable of providing the oxymoronic 'unlookedfor conclusion' (*FW* 108.32–33), Joyce drawing upon visual media to support the text's concerns with rumour and epistolary malleability.

'How Burghley shuck the rackushant Germanon' (II.3)

Joyce's reference to 'stereoptican relief' was the second time he had written of the 'stereoptican', as in a December 1923 draft version of I.4 he wrote, 'every schoolgirl by now |¹knows has learnt to know¹| how it was Buckley who struck and the Russian general […] Would we vision her |ª(subconscious editor)ª| with stereoptican relief¹|'.[106] He again removed the 'stereoptican' before final publication, with this not appearing in his typescript *c.* January 1924.[107] In *Finnegans Wake*, Joyce uses the motif of 'Buckley who struck […] the Russian general' multiple times, including in I.4, where 'it was Buckleyself […] who struck and the Russian generals' (*FW* 101.19–21) and in II.3, where the details of 'How Burghley shuck the rackushant Germanon' appear during a dialogue between brothers, Butt and Taff (*FW* 338.2–3). The *'verbivocovisual'* elements of II.3 have typically been read in relation to television or radio but photography is also present, as recognized by Finn Fordham, who notes, 'The one with the "shutter" (the "shooter") is Butt, and yet the "shitter" is the Russian General'.[108] William York Tindall suggests that the 'verbivocovisual' battle between the *Wake*'s brothers is one of 'ear and eye' and argues that the text 'is primarily "graphique", writing in and for itself, [and] sharing little in common with daguerreotype, or any other means of realistically representing the world'.[109] Whilst photographic realism is not evident, Joyce engages with the malleability of the photograph to interrogate the medium's claim to 'realistically' represent 'the world'.

In II.3, Joyce invokes the Crimean War (1853–56) and the daguerreotype in 'Say mangraphique, may say nay por daguerre' to reinforce visual instability (*FW* 339.23). Politicized photography is also suggested in the account of HCE's 'snapper' or snapshot being 'shot in the Rumjar Journaral' (*FW* 341.6–7). The 'Rumjar' or Russian 'Journaral' hints at the political implications of photography first used by Joyce in *Stephen Hero,* where Stephen observes the 'two photographs, one of the Tsar of Russia, the other of the Editor of the *Review of Reviews*' (*SH* 103), and in *A Portrait,* where the 'photograph of two soldiers' intrudes on his sexual experience (*P* 86). In each incident with Stephen, photography cannot be trusted, with Joyce magnifying this photographic malleability in the *Wake*. In the 1830s, the daguerreotype was the predominant form used for photographic portraits, before the introduction of smaller and portable cartes de visite in the late 1850s. The latter images were regularly traded in the 1860s and although this pastime declined in popularity, Lafayette's in Dublin were still selling cartes de visite using the new silver gelatin printing process *c*. 1902.[110]

Each daguerreotype was extremely fragile and unique in its formation. In 1839, Louis-Jacques-Mandé Daguerre described his silver plate daguerreotypes as 'not merely an instrument which serves to draw Nature; on the contrary it is a chemical and physical process which gives her the power to reproduce herself'.[111] Despite photography's claims to rival nature, the photographic image could be distorted and was temporal, as recognized by Joyce in *Ulysses*. In the fusion of multimedia in II.3, the '*teleframe*' plays 'the *charge of a light barricade. Down the photoslope*' (*FW* 349.8–10). Joyce invokes the 1854 Charge of the Light Brigade at the Battle of Balaclava at the Crimean War, the second military conflict to be photographed after the Mexican-American War (1846–8). Due to lengthy exposure times and the dangers involved, photographers at these battles would have been unable to capture live action. In the Mexican-American War, an unnamed photographer took approximately fifty daguerreotypes of soldiers, civilians and burial sites. The Crimean War saw British and French armed forces declare war on the Russian Empire on 28 March 1854, in support of Turkey's stance against Russia's invasion of Ottoman territory. Military action had previously been captured via illustration and text, as when the Irish wartime reporter, Sir William Howard Russell was despatched to the Crimea for London's *The Times*, 'for the purpose of satisfying the public thirst for early and authentic information as to the momentous events which were daily expected to take place'.[112] Russell's wartime accounts exposed the horrors of military mismanagement, 'the most disgraceful and disastrous episode in our military history' and 'the cruel strokes of neglect and the fatal evils of mal-administration'.[113] British publishers and art dealers, Thomas Agnew & Sons sought to counteract criticism of military ineptitude and capitalize on public interest in the war by funding Roger Fenton's trip to the Crimea, with the intention of selling his photographs and using these as source material for the oil painter, Thomas J. Barker. Their sale of Fenton's photographs was not a success, as these proved too expensive. Officers photographed in the Crimea were able to purchase images from Fenton, which they then sent home by post.

Fenton left for the East in 1855, accompanied by his assistant, Marcus Sparling and a second helper, William, whose surname is unknown.[114] His work was 'slow' and was challenged by the 'the labour' and 'the dust and heat still more by the cows of all sorts who flock[ed] round'.[115] He was unable to cross enemy lines and was prevented from photographing the dead or live conflict due to his photographic van attracting Russian artillery interest.[116] In an 1855 letter to his wife, he described the challenges he faced in producing photographs and sketches: 'The views here were not very good pictures as nobody being in front I could make no foregrounds & the town is so far off that in itself it is no picture.'[117] After his return, Fenton's images were displayed in Ireland. In 1856, the *Freeman's Journal* advertised an exhibition of 350 of his photographs 'of the Heroes of the War, the Encampments, Valley of the Shadow of Death, Plains of Balaklava, Inkermen, the Redan and Malakoff groups of General Officers and their Staffs', which were shown at the Royal Hibernian Academy, Dublin.[118] Irish newspapers used photography to critique military engagement and in an 1908 feature, the *Weekly Irish Times* included photographs of Belfast, Crimean War veterans to expose the fate of those 'woefully neglected by the nation whose honour and prestige they had helped to save [...] [as] veterans of the [...] heartbreaking campaign in the bleak Crimea'.[119]

In II.3, Taff describes the battleground whilst in conflict with Butt as 'A cheap decoy! Too deep destroy! Say mangraphique, may say nay por Daguerre!' (*FW* 339.23). In doing so, he engages with debates over the interrelationship between art and photography since photography's inception. He further advocates for daguerreotypes as an alternative to cheaper, more inauthentic media. These daguerreotypes cannot have been captured by Fenton at the Crimea, since he instead used the calotype process involving glass, photographic negatives, rather Louis-Jacques-Mandé Daguerre's fragile silver sheets. The accusation of 'A cheap decoy! Too deep destroy!' levelled against Buckley (*FW* 339.22–23), posits him against the supposed validity of the daguerreotype. It is only after reference to 'daguerre' that the photograph is captured, thanks to the appearance of 'Erminia's capecloaked hoodoodman! First he s s st steppes. Then he st stoo stooppt. Lookt' (*FW* 339.29). The 'capecloaked hoodoodman' invokes images of the black cloth used in early photography, with the stammer in the 's s st' revealing that this is not a scene to be fully trusted.

Butt responds to Taff's question of, 'What see, buttywalch?' (*FW* 338.9) with 'Sea vast a pool!' (*FW* 333.14). In doing so, he alludes to the Crimea's Siege of Sevastopol (1854–5), which enabled British and French troops to capture the Russian naval base. In Joyce's portrayal of Taff's response to 'Daguerre', he plays on General Pierre Bosquet's comment at the Battle of Baclava's Charge of the Light Brigade, 'C'est magnifique, mais ce n'est pas la guerre: c'est de la folie [it is magnificent, but it is not war; it's madness]'. Alfred Tennyson immortalized this military action in his poem, 'The Charge of the Light Brigade' (1854). It was also captured by Fenton in his photograph, 'Valley of the Shadow of Death' (1855), which depicts a sparse landscape of discarded 'cannonball wappents' (*FW* 339.10). In the *Wake,* Joyce's suggestion that the 'decoy' lacks the validity and status of the 'Daguerre' echoes the cultural status attributed to wartime photography, with the *Freeman's Journal* reporting on Fenton's Crimean photographs in 1856:

> The art of photography has certainly never before been applied to a more important purpose than the production of these pictures, which will be amongst the most interesting and truthful records of the great struggle which may now, we trust, be considered at an end.[120]

Had he known that Fenton had in fact not used daguerreotypes, Joyce may have deliberately invoked 'Daguerre' with reference to the Crimea in II.3 to expose the absurdity of this comparison (*FW* 339.23). Since this was not regularly covered in news reports, it is more likely that Joyce chose the validity of the 'Daguerre' to highlight the challenges of comprehending the *Wake*'s 'mangraphique' media and the absurdity of the conflict between the two brothers where photography has replaced the 'war'.

Anaglyph technology (III.1)

In 1851, the transformative potential of the stereoscope and lantern technology led London's *Art-Journal* to declare, 'the representation is nature itself again, omitting all defects and incorrectness in the drawing which can never be avoided in painting a picture on the small scale required for the old slides'.[121] In III.1, Joyce questions the ability for the stereoscope to replicate nature in one of a series of questions put to Shaun whilst under interrogation:

> But could you, of course, decent Lettrechaun [...] read the strangewrote anaglyptics of those shemletters patent for His Christian's Em? —Greek! Hand it to me! Shaun replied, plosively pointing to the cinnamon quistoquill behind his acoustrolobe.
>
> (*FW* 419.16–21)

The 'anaglyptics' suggests both the art of sculpting in low relief to leave a non-sculpted section exposed and the anaglyph stereoscopic process invented by

Louis Arthur Ducos du Hauron in 1891. In an anaglyph stereo card, two near-identical images are printed alongside one another in complementary colours, allowing them to be viewed as a single, coloured image. These images were initially used with the 'artificial light of the [magic] lantern', before Ducos du Hauron decided 'The effect will be so much the more striking, inasmuch as there is nothing of the appearance of a show, phantasmagoria, or entertainment of any kind about it – i.e., neither darkness, screen, nor magic lantern'.[122] The anaglyph process is likely to have appealed to Joyce given its roots in stereoscopic experimentation and its use as a precursor to film.

Ducos du Hauron announced that he would relinquish the rights to his anaglyph patent should someone 'print and publish an anaglyph image of the moon suspended in space', a challenge that was met by *The Illustrated London News* in 1921.[123] Alongside printing wood-engravings of Fenton's Crimean War photographs prior to the inclusion of photographs in newspapers from the mid-teens, they featured anaglyph photographic stereo cards in their pages throughout the 1920s. Their 29 March 1924 edition includes 'Seen in Stereoscopic Relief if Viewed through Red and Green Films: Occupants of the New "Zoo" Aquarium'.[124] In order to view these images in their intended form, the reader had to send off for a 'portable stereoscope, adapted for use in books', costing 'three-halfpence stamps for "Inland" postage and two pence and a halfpenny for "Foreign" postage'.[125] In III.1, Joyce invokes George Berkeley, writing, 'I'm not at all surprised the saint kicked him whereby the sum taken Berkeley showed the reason genrously' (*FW* 423.31–33). As Cleo Hanaway-Oakley has acknowledged, 'for both Berkeley and Stephen, three-dimensionality is mental rather than physical'.[126] Joyce's reference to Berkeley and 'the saint [that] kicked him' alludes to Dr Johnson reportedly 'kicking [a] stone to refute Berkeley's immaterialism'.[127] In writing of the saint 'kicking him' amidst Shaun's critique of the *Wake*'s letter, Joyce equates him with Dr Johnson and highlights the continued conflict between Shem and Shaun.

In Shaun's stance as he appears 'like the good man you are, with your picture pockets turned knockside out', Joyce interrogates the act of visual comprehension, which is further threatened by the presence of 'the rake of the rain' (*FW* 428.23–24). Shaun's 'picture pockets' could be picture postcards, carried in his role as a postman and transporter of 'decent Lettrechaun' (*FW* 419.16). His 'picture pockets' suggest the same movement of photographs evidenced in *Ulysses*, where Bloom keeps Molly's image in his 'pocketbook' (*U* 16.1423–65) and by Joyce, who carried 'in his pocket photographs of the portraits by Tuohy of his father, himself, and – James Stephens' (*JJ* 592). In Shem's account of his brother,

Joyce portrays the 'thrice truthful teller, Shaun of grace' (*FW* 424.14) as 'rubbing his magic lantern' (*FW* 421.22). Shaun describes the *Wake*'s letter as containing details of HCE's encounter with the 'two madges on the makewater. And why there were treefellers in the shrubrubs' (*FW* 420.7–8). Yet despite this insight and his attempts at 'rubbing his magic latern to a flow of full consciousness' (*FW* 421.21–22), he is unable to fully verify the letter's contents, stating, 'I would not care to be so unfruitful to my own part as to swear for the moment positively as to the views of Denmark' (*FW* 421.27–29). Given the shared focus in I.5, II.3 and III.1 on the letter and image's fluid and indecipherable contents, it is unsurprising that by the end of III.1, Shaun's 'lamp went out as it couldn't glow on burning, yep, the lmp went out for it couldn't stay alight' (*FW* 427.15–16). Visible meaning has been lost, with Joyce using the malleability of the stereoscope to challenge the Wakean possibility of ascertaining the full details of HCE's crime.

3

'it simply wasn't art in a word': Leopold Bloom, photography and artistic and erotic debate

Shortly after arriving in Paris on 3 December 1902, James Joyce visited the Photo-Cartes studio located on 28 Boulevard Poissonnière, where he had his photograph taken (*JJ* viii). The studio was owned by Fernand Désiré Fleury and Baldomar, the latter figure who was praised for his use of William Fox Talbot's calotype process, in which multiple photographic prints could be produced.[1] Joyce had his portrait printed on three picture postcards, sending one to his family and the other two to Vincent Cosgrave and John Francis Byrne (*JJ* 115). Despite having 'no money' to go 'to the theatre' or 'buy books' (*LII* 38), Joyce deemed the photographic session economically worthwhile. Using his images to portray a sense of European refinement in his 'Latin quarter hat' (*U* 1.519), he asked his family to inform those asking after him that he was doing 'Very Nicely, thank you' (*LII* 21). After returning to Dublin and departing again for Paris in January 1903, Joyce contemplated aesthetics in his Paris notebook, recording quotations from Aristotelian and pseudo-Aristotelian works.[2] In an undated entry *c.* March 1903, he writes:

> Question: *Can a photograph be a work of art?*
> Answer: A photograph is a disposition of sensible matter and may be so disposed for an aesthetic end but it is not a human disposition of sensible matter. Therefore it is not a work of art.
>
> (*OCPW* 104)

As critics have acknowledged, this formed part of a series of eight enquiries, in which he also questioned, 'I desire to see the Mona Lisa. Is it therefore beautiful or is it good?' and 'Spicer-Simson has made a bust of his wife. Is it lyrical, epical, or dramatic?'[3]

In situating concerns over photography's aesthetic value alongside reference to the Mona Lisa and Spicer-Simson's wife, Joyce exposes the way in which his literary engagement with photography is frequently underpinned by a preoccupation with the female form, where it is 'woman [who] is beauty of course' (*U* 18.559–60). As in Leopold Bloom's thought of wife, Molly's curves in her photograph that 'Marble could give the original, shoulders, back, all the symmetry, all the rest. [...] Whereas no photo could because it simply wasn't art in a word' (*U* 16.1451–55), Joyce renders this visual medium incapable of representing female beauty, unlike 'those Grecian statues, perfectly developed as works of art' (*U* 16.1450–51). Tracing the interrelationship of photography, art and eroticism via Bloom's picture of Molly, Lafayette's photographic studio and the photography of nude, female models in *Ulysses* and the *Wake* reveals the medium's duality. Photography enhances Bloom's sexual fantasies whilst also signalling aesthetic and marital lacking. Photographs and advertisements in one of Gerty MacDowell's chosen magazines, the '*Lady's Pictorial*' (*U* 13.151) attest to the status attributed to visiting a photographer's studio and the 'art' of photographic retouching.

Photography was informed by artistic techniques since its inception. Painters and illustrators used the camera obscura, a precursor for the first photographic camera to frame and trace static images, typically of landscapes or natural settings. The first known 'fixing' of the camera obscura's image was carried out by Nicéphore Niépce, who used a camera obscura coated with bitumen of Judea to secure his image with light, titling this, 'View from the Window at Le Gras' (*c.* 1826). Niépce termed the progress of using light to 'fix' an image 'héliographie' or 'light writing'. Describing how a visitor to Joyce's flat had referred to a painting as a photograph, Frank Budgen recalls the author commenting, "'It isn't the usual word, but surely light-writing is a beautiful word to apply to a painted picture'".[4] Neither 'héliographie' nor its direct translation 'heliography' occur in *Ulysses*, but the text does reference the heliotrope, as do *Dubliners* and *Finnegans Wake*. In the latter text, Joyce uses the '*Hippohopparry helioscope*' (*FW* 341.22–23) and '*heliotropical noughttime*' (*FW* 349.6) to create a multimodal fusion of art, photography and television in the same chapter reference 'daguerre' (*FW* 339.23).

In 1839, Louis-Jacques-Mandé Daguerre launched his photographic process to the French Academy of Sciences.[5] Seven months later, his audience also included the French Academy of Fine Arts. Despite societal recognition of photography's scientific and artistic value, the French Society of Photography were not permitted to exhibit their photographs at the annual Paris Salon until twenty years later, in 1859.[6] This inclusion of photography prompted a scathing response from Charles Baudelaire, who critiqued the general public's belief that 'Art is, and cannot be other than, the exact reproduction of Nature'.[7] For

Baudelaire, photography was capable of acting as a 'servant of the sciences and arts' or as an 'astronomer's hypotheses' but it had not earned its place at the Salon.⁸ In 1865, Dublin's International Exhibition featured photography for the first time, arguing that the medium was 'deserving of a special place'.⁹ Reporting on its inclusion, *The Irish Times* suggested that photography had 'entered the province of the Fine Arts and obtained a room for itself'.¹⁰

In 1866, *The Irish Times* praised the skills of Dublin-based, photographic artists, Nelson and Marshall, writing:

> The last days of portrait painting after the old method have come. By dint of great perseverance, energy and skill, the Messrs. Nelson and Marshall, of 11 Upper Sackville street, have brought the art of photography to such a state of perfection that they are now producing magnificent pictures of extraordinary size.¹¹

Mr Schroeder of 28 Grafton-Street was similarly commended for his 'new enlarging process', capable of imbuing his photographs with 'artistic qualities [that] render them singularly attractive'.¹² Dublin photographers enjoyed much success outside of Ireland and in 1895, Messrs. Warnes and Son of Grafton Street, Dublin were 'awarded the gold medal in London' for 'Honours in Art Photography'.¹³ Studios seized upon the advertorial appeal of the art photographer and marketed themselves as able to produce 'First-Class Art Photography'.¹⁴ Joyce's 1903 concept of the photograph as able to be 'disposed for an aesthetic end [...] [but] not a work of art' (*OCPW* 104) was echoed in artistic and critical debate. In 1906, *The American Amateur Photographer* reported:

> The sculptor, the painter, the photographer, *they* may be artists and their works may be works of art, but if so, their work is artistic because they are artists, not because of their respective use of marble, paint, and dry plate. Art is in persons, not in things or mechanical actions.¹⁵

This acknowledgement of the mechanical nature of photography was shared by a columnist in New York's *The Photographic Times* in 1899, who proposed, 'Whatever subtlety of tones, of drawing, there are in the photograph, these are the work of a machine'.¹⁶ The aesthetic value of the image was to be attributed to the '*artist*' engaged in 'hand-work' or retouching, rather than the person operating the camera.¹⁷

In *Ulysses*, Bloom's photograph of Molly has been taken at Lafayette's, 'Dublin's premier photographic artist' (*U* 16.1435–36). The studio was founded by James Stack Lauder in 1880, after he was inspired by the success of his father's photographic studio. His business was located at 30 Westmoreland Street, next to his father's studio, Lauder Brothers.[18] In his choice of brand name and references to himself whilst trading as Jacques Lafayette, he sought to capitalize on the French origins of photography, rather than any French heritage.[19] He used 'Lafayette (Late of Paris)' in images and advertisements, seeking to invoke Parisian art culture and his training in painting in this city. He saw near-immediate success and in 1887 was awarded the Royal Warrant from Queen Victoria as 'Her Majesty's Photographer in Dublin'.[20] This was subsequently renewed by King Edward VII and King George V.[21] His popularity means that whilst Molly visits Lafayette's, she may not have been photographed by its owner. Bloom's '2 fading photographs' of Maud Branscombe and Queen Alexandra could have been taken by Lafayette (U 17.1778–79), since he captured images of the Queen during the late nineteenth and early twentieth centuries. These would not have been taken at their Dublin studio and instead would have been captured at royal households or locations. Bloom's image of the Queen could have been a photographic postcard. Queen Alexandra was photographed in her Doctor of Music Robes by Lafayette in 1885.[22] The image was registered for copyright as a picture postcard and by 1900 had sold 80,000 copies.[23]

In 1893, *The Irish Times* encouraged students of 'photographic art' to visit Lafayette's to 'inspect the beautiful collection of portraits which he is about forwarding to the Chicago Exhibition'.[24] Lafayette sent *c*. 125 portraits to the Chicago Exhibition, all 'with one exception [...] direct from life' and produced 'upon the exceptionally large scale of 35 × 21 inches'.[25] The images would have been hand coloured by a photographer's assistant, 'black, sapia, and Bartolozzi red, all being absolutely prominent'.[26] Sir James Clerk Maxwell introduced the principles of colour photography in an 1861 lecture, demonstrating how one colour photograph could be shown through use of red, blue and green metallic salts; these were included as filters with three photographic slides, which were then projected through three optical lamps to form one image.[27] His discovery did not begin to have practical use in everyday photography until the early twentieth century and the post-production, hand colouring of photographic negatives remained the cheaper, preferred option. In showcasing his fine art photographs, Lafayette sought to demonstrate that the camera could be used 'in skilful hands to produce true works of fine art as well as ordinary portraiture'.[28] His photographs were well-received and he was awarded 'Gold Medals' and 'enthusiastic commendations' from art critics and the press in London, Dublin and New York.[29]

Lafayette was at the cutting edge of photographic technology and used flash light photography to capture images of 'Their Royal Highnesses the Duke and

Duchess of Connaught and Price Arthur of Connaught' in 1902.³⁰ He combined photographic and artistic practices, carving ivory miniatures on top of printed photographs in 1904 and advertising them as 'a piece of really artistic work'.³¹ Lafayette's was not used exclusively for photography and in 1906, Mr. Sydney Rowley, a pupil of artist and film-director Sir Hubert von Herkomer exhibited oil paintings at the studio. Responding to an exhibition of his paintings, *The Irish Times* described how Dublin citizens could be 'content with the work of our own artists without going to the London and Paris studios'.³² The studio's photographs were reproduced in popular magazines, such as Gerty's choice of reading material, the '*Lady's Pictorial*' (*U* 13.151), who featured a photograph of the author, Hon. Mrs Henniker by Lafayette in their 23 June 1900 edition.³³ In 'The Corruption of Gerty MacDowell', Walter Kendrick argues that Gerty 'enters *Ulysses* already ruined, not by obscenity but by the kind of magazine fiction that is intended specifically for young women like her'.³⁴ Her other regular reading material is the 'Princess Novelette', which was illustrated, rather than containing photographs (*U* 13.110).

By the early twentieth century, the *Lady's Pictorial* (1881–1921) included photographic snapshots of couples, products, animals and sports teams, although pre-1904, photographs were predominantly used on their front cover. A special issue on 'Queen Victoria: In Memoriam' dated 2 February 1901 features an image of the Queen on its cover.³⁵ These photographs would have been produced using the halftone printing process. This printing technique was used very rarely but it was 'more in evidence in the "Lady's Pictorial"' from the 1890s 'than in any other journal of that date'.³⁶ Readers were regularly invited to send in their photographs to the magazine. These were often printed in 'News' items, such as in their 'Weddings' announcement feature.³⁷ In the *Pictorial*'s advertising supplements, women appear in photographs in corsets and petticoats in a variety of staged poses. A 1907 advertisement promises that 'Tailor-made Corsets, which are obtainable in upwards of fifty types at all prices [...] [will] suit slender, medium, well-developed, or extra full figures'.³⁸ These advertorial features are likely to have inspired Gerty's choice of 'finespun hose with highspliced heels and wide garter tops' (*U* 13.170–71), which prove pivotal in attracting Bloom's gaze to 'her every contour' (*U* 13.564). Joyce began the earliest surviving draft of 'Nausicaa' in 1919, so could have seen these images.³⁹ After Gerty considers Bertha Supple's story of a man who was found to have had 'pictures cut out of papers of those skirtdancers and highkickers' (*U* 13.703–04), she recalls that 'Winny Rippingham [was] so mad about actors' photographs' (*U* 13.712–13). Joyce's placing of these thoughts so close to one another mimics the pages of the

Pictorial, where advertisements for underwear and images of celebrated figures appeared in close proximity. This interplay between Gerty's narrative and the magazine's contents demonstrates Joyce's sustained engagement with consumer culture and the ability for photography to act as a coveted means of enhancing social status and aesthetic worth.

On 2 November 1907, Princess Alexander of Teck was featured on the front cover of the *Lady's Pictorial*, reflecting the magazine's intended demographic.[40] The periodical was 'aimed squarely at middle class women' and sought to rival *The Queen* magazine (1861–1970), a popular source of entertainment for keen royalists.[41] The magazine's subtitle, 'A Newspaper for the Home' is appropriate given Gerty's preoccupation with her ideal domestic space. Since she pays 'Three and eleven […] for those stockings in Sparrow's of George's street' (*U* 13.499–500), an 'an unusually expensive pair', she is likely to have been able to afford the sixpence purchase price for a standard edition of the magazine or one shilling for a special issue.[42] If finances proved more challenging, she would have been assisted by the increasing availability of reading matter during the early twentieth century, 'not only in the cheap press but also through school prizes, second-hand bookstalls, and libraries, including the early free public libraries'.[43] Having a photograph taken at a studio was aspirational and magazines advocating for the artistry of photography continued to market the act of being photographed as a popular and covetable pursuit.

As Mark Osteen has acknowledged, 'Buried in the lower-middle class, with limited education and little access to other sources of information, Gerty is precisely the kind of person most susceptible to advertising'.[44] Gerty owns 'A neat blouse of electric blue selftinted by dolly dyes (because it was expected in the *Lady's Pictorial* that electric blue would be worn)' but her blouse is 'selftinted' (*U* 13.150–51). Unlike Annie's 'pale blue summer blouse' in 'A Little Cloud' in *Dubliners,* which cost Little Chandler 'ten and elevenpence' (*D* 78), Gerty is forced to be inventive in order to obtain a similar item. Annie is photographed at a studio, but Gerty recalls that on her 'mother's birthday' they were to have had a group photograph taken, before Mr Dignam 'died suddenly and was buried' (*U* 13.315–18). Gerty adds a matching 'chenille' to her blouse which had been bought 'at Clery's summer sales, the very it, slightly shopsoiled but you would never notice, seven fingers two and a penny' (*U* 13.158–60). Annie possesses the item in its authentic form but similarly projects an image of herself via her clothing that is at odds with her economic and domestic situation. The 'dolly dyes' become a further means of Gerty visualizing her desired social status. Her movements as she poses with 'pretty lips pouted awhile but then […] glanced up and broke out into a joyous little laugh' see her position herself in a series of photographic tableau (*U* 13.125–26), designed to mask her fear that 'the years were slipping by for her, one by one' (*U* 13.649).

Joyce's 1917 notebooks and 1921 fair copies of *Ulysses* postdate Alfred Stieglitz's photo-secession movement, in which he advocated for photography to be recognized as a pictorial, art form. Stieglitz published and edited his *Camera Work* journal between 1903 and 1917 and devoted a special issue to Gertrude Stein in 1912.[45] This included her essay responses to works by Picasso and Matisse and photographs and drawings by Eugène Druet, Kahn Weller and Stieglitz.[46] Stein donated a copy of her special issue to Sylvia Beach's Shakespeare and Company bookstore shortly after their November 1919 opening.[47] Joyce could have viewed this issue at Beach's bookstore given his 1920 move from Trieste to Paris, although he is not formally recorded as having borrowed this work. *Camera Work* was not devoid of commercial photography and Stieglitz was reliant upon advertising revenue to fund his publication. Stein's special issue features advertisements for George Eastman's Kodak cameras and Kodak printed paper marketed at fine art photographers, along with an advertisement for P. & S. Semi-Achromatic Lenses informing the reader 'These are the lenses that make portraits that rival paintings'.[48]

Nude models were used in art photography from the mid-nineteenth century, as shown in Figure 3.1. In this image, the photographer captures a tendency in nude, art photography to utilize classical tropes, fusing Grecian-style imagery with drapery inspired by art and sculpture. Detailing the inclusion of A. B. Langfield's *c.* 1900 'A Greek Girl' photograph at the 1900 Philadelphia Salon, an image described as a 'quiet study of the nude in the open air', photographer and art critic, Joseph T. Keiley argued that he 'saw nothing distinctly Greek about the model'.[49] The title, he presumed, had been chosen to mitigate against criticism, since 'education and habit have accustomed us to associate the idea of nudeness with Greek art'.[50] Keiley noted the 'strong feeling against the making of pictures of the nude by means of the camera' but proposed 'Within proper limitations, the study of the nude in photography is desirable'.[51] Male models were usually used in classical art studies, but in a series of 1890's articles on the nude for *The Photogram* magazine, Victorian art critic, Joseph Gleeson White revealed 'An Irish amateur, W. H. A. Collins, has taken several excellent studies of the female nude by the rocks on the seashore, studies which have been publicly exhibited in the London Salon, and are wholly innocent'.[52] The magazine deemed the 'seashore with its curving line of beach, and its still more subtly rounded waves' best suited to complimenting the naked form, as opposed to 'woodland scenery or

Figure 3.1 Unknown Photographer, Draped Female Nude, *c.* 1855. Digital image courtesy of the Getty's Open Content Program.

but a few river-banks'.[53] Such locations were not devoid of covert photography and in 1898, the *British Journal of Photography* wrote, 'One often hears and reads of the "hand-camera-fiend" who "snap-shots" [*sic*] ladies as they emerge from their morning dip at the seaside, or loving couples quietly reading under a shady rock'.[54]

Alongside appearing in fine art photographs, nude models were often used as aids for artistic and illustrative studies. In 1893, Gleeson White wrote, 'photographs of the Nude are [...] not to be considered as pictures but merely as charts for references, or working drawings'.[55] These nudes provoked in the lower classes 'the most rooted dislike [...] Athletes and public schoolmen [...] [being] more broad-minded'.[56] Artists would not have mandated the use of cameras at studios but photographing models enabled them to better restage and return to compositions. Models photographed at art academies could not always retain control over their image and in 1931, artist's model, Mme. Viviane Cepa claimed £240 damages after finding a picture postcard of her posing nude for sale in Paris.[57] Though she had 'posed before many art students daily', she successfully argued that this did not give 'the photographer the right to exhibit her photograph to the public', with the judge ruling in her favour.[58] Responding to debates surrounding nude, artistic studies, Alison Smith reveals that 'While photographs of male nudes were accepted as a serious aid to academic study, female studies could not be so easily prised apart from the more debased uses of photography'.[59] Joyce was familiar with the erotic implications of artists' studios and references George du Maurier's *Trilby* (1895) in his work, a novel depicting the fate of Trilby O'Farrall, a half-Irish, artist's model who is hypnotized by musician, Svengali whilst working in Paris. In *Stephen Hero* (1944), published posthumously, Wells asks Stephen Dedalus 'had he read *Trilby*', before responding, 'Famous book, you know; style would suit you, I think. Of course it's a bit... blue. [...] Paris, you know... artists' (*SH* 68). Stephen considers, 'the young men in the college regarded art as a continental vice [...] really art was all "rot": besides it was probably immortal; they knew (or, at least, they had heard) about studios' (*SH* 35).

In *Trilby*, 'One of the photographs represents her in classical dress, with her left foot on a stool, in something of the attitude of the Venus of Milo'.[60] Joyce similarly fuses eroticism with mock displays of classicism in *Ulysses*, where in the 'Circe' episode, '*The keeper of the Kildare street museum*' drags '*a lorry on which are the shaking statues of several naked goddesses, Venus Callipyge, Venus Pandemos, Venus Metempsychosis*' (*U* 15.1703–06). After Trilby and Svengali's arrival in London, 'Her photograph' is described as being 'in the shop-windows' and 'in front of the windows of the Stereoscopic Company in Regent Street'.[61] Du Maurier satirized this visual and erotic spectacle in an 1888 illustration for *Punch* magazine, in which an elderly aunt is shown saying to her young niece, 'Ugh! When I was your age, Matilda, ladies of rank and position didn't have their photographs exposed in the shop-windows'.[62] Photographs were displayed in the windows of Dublin's photographic studios and Joyce's brother, Stanislaus recalls how after 'passing a photographer's studio' in their youth, he had commented on 'the *embonpoint* of the ladies pictured in the window' (*JJ* 134). Joyce transfers this comment to *Ulysses*, where Bloom looks 'away thoughtfully with the intention of not further increasing the other's possible embarrassment while gauging her symmetry of heaving *embonpoint*', after showing Molly's photograph to Stephen (*U* 16.1466–68).

Late-nineteenth- and early-twentieth-century illustrators for *Punch* magazine included du Maurier and Edward Linley Sambourne, the latter figure who had progressed to principal cartoonist by 1901. Joyce alludes to the magazine's illustrations in *Stephen Hero,* where Madden tells Stephen, 'No West-Briton could speak worse of his countrymen. You are simply giving vent to old stale libels – the drunken Irishman, the baboon-faced Irishmen we see in *Punch*' (*SH* 62). Sambourne began using photography to aid his illustrations in the 1870s, in part due to the tight deadlines involved at the magazine, where commissions were received on Wednesdays and final cartoons required to be returned by Friday.[63] He had members of his household act as clothed models and was himself photographed in costume, when his assistant would take the shot.[64] Sambourne was a passionate advocate for photography and one of the founders of London's Camera Club, whose portfolio includes nude and partially draped models. In *c.* 1887, *Punch* featured an anonymous poem including the lines, 'They will fly when they see me, and ne'er stop to chat, | For I carry a camera up in my hat'.[65] Sambourne's interest in the female form saw him capture furtive photographic street scenes of women using a handheld, detective camera designed to resemble a pair of binoculars.[66] In his composition of *Ulysses* and the *Wake*, Joyce was writing within a culture in which art photography and surreptitiously captured images of women frequently enabled the viewer to transgress societal norms.

The Post Office Protection Act of 1908 prevented indecent photographs from being sent by post and in 1909, Walter M'Intosh, of Rydevale Road, London was summoned to court for sending a postal packet containing offensive images and possessing 130 indecent photographs.[67] In prosecuting, Herbert Muskett described how M'Intosh had 'traded as the Fine Art Photographers' Publishing Company'; the majority of his business was found to be genuine but his catalogue also contained erotic 'stereoscopic slides' of 'artistic life studies; artists' model and [the] female figure'.[68] The defendant argued that the 130 images seized were only a small part of a larger stock of over 30,000 'artistic and unobjectionable' photographs but 'agreed to destroy the images and pay costs'.[69] For Joycean scholars, the surname of the defendant is likely to playfully evoke *Ulysses*' man 'in the macintosh' (*U* 6.805), who first appears in the 'Hades' episode composed in 1918, where he is incorrectly recorded by reporter Joe Hynes as 'M'Intosh' (*U* 6.895). Joyce may not have viewed the photograph as 'a work of art' but he recognized its value in being 'disposed for an aesthetic end' and merged art and photography in his own visual collections (*OCPW* 104). At his Triestine flat, he had on display three photographs of sculptures of women at different life stages by the artist, Ivan Meštrović, having 'cut them from a catalogue, sent them to be framed, and then inscribed his own titles below them' (*JJ* 381). He kept a 'photograph of a Greek statue of Penelope' on the wall of his Zürich accommodation, joking to Frank Budgen, '"she is trying to recollect what Ulysses looks like. You see, he has been away many years, and they had no photographs in those days"' (*JJ* 430).

Joyce engages with debates over the interrelationship between photography and art throughout his literature, including Pope Leo XIII's 'L'Arte fotograficà' (1867) in *Dubliners*, as analysed in Chapter 1 of this project and depicting Shaun in the guise of Jaun lecturing Issy on the dangers of posing 'in your nudies [...] [before] the usual bilker's dozen of dowdycameramen' in III.2 of *Finnegans Wake* (*FW* 434.43–435.10). In *Ulysses*, Bloom recalls his lack of 'complete carnal intercourse' with Molly (*U* 17.2278), with sexual intimacy instead occurring when he kisses 'the plump mellow yellow smellow melons of her rump' (*U* 17.2241). Despite his photograph of Molly signifying absence, his ownership and revealing of the image to others paradoxically enables the couple to maintain an element of corporeality, Bloom clearly having regularly carried this about given its 'slightly soiled' effect (*U* 16.1465). In situating Bloom as a 'bit of an artist', whilst portraying him engaging with Molly's image and pornographic photo cards, Joyce uses his protagonist to interrogate photography's aesthetic value and the erotic potential of more 'lowbrow' images. An examination of Bloom's photographic collection and nude, female models in *Ulysses* and *Finnegans Wake* (III.2) reveals Joyce's sustained interest in women and photography and his frequent situating of Molly as part of Bloom's trilateral, photographic fantasies.

'Lafayette of Westmoreland street, Dublin's premier photographic artist'

Bloom's photograph of Molly is the only image in *Ulysses* to have been purchased and obtained of one of the text's central protagonists. Milly has had her photograph taken by Mr Coghlan at his studio in Mullingar and 'Will send when developed' (*U* 4.402) and her presence is hinted at in the 'very picture' in Alec Bannon's locket (*U* 14.753–55) but no other images of the Blooms exist, bar Leopold's 'photo of the lady now his legal wife' (*U* 16.1440–41) and his 'indistinct daguerreotype' of his father and paternal grandfather (*U* 17.1875). The solitary nature of Molly's photograph enhances its significance, as does its 'slightly soiled' effect (*U* 16.1465), which has been caused by Bloom having carried it in his 'pocketbook' (*U* 16.1423). With a cabinet print measuring approximately 14 cm × 19.3 cm and the photograph of Molly being portable, this is likely to have been a carte de visite with a smaller measurement of roughly 6.4 cm × 9.5 cm. In 1902, a dozen cartes de visite cost twenty-one shillings at Lafayette's.[70] Bloom's image of Molly shows her:

> in the full bloom of womanhood in evening dress cut ostentatiously low for the occasion to give a liberal display of bosom, with more than vision of breasts, her full lips parted and some perfect teeth, standing near, ostensibly with gravity, a piano on the rest of which was *In Old Madrid*.
>
> (*U* 16.1429–32)

The musical items signify her role as a 'concert' singer (*U* 11.485–86), the image having been taken 'In or about ninety six' (*U* 16.1438). The use of symbolic objects in photography was common and Joyce was photographed at Lafayette's prior to his departure to Clongowes Wood College looking at a large photographic poster featuring images of college priests to mark this educational endeavour.[71] The importance of the '*In Old Madrid*' sheet music is revealed earlier in 'Sirens', where Bloom thinks of Molly's 'Spanishy eyes' and the couple having met in Gibraltar, when 'she sang. [...] Under a peartree alone patio this hour in old Madrid one side in shadow Dolores shedolores. At me. Luring. Ah, alluring' (*U* 11.730–74). The photograph's 'display of bosom' makes visible Bloom's recollection of the 'Bosom I saw, both full, throat warbling' (*U* 11.731–32) and contains a visible suggestion of eroticism not currently shared between the couple.

The image of Molly was taken whilst the couple were residing at Holles Street, Dublin, when Bloom had 'lost the job in Helys' and she was 'selling the clothes and strumming in the coffee palace' (*U* 18.561–62). By 16 June 1904, Bloom's daily earnings are roughly comparable to the £1 7s 6d now earnt by Molly per concert performance with Blazes Boylan.[72] With the couple having obtained the photograph during financial destitution, this image could have been arranged by a promoter as advertorial material for her role 'playing the piano in the coffee palace on Saturdays for a very trifling consideration' (*U* 11.485–86). Had the owners of the 'coffee palace' purchased a dozen cartes de visite, the Blooms may have been given one of these to keep. Photographs of celebrated figures proved popular in the early twentieth century and Joyce procured an image of the actress, Eleanora Duse after seeing her perform in London in May 1900; he subsequently kept this on his desk (*JJ* 77). Joyce saw Duse perform again in 1908, deeming her 'aged and broken' in comparison to the performance in his youth (*JJ* 226). He applies this notion of aesthetic transience to *Ulysses*. Bloom may think of his idea of having a 'gramophone in every grave', 'Remind[s] you of the voice like the photograph reminds you of the face' (*U* 6.966–67), but after showing Molly's image to Stephen, he recognizes that her image has become dated and considers, 'Besides he said the picture was handsome which, say what you like, it was though at the moment she was distinctly stouter' (*U* 16.1479–80). Unlike Little Chandler, who thinks of Annie's portrait, 'The composure of the eyes irritated him. They repelled him and defied him' (*D* 78), Bloom's issue is not with finding ugliness in Molly's image but instead in its inability to fully showcase his wife's beauty.

Given the Blooms' increased earnings by 1904, their decision not to obtain a more up-to-date image reveals Joyce's use of photography to highlight an absence. The visual medium is deemed incapable of capturing Molly's curves and Joyce imbues the image with a sense of photographic haunting in its evocation of the past. In 'The Dead', Gabriel Conroy is absent from the photograph of his mother and brother and thinks after his proto-photographic framing of Gretta, 'He did not like to say even to himself that her face was no longer beautiful but he knew that it was no longer the face for which Michael Furey had braved death' (*D* 223). Though his protagonists' lack of more recent photographs could be attributed to cost, Joyce's decision to focus on earlier, outdated images, from which those viewing them are absent highlights the sense of decline that he frequently ascribes to photography. After Bloom receives a letter from Martha Clifford, he wonders if it might include a 'photo perhaps. Hair? No' (*U* 5.80–81). Their correspondence heralds the possibility of erotic exchange, but a photograph is not included and with the Blooms having last had 'complete carnal intercourse' some '10 years, 5 months and 18 days' ago (*U* 17.2278–83), he is left to reflect of Molly's photograph, 'I was happier then. Or was that I? Or am I now I? […] Can't bring back time' (*U* 8.608–10).

One of the first street photographers, Jacques Henri Lartigue (1894–1986) wrote of his experiences with the camera, 'you can only rely on your own intuition and reflexes! The shutter must be an extension of the eye: ready to respond instantly to whatever attracts it.'[73] Recalling a lost opportunity to photograph a woman in 1910, he described how:

> She walks on, approaching, and the closer she comes, the prettier she is. She has rouge on her lips, although she's not on the stage of a theatre. She's holding a large muff, and has such a pretty face under her broad hat that the regret for a missed photograph begins to grow in me. It's more than a regret: it's something that makes me almost ill.[74]

Bloom shares Lartigue's fascination with the minutia of the female form and experiences regret when his observation of a woman 'Getting up in a minute' is thwarted by 'A heavy tramcar honking its gong [that] slewed between' (*U* 5.124–31). As he watches the woman outside The Grosvenor Hotel, he thinks, 'Stylish kind of coat with that roll collar, warm for a day like this, looks like blanketcloth. Careless stand of her with her hands in those patch pockets' (*U* 5.101–03). In his covert recording, he occupies an observatory position, his actions reminiscence of the scopophilic potential offered by handheld, detective cameras. Bloom's framing of the woman outside the hotel follows his explicit thought of Martha's letter and its potential inclusion of a photograph, where in the absence of an image, he is left to generate his own erotically charged scene.

Writing on the evolution of handheld 'detective' cameras, Sandra S. Phillips observes how 'The issue of privacy evolved as a pressing and common concern'.[75] This was a theme highlighted in 1887 by the French amateur photographic journal, *L'Amateur Photographe*, where a contributor described how 'Any person one meets could be photographed without suspecting it' and 'It is certain that the general use of this little camera could take some very bad turns'.[76] In an additional display of streetside voyeurism, Bloom recalls, 'Girl in Eustace street hallway Monday was it settling her garter. Her friend covering the display of. *Esprit de corps*. Well, what are you gaping at?' (*U* 5.132–35). With the introduction of new modes of surreptitious photography, scenes that would have previously remained unseen moved into the realm of public viewing, generating what Justin Carville terms the 'anxiety-inducing ocular exchange'.[77] Given that Molly's image has been taken *c.* 1896, she would have been able to enjoy Lafayette's updates to his studio, with an 1895 advertisement revealing 'sitters are now photographed by the "Snapshot" process, the exposure being reduced to the twenty-fifth part of a second'.[78] Outlining additional improvements in the same advertisement, they noted that 'extraordinary rapidity enables him [Lafayette] to dispense entirely with the offensive headrest, which in his Studios is now obsolete' and

Figure 3.2 Lafayette Photography, Queen Alexandra, 1902. Courtesy of Lafayette Photography, Dublin.

'For Outdoor Photography a qualified Artist is retained'.[79] Lafayette's claim to photographic artistry is evident in *Ulysses*, where Joyce acknowledges the studio's reputation as 'Dublin's premier photographic artist' (*U* 16.1435–36). Molly would have had to remain still whilst her image was captured but reductions in exposure times would have enabled a greater fluidity to this studio session.

Hidden behind the cover of the front page of their 11 March 1911 edition, *Photo Bits* magazine advertised the sale of 'Unique Snap Shots [...] [in a]

Splendid sample packet'.[80] The fact that they were to be 'sent privately' suggests their erotic content. Bloom may keep his 'erotic photocards' in a locked 'first drawer' but this appears to be a practicality, since his drawers are also filled with everyday items and more conventional 'photographs of queen Alexandra of England and of Maud Branscombe, actress and professional beauty' (*U* 17.1774–80). Despite the male, photographic heritage suggested in Bloom's father's '2nd cousin' Stefan having operated a photographic 'portrait atelier' (*U* 17.1876–77), his relationship with visual culture is frequently informed by his preoccupation with women, as in his encouragement of Milly in photography and his ownership of photographs. Given her status, Bloom's image of 'queen Alexandra' would have been taken by Jacques Lafayette, rather than another studio worker, as in the 1902 photograph shown in Figure 3.2. Lafayette took this photograph at Sandringham House, Norfolk, after he was granted the Royal Warrant. The image would have been available to purchase at his Dublin studio.

'He dwelt, being a bit of an artist in his spare time, on the female form'

Imagining his ideal 'Bloom Cottage' or 'Bloom of Flowerville', Bloom considers 'What syllabus of intellectual pursuits was simultaneously possible? Snapshot photography' (*U* 17.1580–89). He may not conceive of the photograph as a work of art, 'it simply wasn't art in a word' (*U* 16.1451–55), but it still holds merit for him as a perceived 'intellectual' pursuit in its commodified, 'snapshot' form. Bloom's subsequent list of 'lighter recreations' includes an 'Indoor: [...] lecture of unexpurgated exotic erotic masterpieces' (*U* 17.1599–1601). Unlike his 'lighter recreations', 'Snapshot photography' is deemed worthy of intellectual consideration comparable with the 'study of religions' and 'the celestial constellations' (*U* 17.1589–91). Joyce's use of 'Snapshot' suggests a gentle mocking of his protagonist, since by the 1890s, a 'snapshot' photograph typically referred to an image 'taken with a very brief exposure' or 'by an unsophisticated amateur, using a simple camera'.[81] In *Ulysses*, Joyce plays with the erotic innuendo of the 'brief exposure', with Milly referred to in conversation between Buck Mulligan and a young bather as 'Snapshot, eh? Brief exposure' (*U* 1.686) and Bloom imaging, 'Mutoscope pictures in Capel street: for men only. [...] Do they snapshot those girls or is it all a fake?' (*U* 13.794–96). The medium paradoxically functions as an erotic signifier whilst also denoting absence, as when Bloom considers his resemblance to 'the attitude depicted in a snapshot photograph made by Percy Apjohn' during a bedroom scene with Molly (*U* 17.2316–18), in which he also acknowledges their continued absence of 'carnal intercourse' (*U* 17.2283). Apjohn is a friend from Bloom's youth, who was later '(killed in action, Modder River)' at the Boer War (*U* 17.1251–52). His presence during the bedroom scene evokes a similar sense of haunting as that of 'Michael Furey' in 'The Dead' (*D* 223), where Gabriel thinks, 'The time had come for him to set out on his journey westward' (*D* 225). Rather than encouraging departure, the image of 'Apjohn' instead causes Bloom to turn inwards, his thought that 'He rests. He has travelled' (*U* 17.2320) seeing him draw closer to Molly, 'At rest relatively to themselves and each other' (*U* 17.2307).

Bloom's status as an artist is ambivalent. The addition of 'in a word' when he thinks, 'no photo could because it simply wasn't art in a word' (*U* 16.1455–55) adds an element of uncertainty to his aesthetic theory not evident in Joyce's Paris notebook, in which he writes, 'Therefore, it is not a work of art' (*OCPW* 104). This ambiguity over photography's aesthetic value is apparent in Bloom's wider, artistic contemplation, as when he reflects after viewing Molly's photograph, 'He dwelt, being a bit of an artist in his spare time, on the female form' (*U* 16.1448–49). The suggestion that he is a *bit* 'of an artist' is echoed in Lenehan's thought that he is 'a cultured allroundman [...] There's a touch of the artist about old Bloom' (*U* 10.581–83). Given that Joyce writes of Lenehan in *Dubliners*, 'Most people considered Lenehan a leech' (*D* 44) and 'his eyes made a swift anxious scrutiny of the young woman's appearance' (*D* 49), his ability to assess Bloom's artistry is rendered doubtful, yet Joyce adds these ambiguous quantifiers throughout these suggestions, 'in a word', 'a bit' and 'a touch'. In *A Portrait of an Artist as a Young Man*, Joyce copies part of his aesthetic treatise near-verbatim, describing Stephen Dedalus asking Lynch '*If a man hacking in fury at a block of wood make there an image of a cow, is that image a work of art?*' (*P* 180). In his Paris notebook, this question is recorded as, '*If a man hacking in fury at a block of wood make there an image of a cow (say) has he made a work of art?*' (*OCPW* 104). In transferring this creative query to *A Portrait*, Joyce removes the more ambivalent '(*say*)', granting his semi-autobiographical protagonist a level of aesthetic conviction not wholly assigned to Bloom.

Comparing himself to Stephen, Bloom deems his 'temperament' as 'scientific' and Stephen's as 'artistic' (*U* 17.559–60). In occupying a status as only as a 'bit' of an artist, Bloom is better able to enjoy his engagement with photography's erotic and aesthetic potential in the medium's more popular, commodified forms.

Bar the hallucinatory 'Circe' episode, he does so without the sense of shame Stephen experiences in his contemplation of his 'sootcoated packet of pictures', which he hides 'in the flue of the fireplace' (*P* 97). Reflecting on his 'packet of pictures', Stephen recalls how in their 'shameless or bashful wantonness he lay for hours sinning in thought and deed' (*P* 97). As an avid reader of *Photo Bits*, Bloom would have been able to purchase pictures of women via the magazine's advertorial pages, with these images, socially considered to be 'shabbty little imagettes, pennydirts and dodgemyeyes you buy in the soottee stores' still enjoyed by members of the public (*FW* 25.2–3).

'the inspired pencil of Lafayette has limned for ages yet to come'

Joyce skilfully parodies English stylistic prose in *Ulysses*'s 'Oxen of the Sun' episode, where he portrays Bloom as:

> that vigilant wanderer, soiled by the dust of travel and combat and stained by the mire of an indelible dishonour, but from whose steadfast and constant heart no lure or peril or threat or degradation could ever efface the image of that voluptuous loveliness which the inspired pencil of Lafayette has limned for ages yet to come.
>
> (*U* 14.1213–22)

As Fritz Senn notes, this reference to 'Lafayette' functions as a 'delayed identification', as the reader only later learns in 'Eumaeus' that Molly's photograph has been taken by 'Lafayette of Westmoreland street' (*U* 16.1435).[82] In the description of Molly's portrait, the word 'soil' reoccurs in different variants, as Bloom considers, 'In fact the slight soiling was only an added charm like the case of linen slightly soiled' (*U* 16.1468–70). The reader is again forced to act as detective, connecting the 'linen slightly soiled' with his earlier thought in 'Eumaeus' that 'candour compelled him to admit he had washed his wife's undergarments when soiled in Holles street and women would and did too a man's [...] if they really loved him' (*U* 16.716–19). As with Bloom's self-identification with 'Apjohn', Joyce further aligns his protagonist with the photographic image in 'Oxen', where his having been 'soiled by the dust of travel' (*U* 14.1218) foreshadows the 'slight soiling' of Molly's photograph (*U* 16.1468). In setting 'Oxen' in the maternity hospital on 'Holles' Street (*U* 14.1) and featuring both photograph and 'soiled' in 'Eumaeus' and 'Oxen', Joyce emphasizes the importance of the visual medium in highlighting a time at which, despite being 'on the rocks' (*U* 11.485), Molly was in 'the full bloom of womanhood' (*U* 16.1429).

In his use of 'shopsoiled' in 'Nausicaa' (*U* 13.160) and his descriptions of Gerty and her friends as 'seated on the rocks' (*U* 13.09), Joyce emphasizes the eroticism associated with Bloom's observation of women and the way in which this spans multiple characters. In Gerty's stance on the strand, she attempts to mimic the pages of her chosen magazines and present herself as 'a radiant little vision, in sooth, almost maddening in its sweetness' (*U* 13.511–12). Gerty and her 'girl friends' would have been able to read about the transformative potential of photography in the *Lady's Pictorial*, where in 1907, M. Blanchard, Complexion Specialist, Edinburgh advertised her face creams as able to replicate 'scientifically exact tintings, in all their perfection [which can only] be produced. By Colour Photography'.[83] Blanchard's declaration that her beauty products could rival the effects of hand colouring photographs highlights the popularity of photographic retouching at the turn of the century. Joyce's description of that 'voluptuous loveliness which the inspired pencil of Lafayette has limned for ages yet to come' (*U* 14.1221–22) further testifies to the ability for images to be edited and retouched. Reporting on the 1873 American Convention and Exhibition of the National Photographic Association, the *British Journal of Photography* described the local secretary ending with an impassioned plea: 'The public in the end [will] tire of and detest the falseness of so much touching. Nature, and not "*finish*," will be required of us'.[84] Concerns were raised about the effects of these techniques on photography, with the secretary arguing that it was only through a reduction in retouching that photographers could avoid mimicking 'the manner and tracks of painters or engravers' and 'become *artists* in [...] [their] own right'.[85] Lafayette was known for his illustrative style of photography but was criticized by exhibition judges in the late nineteenth century for 'over-retouching negatives', to the extent that his images occasionally 'lost their distinctive photographic quality'.[86]

Had Joyce had access to the July 1899 edition of *The Book Buyer: A Monthly Review of American and Foreign Literature*, he would have been able to read that the 'face' of *Punch* magazine, 'limned a little later by the inspired pencil of Richard Doyle, has since become familiar all around the world'.[87] Illustrator, Doyle was responsible for the branding of *Punch*'s front cover and his designs remained in use until the mid-twentieth century. Lafayette did not use the phrase the 'inspired pencil [which] has limned for ages yet to come' in their advertising but the studio was referred to in relation to 'limned', variously meaning to depict in painting or words or to illuminate. In a 28 February 1907 article in *The Irish Times* on 'Oil Paintings at Lafayette's', the reporter described paintings by artist, Mr. Sydney Rowley as 'likenesses [...] in each instance faithful. Some are better than others'.[88] They further noted, 'Mr. North's well-known figure and genial countenance are faithfully limned. [...] These portraits, we believe, were all painted in Lafayette's Studio.'[89] Joyce used *The Irish Times* as source material for *Ulysses* and published 'THE MOTOR DERBY: Interview with the French Champion (from a correspondent)' via Paris in their 7 April 1903 issue.[90] Since he was familiar with the *Times*, he could have reasonably taken his inspiration for 'limned for ages yet to come' and 'the face it was a speaking likeness in expression' (*U* 16.1444) from their 1907 article, as well as possibly drawing upon his knowledge of *Punch* magazine. In the sixteenth century, portrait miniatures were initially referred to as 'limnings'. These were small enough to be portable and were hand coloured, suggesting that Molly's photograph has also been retouched.

In 'Oxen of the Sun', Buck Mulligan prophesies that 'Kalipedia' – the study of beauty – should include:

> plastercast reproductions of the classical status such as Venus and Apollo, artist coloured photographs of prize babies, all these little attentions would enable ladies who were in a particular condition to pass the intervening months in a most enjoyable manner.
>
> (*U* 14.1254–56)

In portraying Mulligan associating the 'artist' colouring of photographs with 'plastercast reproductions of the classical statues' and deeming these capable of remedying 'infant mortality' (*U* 14.1240–41), Joyce satirizes the aesthetic status attributed to these items. Mulligan criticizes the 'revolting spectacles offered by our streets, hideous publicity posters' (*U* 14.1246), here suggesting the recurring motif of Marie Kendall, whose poster is variously: displayed outside 'Dan Lowry's musichall' (*U* 10.495), smiles 'upon William Humble, earl of Dudley, and upon lieutenantcolonel H. G. Heseltine, and also upon the honourable Gerald Ward A. D. C.' (*U* 10.1221–23), is stared at by a typist (*U* 10.380) and is acknowledged by Patrick Dignam, who notices 'the image of Marie Kendall, charming soubrette, beside the two puckers' (*U* 10.1141–42). In near-personifying the image of Kendall, and critiquing 'publicity posters' in 'Oxen', Joyce draws attention to the hierarchy of aesthetic value applied to photography in its popular, commodified forms.

Kendall was a well-regarded, music-hall performer. She appeared on the bill at the Empire Palace Theatre, Dublin in 1903 alongside 'Edison's Grand Pictures' of 'Trial Speeds in the Park' and 'Weighing Cars at Naas'.[91] These 'Grand Pictures' were not actually operated by Thomas Alva Edison and the Edison Manufacturing Company of America and the cinematic company brought an injunction against the Star Theatre of Varieties, Dublin, after arguing that their newspaper advertisement had been 'untrue and misleading'.[92] Master Dignam's description of Kendall as like 'One of them mots that do be in the packets of fags' (U 10.1142) attests to the way in which cigarette advertisers sought to capitalize on the erotic potential and visual allure of female models and celebrated figures in the late nineteenth century. Since the late 1880s, photographs of female celebrities were used in windows and stores of apothecaries' shops to attract passing consumers, before these were added to 'packets of fags' as a practical method of stiffening paper cigarette containers.[93] Cigarette cards were often produced in sets of collectable images and provided purchasers with a popular and affordable way of obtaining photographs. With 'mots' slang for 'loose women or prostitutes', their inclusion in *Ulysses* reveals Joyce's sustained engagement with photography in multiple, printed forms and his frequent eroticism of women via media.[94]

Bloom's pornographic photocards

In 'Circe', Joyce returns to questions of photographic retouching and 'artist coloured photographs', as the Nymph pictured in the Blooms' photograph of 'The *Bath of the Nymph*' (U 4.369) steps out of the picture and accuses Bloom of having 'bore me away, framed me in oak and tinsel [...] And with loving pencil you shaded my eyes, my bosom and my shame' (U 15.3263–65). In an exploration of the supplementary photographic material included with *Photo Bits* magazine between 1902 and 1909, Tess Marsh details the 'numerous photographs that appear during the years when the supplements were included' and their preoccupation with eroticized versions of classical motifs.[95] The description of the Nymph as having been 'shaded' with 'loving pencil' demonstrates the vogue for colour retouching of images and posits Bloom as the photographic artist responsible for her 'esthetic execution' (U 16.1436). Bloom is encouraged in his visual appraisal of the Nymph by his position as a proto-artist and, as with his preoccupation with Molly's 'opulent curves' (U 16.1447), it is her 'classic curves, beautiful immortal' he admires (U 15.3268–69). His desire for female 'curves' is further suggested in *Sweets of the Sin,* the romantic, semi-pornographic book that he purchases for Molly in 'Wandering Rocks', with which he pauses at the lines, *'Her mouth glued on his in a luscious voluptuous kiss while his hands felt for the opulent curves inside her deshabille'* (*U* 10.611–12). His reading yields a corporeal reaction, as 'Warmth showered gently over him, cowing his flesh' (*U* 10.619).

Bloom's image of the Nymph becomes near-synonymous with spirituality, as he reveals, 'I was glad to look on you, to praise you, a thing of beauty, almost to pray' (*U* 15.3267–78). After the 1859 Paris Salon, Charles Baudelaire decried the public's 'praise' of photography, writing:

> a revengeful God has given ear to the prayers of this multitude. Daguerre was his Messiah. And now the faithful says to himself: 'Since photography gives us every guarantee of exactitude that we could desire [...] then photography and Art are the same thing.[96]

Joyce may portray Bloom positioning the Nymph as an object of 'praise', but he is able to distinguish between 'photography and Art', noting of Molly's portrait 'it wasn't art in a word' (*U* 16.1454–55). Alongside his aesthetic assessment of photography, Bloom owns several pornographic photocards and is accused by 'THE HONORABLE MRS MERVYN TALBOYS' in 'Circe' of having 'sent me in double envelopes an obscene photograph [...] It represents a partially nude señorita, frail and lovely (his wife, as he solemnly assured me, taken by him from nature)' (*U* 15.1065–69).

The details of Bloom's 'obscene photograph' are revealed in 'Ithaca', where his 'first drawer unlocked' (*U* 17.1774) contains:

> 2 erotic postcards showing a) buccal coition between nude señorita (rere presentation, superior position) and nude torero (fore presentation, inferior position) b) anal violation by male religious (fully clothed, eyes abject) of female religious (partly clothed, eyes direct), purchased by post from Box 32, P. O., Charing Cross, London, W. C.
>
> (*U* 17.1809–13)

In 'Circe', Mrs Talboys' accusation that the snapshot of the 'nude señorita' depicts 'his wife' Molly, 'taken by him from nature' posits Bloom as the photographer of the '2 erotic postcards', paradoxically magnifying his erotic fantasies and fear of cuckolding. Molly identifies with Bloom's pornographic collection and considers, 'Im a little like that dirty bitch in that Spanish photo he has nymph' (*U* 18.564–65). In doing so, she combines thoughts of the Bath of the Nymph and the 'nude señorita' with her Gibraltar heritage, Bloom having previously asked Stephen after showing him her picture, 'Do you consider, by the by [...] that a Spanish type?' (*U* 16.1425-26). Joyce depicts the fetishization of exotic imagery, as when Little Chandler recalls 'what Gallaher had said about rich Jewesses. Those dark Oriental eyes [...] how full they are of passion, of voluptuous longing' in *Dubliners* (*D* 78) and Gerty thinks of Bloom, 'She could see by his dark eyes and his pale intellectual face that he was a foreigner, the image of the photo she had of Martin Harvey' (*U* 13.415-17). This vogue for the exotic was shared in Victorian photography, with Gleeson White arguing in 1893, 'In photographs we certainly find that the olive skins of Italy yield often a more pleasant picture than the dead white of the Anglo-Saxons'.[97]

Joyce presents erotically charged characters in *Ulysses* as interchangeable, as when Bloom mistakenly thinks of Charles Stewart Parnell's mistress, Katherine 'Kitty' O'Shea that she too, 'was spanish' (*U* 16.1413). O'Shea appears in photographic form when Henry Campbell suggests, 'She loosened many a man's thighs. I seen her picture in a barber's' (*U* 16.1355-56). In the late nineteenth and early twentieth centuries, American publication, *The National Police Gazette* was renowned for featuring 'sexualised women *without* their consent', in images showing them being 'peeped upon through keyholes, spied on in their bedrooms'.[98] In a postcard to his Aunt Josephine, sent from Trieste on 17 June 1920, Joyce sought to acquire a recent copy: 'As regards the gazette or police news or whatever the devil it is it was always on sale in low newsagents. You must be misinformed unless it is a brandnew regulation' (*LII* 471-472). Alongside a focus on 'manliness', the *Police Gazette* printed photographs of 'pretty dancing girls' and invited their readers to purchase pictures of 'Some great actresses'.[99] The newspaper is referenced in 'Cyclops', where the men in Barney Kiernan's are described as 'giggling over the *Police Gazette* with Terry on the counter' (*U* 12.1165-66). The magazine was typically available in male-only environments and subsequently became known as the 'barber's bible', as Joyce alludes to in 'her picture [being] in a barber's'.[100] Like Joyce's association of Marie Kendall with 'mots', his portrayal of Campbell commenting on O'Shea having 'loosened many a man's thighs' demonstrates his continued sexualization of women in photography. O'Shea's image is infused with eroticism and classicism, as acknowledged by Richard K. Bass, who notes that this line functions as a Homeric parallel of 'Helen [...] [having] loosened the knees of many warriors'.[101]

'May I bring two men chums to witness the deed and take a snapshot?'

Bloom moves from ownership of pornographic photographs to facilitating their production in 'Circe'. After Blazes Boylan tells him, 'You can apply your eye to the keyhole and play with yourself while I just go through her a few times' (*U* 15.3788–89), Bloom asks 'May I bring two men chums to witness the deed and take a snapshot?' (*U* 15.3791–92). This hallucinatory encounter makes visible Bloom's earlier thought of 'Peeping Tom through the keyhole' (*U* 8.449), a motif that Marco Camerani recognizes may have been informed by the 'through the keyhole' cinematic genre, which included 'movies based on the same plot: a peeping tom [...] peeps through the keyholes of different rooms discovering girls undressing – who are often aware of being looked at'.[102] As well as functioning as a cinematic trope, 'through the keyhole' films were used at mutoscope parlours, as acknowledged by Katherine Mullin.[103] This visual motif appeared across media in late-nineteenth-century art, in Moritz Stifter's *c.* 1890 oil painting, 'Erotica Keyhole' and Hans Zatzka's *c.* 1890–1900 painted series 'A Look through the Keyhole (Un Regard par le Trou de la Serrure)', both of which highlight the erotic potential of transgressing these private spaces. Bloom's request to Boylan that he 'take a snapshot' through the keyhole sees Joyce associate this motif with photography. The act of photographing the scene through the keyhole suggests Joyce's up-to-date knowledge of camera technology, since by the early twentieth century, photographers could capture images in a fraction of a second using handheld devices.[104]

Joyce refers to the erotic possibilities of snapshot photography in 'Telemachus', where Milly, as yet unnamed, is referred to as 'Snapshot, eh? Brief exposure' (*U* 1.686) and in 'Nausicaa', when Bloom wonders whether they 'snapshot those girls' for the mutoscope (*U* 13.795). Unlike Mulligan's vision of Kalipedia, where 'Snapshot photography' parodically functions as an 'intellectual' pursuit (*U* 17.1580–89), Bloom's engagement with instantaneous photography is imbued with pornographic potential. In encouraging him to apply his 'eye to the keyhole' (*U* 15.3788), Boylan enables his participation in this sexual scenario, albeit at an observational distance. Kimberly J. Devlin has acknowledged the men's mutual, erotic engagement, arguing that 'Bloom's vision also dramatizes the possibility that Molly and Boylan are very much aware of his voyeuristic presence, that they are watching him watch, that the viewing subject is also the viewed object'.[105] Bloom's ability to 'snapshot' the scene would have been enhanced by the popularity of detective cameras, which were marketed from the late nineteenth century as enabling photographers to capture 'that which seems unsnappable and which public exigencies often demand[ed] should not be snapped', albeit with varying degrees of success.[106]

The 1911 edition of *Encyclopaedia Britannica* owned by Joyce contains extensive details on the history and evolution of photography, including on the 'detective camera'.[107] The entry notes 'it was not until 1881' when 'rapid gelatin dry plates were available that T. Bolas brought out his "detective" camera'.[108] It further outlines how detective cameras were disguised as 'books' and 'watches' throughout the 1880s.[109] It was not unusual for court trials to include photography and in 1864, Irish Courts deemed photographs 'admissible in evidence', stating 'The photographer must prove that he or she took the photograph [...] [but] the person who took the photograph does not need to be a professional photographer'.[110] Amateur photographers could capture 'evidence' using detective cameras and in 1899, the Demon Detective Camera was marketed as for 'The artful maiden, the wily detective, the wronged wife [who] will all now collect damning evidence'.[111] In 'Ithaca', Bloom thinks, 'Divorce, not now. Exposure by mechanical artifice (automatic bed) or individual testimony (concealed ocular witnesses), not yet' (*U* 17.2202–03). Had Bloom pursued divorce from Molly by exposing her infidelity with Boylan, his case would have been strengthened by possession of photographic evidence, particularly a snapshot captured through 'the keyhole' (*U* 15.3788).

Joyce could have been inspired in his depiction of Bloom's keyhole scene by the contents of *Photo Bits*. On 11 March 1911, the magazine published a 'dainty snapshot' taken 'in the privacy of a pretty little maisonette not a hundred miles from Piccadilly Circus'.[112] The woman's pose in the photograph in a sheer swath of fabric is designed to enhance the titillation associated with the invasion of this domestic space.[113] Bloom's keyhole request situates him within a male-centric culture of covert photography and 'Peeping Tom' imagery, but Joyce subverts this gendered dichotomy by having Kitty, Mina Kennedy and Lydia Douce join him, rather than the 'two men chums' he originally requests (*U* 15.3791). This change in the gendered, power dynamic speaks to the way in which photography both aids Bloom's sexual fantasies and reminds him of his lack of marital intimacy. Initially, there is no indication that Bloom is actually able to look 'through the keyhole' and instead Mina Kennedy exclaims, 'O, he simply idolises every bit of her! Stuck together!' (*U* 15.3800–01), whilst Lydia Douce remarks that 'he's carrying her round the room doing it! Ride a cockhorse. You could hear them in Paris and New York' (*U* 15.3803–04). The keyhole view becomes a '*verbivocovisual*' spectacle (*FW* 341.18), in which Joyce's multisensory focus on the visual and auditory nature of the scene culminates in 'BOYLAN'S VOICE' and 'MARION'S VOICE' being heard through the door, as Bloom finally, '(*his eyes wildly dilated, clasps himself*)' directs 'Show! Hide! Show! Plough her! More! Shoot!' (*U* 15.3808–16).

'hell write about me lover and mistress publicly too with our 2 photographs in all the papers'

Molly accuses Bloom of 'always skeezing at those brazenfaced things on the bicycles' (*U* 18.289–90) and engages in her voyeuristic fantasies in private. Imagining a potential relationship with Stephen, she considers:

> besides hes young those fine young men I could see down in Margate strand bathingplace from the side of the rock standing up in the sun naked like a God or something and then plunging into the sea with them why arent all men like that
>
> (*U* 18.1345–48).

The possibility of capturing photographs in 'bathingplace[s]' was such that by 1893, a 'Vigilance Association' was formed in England whose task it was to thrash 'cads with cameras who go about in seaside places taking snapshots of ladies emerging from the deep'.[114] The Association typically focused on male 'cads' and their cameras but Molly's image of the men 'naked like a God or something' suggests her knowledge of the voyeuristic potential of this setting. After thinking of 'those fine young men [...] down in Margate strand bathingplace' (*U* 18.1345–46), she turns to photography and transforms her thoughts of Stephen into a fantasy of being publicly observed:

> Ill make him feel all over him till he half faints under me then hell write about me lover and mistress publicly too with our 2 photographs in all the papers when he becomes famous O but then what am I going to do about him though
>
> (*U* 18.1363–67).

Joyce's reference to the '2 photographs' connects Molly's sexual fantasies with Bloom's, recalling his very specific '2 fading photographs of queen alexandra of England and of Maud Branscombe' and his '2 erotic photocards' (*U* 17.1778–1809).

Molly's desire to have her private affairs made public is not new, as she thinks of her prior relationship with Lieutenant Mulvey:

> what I did with her beloved husband before he ever dreamt of her in broad daylight too in the sight of the whole world you might say they could have put an article about it in the Chronicle
>
> (*U* 18.827–30)

The first newspaper to be illustrated throughout with photographs was the *Daily Mirror* in 1904, and with Molly's relationship with Mulvey dating back to 1886, it is only in her later, imagined liaison with Stephen that photography forms part of this scenario.[115] Despite the absence of potential newspaper images, Molly makes use of 'Mulveys photo' in reality, including this in a book that she lends to Bloom so that he can see she 'wasnt without' (*U* 18.655–56). She recalls that her intimacy with Mulvey had been carried out 'in broad daylight too in the sight of the whole world' (*U* 18.828–29), yet paradoxically recognizes, 'the days [were] like years not a letter from a living soul except the odd few I posted to myself with bits of paper in them so bored sometimes' (*U* 18.698–99).

Molly remembers in her childhood, 'Im sure that fellow opposite used to be there the whole time watching with the lights out in the summer and I in my skin hopping around I used to love myself then stripped at the washstand' (*U* 18.920–23). Just as Gerty performs for Bloom's gaze, Molly fantasizes about being watched by others, albeit noting that she 'put out the light' when it came 'to the chamber performance' (*U* 18.923–24). In III.4 of the *Wake,* the presence of the 'man in the street' (*FW* 583.16) renders it possible that intercourse between Humphrey Chimpden Earwicker (HCE) and Anna Livia Plurabelle (ALP) viewed through their blind will be subject to 'Photoflashing it far too wide' (*FW* 583.15–16). Since the scene will 'be known through all Urania soon' (*FW* 583.16), Joyce likely anticipates these appearing in newspaper print. In I.3, Joyce reconfigures Molly's childhood memory of being observed by 'that fellow opposite' in his description of Luperca Latouche, who 'one day while dodging chores […] stripped teasily for binocular man and that her jambs were jimpjoyed to see each other' (*FW* 68.1–2). Where previously 'certain intimacies […] [were] lease to imagination' (*FW* 68.6–7), she now faces the possibility of being photographed, with the 'dodging' invoking Charles Lutwidge Dodgson, whose photography is explored in Chapter 4 of this project. Given the popularity of binocular-style detective cameras, the 'binocular man' hints at the presence of a photographer. At the turn of the century, W. W. Watson and Sons of London advertised their Stereoscopic Binocular Camera as the 'ideal' Detective Camera 'to catch native subjects in perfectly natural poses, without arousing any suspicion in their minds that they are being photographed'.[116]

'he said I could pose for a picture naked'

In 'Penelope', Molly thinks, 'The woman is beauty of course thats admitted when he said I could pose for a picture naked to some rich fellow in Holles street' (*U* 18.559–61). Bloom's suggestion that Molly 'pose for a picture naked' could have involved her sitting for a painter, rather than a photographer, but the interrelationship between photography and art was such that many painters still relied upon the camera 'to preserve records of their subjects, […] in lieu of tedious preliminary studies'.[117] In 1901 and 1911 Irish census records, only one Holles Street, Dublin resident is recorded as having an explicit, photographic connection, this being Mary Murray, whose occupation is recorded as a 'photographer's assistant'.[118] By 1911, several households of painters resided on the road, including John Deegan and Nealie Deegan at 4.3 and William and Annie Corcoran at 27.8.[119] Joyce portrays the Blooms as having resided on Holles Street in 1895–6, during a time of financial poverty in which he had 'lost the job in Helys and I was selling the clothes and strumming in the coffee palace' (*U* 18.561–62). Artists' models were often in a far more perilous situation and were 'almost always impoverished; their bodies often show the effects of child-bearing, malnourishment, and general neglect'.[120]

Female artists' models joined together in professional networks, seeking to progress beyond modelling into 'careers as dancers, actors, and even as artists'.[121] Professional artists' models resided in Ireland and the 1901 Irish census records Phyliss Sutcliffe and Frances Sutcliffe of County Antrim under this professional occupation.[122] More models would have gone unlisted, since this role was associated with social stigma and women were 'treated as little better – or even worse – than a prostitute'.[123] Joyce was aware of this preconception. In a 1900 review of Henrik Ibsen's play, *When We Dead Awaken* (1899), he notes of Irene von Satow, 'It will be considered by some as a blemish that she – a woman of fine spirituality – is made an artist's model'.[124] Women were photographed nude at art and camera clubs, including London's Camera Club, of which *Punch* illustrator, Edward Linley Sambourne was a member.[125] As Mary Ann Roberts has acknowledged, voyeurism was 'endemic' to the Camera Club's 'studies and is made obvious by the vast number of repetitions of poses by a variety of women, far in excess of those needed for reference'.¹²⁶ Photographers were advised to avoid choosing nude models with only 'one or two good points' and it was instead recommended that they select 'professional dancers, who were trained in the all-important question of balance, and in retraining a graceful pose'.¹²⁷

Detailing Joyce's manuscript changes between draft and print editions of 'Penelope', Luca Crispi describes how Molly's phrase, 'he said I could pose' initially appeared as '[he] wanted me to pose'.¹²⁸ Joyce's change between 'he wanted me' and 'he said I could' appears to grant Molly autonomy over the decision to pose naked, yet it is Bloom who is still in charge of this decision, generating another instance in which she is situated in his trilateral, photographic fantasies. In III.2 of the *Wake*, Joyce reimagines the possibility of Molly posing 'naked'. Appearing in the guise of Jaun, Shaun delivers a lecture to his sister, Issy, in which he cautions:

> But now reappears Autist Algy, the pulcherman and would-do performer, *oleas* Mr Smuth, stated by the vice crusaders to be well known to all the dallytaunties in and near the ciudad of Buellas Arias, taking you to the playguehouse to see the *Smirching of Venus* and asking with whispered offers in a very low bearded voice, with a nice little tiny manner and in a very nice little tony way, won't you be an artist's moral and pose in your nudies.
>
> (*FW* 434.34–435.9)

The 'Autist' or artist Algy is accompanied by '*oleas* Mr Smuth', with '*oleas*' suggesting the use of an alias and the presence of 'smut' or pornography. Joyce's reference to Algy as 'in and near' the city of Buenos Aires and their trip to the 'playguehouse' or playhouse recalls Frank's theatrical trip with Eveline in *Dubliners* and his desire to take her to 'Buenos Ayres' (*D* 31). The implications of this destination have been explored by Katherine Mullin, who reveals that by the late nineteenth and early twentieth centuries, the city was heavily associated with sexual trafficking.¹²⁹

Joyce's choice of title of play as 'the *Smirching of Venus*' attests to his continued association of visual culture with classical antiquity and eroticism. In the *Wake*, he builds on Bloom's admiration of the 'Shapely goddesses, Venus, Juno' at the 'library museum' (*U* 8.920–22) and his description of Milly as 'Venus Pandemos. *Les petites femmes*. Bold bad girl from the town of Mullingar' (*U* 14.1494–95). Jaun's warning that 'Autist Algy' may whisper 'won't you be an artist's moral' contains artistic and photographic possibility, as Issy is warned she could find herself posing before 'voluble old masters [...] plus the usual bilker's dozen of dowdycameramen' (*FW* 435.6–9). In Joyce's allusion to the painters 'hogarths like Bottisilly and Titteretto and Vergognese and Coraggio' (*FW* 435.7–9) and the 'dowdycameramen', he highlights the cultural moment in which he was writing, in which photographers utilized artistic tropes in nude photography to encourage respectability and attempt to evade prosecution. As with Molly's self-identification with Bloom's pornographic images, the appearance of Shaun as Jaun emphasizes the frequent interchangeability of Joyce's protagonists in their engagement with visual culture. Joyce may not have deemed the photograph 'a work of art' (*OCPW* 104), but this medium allows him to critically engage with its aesthetic and erotic potential, where it is 'woman [who] is beauty of course' (*U* 18.559–60).

4

James Joyce's 'Photo girl[s]'

James Joyce's relationship with photography was frequently mediated via women. In 1926 and 1928, American photographer, Berenice Abbott captured images of Joyce and his partner, Nora and their daughter, Lucia in her Parisian studio and at their home. In 1938 and 1939, Gisèle Freund photographed Joyce and his family in the same city. Freund's dissertation on French photography was published by Adrienne Monnier and in 1939, one of her portraits of Joyce appeared in colour on the cover of *Time* magazine. Freund's father encouraged her interest in photography and purchased a camera for her at aged fifteen. In 1935, Joyce procured a new camera for his daughter, Lucia, writing in Italian in a letter dated 29 September, 'I enclose a few rather wretched photographs and, by the way, you will receive from Mrs Curran (just now in London) a new camera which, I hope, will prove useful and enjoyable' (*LIII* 374). This purchase was likely intended to encourage Lucia's creativity and well-being, as although Joyce ended his letter, 'We are extremely glad to have the news of your progress' (*LIII* 374), this post-dated her 1932 act of violence towards her mother, one in a series of psychological episodes that would see her later permanently institutionalized.

Helen Laird Curran was unable to obtain a camera for Lucia since she had already left London's Euston Hotel, so instead he turned to Harriet Shaw Weaver, in the hope that she could obtain a 'fine camera' (*LIII* 378). This second appeal was successful, and Joyce wrote again to Lucia on 17 October to acknowledge receipt of her photographs:

> We received your post cards and the two photographs also, of you and of Miss Weaver. Thank you. Miss Weaver is always the same and as for you, you look as if you did not care in the least about the *terrestrial globe,* absorbed as you are in your reading and swinging. If only all the inhabitants of the above mentioned rolling ball were so peaceful!
>
> <div style="text-align:right">(<i>LIII</i> 377)</div>

Joyce's assessment of Lucia's photograph speaks to the way in which photographic interpretation is always subjective, the image hiding 'more than it discloses', despite the 'camera's rendering of reality'.[1] The reality of Lucia's situation is more apparent in his letter of 15 June 1934, where he writes again in Italian:

> I see great progress in your last letter but at the same time there is a sad note which we do not like. Why do you always sit at the window? No doubt it makes a pretty picture but a girl walking in the field also makes a pretty picture.
> Write to us oftener. And let's forget money troubles and black thoughts.
>
> (*LI* 342)

In *Dubliners* (1914), Joyce imbues this 'window' scene with this same sense of lethargy, as Eveline 'continued to sit by the window, leaning her head against the window curtain, inhaling the odour of dusty cretonne' (*D* 32) and is cautioned to ' – Look lively' (*D* 30). Joyce signed his letter to Lucia, 'Babbo', his affectionate family nickname and the Italian word for 'father'. In *Ulysses* (1922), Joyce similarly turns to the Italian language in his portrayal of Leopold Bloom's relationship with his daughter, Milly, where the first of his fictional 'Photo girl[s]' (*U* 1.685) writes to her 'Dearest Papli' (*U* 4.397), the latter word a play on 'paparino', the Italian for 'daddy'.

Milly is working as a photographer's assistant in Mullingar but by I.7 of *Finnegans Wake* (1939) has been transformed into the more aggressively minded 'Tulloch-Turnbull girl with her coldblood kodak' (*FW* 171.31–32). In also drawing upon knowledge of Lewis Carroll and reconfiguring his biography in his portrayal of Humphrey Chimpden Earwicker (HCE) and the *Wake*'s daughter figures, Joyce posits photography as hemiplegic, juxtaposing the more innovative tendencies of his 'Photo girl[s]' with the exploitation of young women behind and in front of the camera. Lucia was engaged in photography prior to obtaining her 1935 camera. She captured a series of images of her family in Ostend, Belgium during their 1926 summer stay and is likely to have taken photographs during the family's previous visit to Saint Malo, France in 1924.[2] In the first, detailed analysis of the Ostend pictures, Xavier Tricot highlights how those featuring Lucia would have been taken between 10 and 26 August, before she posted these to Sylvia Beach.[3] Images including Giorgio can be dated to between 5 and 12 September, due to his later arrival.[4] The earlier snapshots of Lucia were probably taken by Nora given Joyce's issues with his eyesight and the interchanging of mother and daughter as the photograph's subject.[5] Lucia's images reveal the family's familiarity with the camera, with one picture showing Nora and Joyce smiling wryly at their daughter and another capturing Giorgio ignoring his sister and continuing eating.[6]

The make of Lucia's camera is unknown but George Eastman's Kodak brand dominated the market at this time. In 1926, an Eastman Box Brownie No. 2 gift set could be purchased for nineteen shillings six pence at all major Kodak dealers, with this package containing a No. 2 camera, two spools of film, a portrait attachment and an album with mounting paste.[7] A single Box Brownie camera had retailed for five shillings since 1900. Noting the popularity of their devices in 1925 over a prior, twenty-year period, Kodak's London store announced the launch of their Baby Brownie camera, featuring a single lens, 'novel shape' and a 'definite "click" both at the instant of exposure and return of the spring release-lever'.[8] The 'click' of the camera recalls Joyce's reference to the stereoscope in *Ulysses,* where 'Click does the trick' (*U* 3.420). Despite competition from amateur photographers, working within the photographic industry remained a socially appropriate and viable career choice for women in the late nineteenth and early twentieth centuries. In 1901, a British occupational survey revealed that 100 women and 700 men were working as London photographers.[9] After publishing these results in *The Speaker: The Liberal Review*, H. J. Falk and M. G. Spencer described the field as 'particularly suitable for women, who have achieved much distinction in it'.[10]

Between 1915 and 1921, more than 100 women owned and directed photographic studios in London and elsewhere.[11] The *Irish Society and Social Review* responded by writing, 'In this profession women generally have more tact than men, and are quick to see and make the most of the setter's good points'.[12] They further commended the new trend of 'father and baby' pictures as particularly suitable for the 'touring woman photographer [who] [...] seems to have come to stay'.[13] Women working in Ireland's photographic industry at the turn of the century would have been predominantly employed in an assistant's capacity but individual, female photographers did achieve success. One of the most prolific in this field was Irish photographer, Jane W. Shackleton. Between 1885 and 1906, she took 'over 1,000 lantern slides and several thousand prints contained in 44 albums'.[14] Shackleton's images include photographs taken 'during family visits to Norway, Germany, Switzerland, Algiers, England and Scotland'.[15] In the 1901 Irish census, 268 women are recorded as working in the photographic industry.[16] By 1911, this number had increased to 301.[17] Conversely, the number of men in the industry increased from 497 to 673 during the same period.[18] These numbers should be treated with caution, as those who trained as artists but later took up photography were often only recorded under their first profession, whilst married women's occupations were frequently left blank due to omissions or the termination of their work after marriage.[19] Despite these limitations, the number of women in the photographic industry attests to a burgeoning field in which Joyce puts Milly and the Tulloch-Turnbull girl to work.

Victorian and Edwardian women would have been encouraged by the wealth of female figures championing photography. In 1886, Princess Frederica of Hanover opened the London Stereoscopic Company's Second Annual Amateur Photographic Exhibition, where 200 of their 2,000 works were produced by women.[20] Queen Alexandra's interest in photography served to increase the popularity of the medium; she acquired a No. 1 Kodak camera after they were introduced to the market in 1889 and was presented with a No. 4 Bull's-Eye Special by the Kodak Company in 1892.[21] She became Queen Alexandra, consort of King Edward VII in 1901. Given Joyce's reference to Bloom's '2 fading photographs' in his 'first drawer' of 'queen Alexandra of England' and 'Maud Branscombe, actress and professional beauty', he likely intended Bloom to have acquired the Queen's image after her change in title, dating this to 1901–4 (*U* 17.1778–79). Work by Princess Frederica and Queen Alexandra behind and in front of the camera reveals the multiplicity of ways in which women were engaging with photography prior to and during Joyce's composition of his 'Photo girl[s]'.

In 1913, the first colour photographs of Ireland were taken by the French, female photographers, Marguerite Mespoulet and Madeleine Mignon-Alba, after they visited the country as part of financier Albert Khan's 'Archives of the Planet' project. Mespoulet and Mignon-Alba's images reveal the strength of work conducted by women and the vogue for ethnographic images of Ireland, where foreign or wealthy photographers, or purchasers commissioning images on their behalf, captured 'local customs, labouring practices and rituals'.[22] Joyce hints at the use of ethnographic photography in *Ulysses,* where Milly 'On the duke's lawn, entreated by an English visitor, [...] declined to permit him to make and take away her photographic image (objection not stated)' (*U* 17.877–78). Joyce allows her to retain partial control over the distribution of her photograph, as when she later reveals, 'Mr Coghlan took one of me and Mrs. Will send when developed' (*U* 4.401–02).

Eastman launched his Kodak Limited Company in 1888. His lightweight and portable devices revolutionized the photographic market. Rather than visiting a photographers' studio, Eastman's customers could capture images on cameras pre-loaded with film. After the roll was finished, they sent their devices to one of Kodak's international factories, who printed and returned their photographs. Women were working for Kodak in Dublin from the mid-teens. The 1911 Irish census lists Catherine Brennan aged twenty-two as working as a 'Book Keeper' for 'Kodaks' in Dublin and Margaret Mary Leonard aged nineteen years as working as an 'Invoice Clerk' at the city's 'Kodak Branch'.[23] The women's office work is not unusual given that the professional photographic market was still dominated by men. Lafayette's posted nineteenth- and early-twentieth-century advertisements for women to learn 'Photographic Printing and the processes connected therewith' but they would have still been working for the studio's owner and principal photographer, James Stack Lauder, who operated as Jacques Lafayette.[24]

In the early 1900s, the Kodak Limited Company had six specialist branches in Ireland, England and Scotland, one of which was located on 89 Grafton Street, Dublin.[25] The Dublin store was initially operated by Hurman, Ltd. Distributors and opened on 21 April 1903. Hurman revealed their arrival in a 1903 advertisement in *The Irish Times*, in which they twice referred to the interrelationship between photography and art by marketing themselves under the headings, 'Photography: The Art of the Age' and 'The Art of the Age: Photography'.[26] In 1904, Eastman acquired their wholesale business and began working in Dublin as Messrs. Kodak, Limited, of 89 Grafton Street.[27] The brand were not shy about marketing and by 1928, their Grafton Street branch featured a prominent storefront with their brand name spanning the width of the building, as shown in Figure 4.1.

In a further appeal to the amateur market, the Dublin store included a long strip banner informing the consumer 'You can learn to use a Kodak in half an hour'. Joyce would have been familiar with this Dublin location, depicting Bloom as walking down 'Grafton Street, gay with housed awnings [that] lured [his] senses' (*U* 8.614) and Blazes Boylan interacting with 'The blonde girl in Thornton's' (*U* 10.299), the latter store at 63 Grafton Street. In Joyce's first draft of I.7 of *Finnegans Wake*, the 'Thornton girl' initially appears '*with her Kodak*' but by final publication, he had changed this to 'The Tulloch-Turnbull girl with her coldblood kodak' (*FW* 171.31–32).[28] His original conflation of the fruiterer and florist with the Kodak camera reveals his awareness of the physical proximity of the two Grafton Street stores and the visual potential of this commercial location.

In 1897, the word Kodak was 'sparkled from an electric sign in London's Trafalgar Square – one of the first such signs to be used for advertising'.[29] The brand's marketing techniques would have arguably appealed to Joyce given his use of 'how hath fanespanned most high heaven the skysign of soft

Figure 4.1 Unknown Photographer, Kodak, 89 Grafton Street, Dublin, 1928. Courtesy of the George Eastman Museum. Used with permission from the Eastman Kodak Company and the estate of Sam Campanaro.

advertisement! But waz iz! Iseut' in the *Wake* (*FW* 4.13–14). Here, the appearance of Issy as 'Iseut' reveals both the advertorial image and the presence of the text's central, daughter figure. Eastman's advertisements ensured his Kodak camera remained part of popular conversation and he introduced the Kodak Girl to his designs after deciding that a picture of a good-looking girl in a magazine would sell 'more than a tree or a house'.[30] He added her blue and white striped dress in 1910, which quickly became distinctive. The Kodak Girl appeared in illustrations, in photographs posed by models and at 'real life' events, such as the 1922 Brighton Carnival, where 'Kodak Girls' sat on a decorated cart.[31] The visual allure of Eastman's branding recalls Bloom's idea for the perfect advertisement, which he imagines would feature a 'transparent showcart with two smart girls sitting inside writing letters, copybooks, envelopes, blottingpaper' (*U* 8.131–33). Just as Joyce writes in *Stephen Hero* that 'The London public will flock to see anything new or strange' (*SH* 90), Bloom recognizes the consumer appeal of his advertorial campaign, noting, 'Smart girls writing something catch the eye at once. Everyone dying to know what she's writing. Get twenty of them round you if you stare at nothing' (*U* 8.133–35). Bloom's design is reflective of the long standing importance of women in advertising, both as visual attractions and prospective consumers.

In an 1891 article, London's *The Photographic News* described the difficulties faced by Prince George of Greece whilst on holiday in America, after he was 'pursued by 150 ladies, all armed with cameras, who persisted in photographing him, despite his protests and his attempts to cover his face'.[32] The columnist noted, 'This is really a social nuisance, which ought to be sternly repressed ... but who can effectually guard against the pertinacity of a lady photographer?'[33] The jocular reference to the photographer's 'pertinacity' highlights the increasing proficiency of women armed with their cameras. They were capable of capturing those who were 'cowardly gun and camera shy' (*FW* 171.33–34), leaving them to fear their image being shared 'far too wide' (*FW* 583.15–16). Modernist writers were quick to respond to the Kodak camera. In Alfred Jarry's short story, 'Passion considérée comme course de côte [The Passion Considered as an Uphill Bicycle Race]' (1894), he writes, 'It is not certain whether a female spectator wiped his brow, but we know that Veronica, a girl reporter, got a good shot of him with her Kodak'.[34]

Joyce refers to Jarry in *Finnegans Wake*, where 'They were plumped and plumed and jerried and citizens and races, and cinnamondhued' (*FW* 288.34–35) and 'He has novel ideas I know and he's a jarry queer fish betimes, I grant you' (*FW* 463.12). In 1899, a 'London Letter' in *The Western Daily Press*, (Bristol) revealed:

> The lady journalist was in full force [...] One young lady on a bicycle took snapshots with a Kodak, and females from the more enterprising suburban 'ladies; shops' made notes on the dresses.[35]

This conflation of the Kodak camera with cycling was enhanced by Eastman's 1897 Bicycle Kodak, which he advertised with the slogan, 'Nothing so fits into the pleasures of bicycling as photography.'[36] In *Jacob's Room* (1922), Virginia Woolf acknowledges the aggressive potential of the female photographer in depicting 'Madame Lucien Gravé perched on a block of marble with her kodak pointed at his head. [...] she jumped down, but not before Jacob had seen her'.[37] Like Joyce, Woolf was photographed by Gisèle Freund, to whom she dedicated an essay on the photography of her great aunt, Julia Margaret Cameron.

In I.7 of the *Wake*, the Tulloch-Turnbull girl's appearance amidst the conflict between Shem and Shaun hints at the presence of Issy in an alternative guise, putting photography at the heart of *Ulysses*'s and the *Wake*'s family units. Joyce's engagement with young girls and visual culture is not confined to the Tulloch-Turnbull girl and he draws upon knowledge of Lewis Carroll's photography of children to inform his literary association of the visual medium with his paternal motif. Lewis Carroll was the penname used by author and photographer, Charles Lutwidge Dodgson (1832–98). In a letter to Harriet Shaw Weaver dated 31 May 1927, Joyce responded to reader accusations that he had been 'imitating' Carroll in 'Work in Progress' by writing, 'I never read him till Mrs Nutting gave me a book, not Alice, a few weeks ago – though, of course, I heard bits and scraps' (*LI* 255). Genetic analysis by Viviana Mirela Braslasu has revealed that these 'bits and scraps' include Belle Moses's biography *Lewis Carroll in Wonderland and at Home: The Story of His Life* (1910). This text contains extracts from Carroll detailing his friendships with Alice Pleasance Liddell (APL) and Isa Bowman.[38] Alice proved the inspiration for *Alice's Adventures in Wonderland* (1865) and his subsequent *Alice* stories, whilst Isa played Alice in the text's 1888 stage adaptation.

In 1872, Carroll commissioned the building of a glass-structured, photographic studio on the roof of his Christ Church College, University of Oxford accommodation, in the grounds of the Great Quadrangle. As in the image of Xie (Alexandra) Kitchin and her siblings shown in Figure 4.2, Carroll sought to capitalize on play and childhood fantasy in his photography by using costumes and toys to enhance his photographic composition. Writing to Sylvia Beach from London on 25 April 1931, Joyce revealed, 'I have lost the book in which I made all my notes for the children's games. Will you please look and if you find it forward registered. I sent you back the book on L. Carroll'.[39] This book could have been Isa Bowman's *The Story of Lewis Carroll, Told for Young People by the Real Alice in Wonderland* (1899) or Carroll and Collingwood's *The Life and Letters of Lewis Carroll* (1898), both of which Joyce borrowed from

Figure 4.2 Lewis Carroll, Saint George and the Dragon, 1875. Digital image courtesy of the Getty's Open Content Program.

Sylvia Beach's Shakespeare and Company, Parisian bookstore on 16 February 1928.[40] Joyce would have been able to consult other major Carrollian works at their store, since their collection also included *Alice's Adventures in Wonderland* (1865), *Phantasmagoria and Other Poems* (1869), *Through the Looking-Glass, and What Alice Found There* (1871), *The Hunting of the Snark* (1876), *Sylvie and Bruno* (1899), and *A Selection from the Letters of Lewis Carroll (The Rev. Charles Lutwidge Dodgson) to His Child-Friends, Together with 'Eight of Nine Wise Words About Letter-Writing'* (1933).[41]

In the same month in which he borrowed Bowman's autobiography and *The Life and Letters of Lewis Carroll*, Joyce published an early draft of what would become II.2 in *transition* journal, where Dolph 'would, so prim, and pick upon his ten ordinailed ungles, retelling humself by he math hour [...] the charmhim girlalove [...] and filthily with bag from Oxatown'.[42] The influence of his source material is apparent, as Bowman had described Carroll referring to himself as 'uncle' and noted his 'great distinction as a scholar of mathematics' whilst studying and later working at the University of Oxford.[43] Carroll's visual work has been much debated outside the context of Victorian art photography, where children were photographed nude in art studies, such as by Carroll's contemporary, Julia Margaret Cameron. His images of children comprise about 50 per cent of his total portfolio and curators such as Diane Waggoner suggest that his work is best understood as an obsessive desire to visualize Romantic ideals of childhood and spiritual purity.[44] Nevertheless, Waggoner also argues that in his attempts to present nude and partially dressed girls as having 'nonsexual bodies that could only be looked at innocently', Carroll must have recognized the 'possibility – and danger – of the erotic'.[45]

Critics have previously explored Milly's role as a photographer's assistant in *Ulysses* but predominantly in relation to her aesthetic function and her relationship with Alec Bannon, rather than via the historicist context of amateur and professional photographic opportunities for women. Joseph Valente argues that Milly represents 'the medium of amorous commerce between Bannon and herself and between Molly'.[46] Jennifer Wicke equates Milly 'with the image rather than the image maker' and suggests that she displays a 'lack of agency in the world'.[47] Katherine Mullin recognizes the importance of George Eastman's Kodak brand to *Ulysses* and compares Milly to Eastman's Kodak Girls 'who brandished cameras in their distinctive blue and white striped costumes and daringly shortened skirts, were flirtatious, adventurous and spirited heroines of modern life'.[48] This chapter acknowledges Milly's visual function and the aesthetic appeal Joyce frequently ascribes to her character but situates her in relation to late-nineteenth- and early-twentieth-century Irish and Triestine photographic culture. Fewer critics have considered the 'Tulloch-Turnbull girl' (*FW* 171.31–32). William Anastasi notes her similarities to Jarry's Veronica and Susan Brienza approaches her character via an exploration of Shem.[49] This is unsurprising given her appearance in I.7, the text's Shem chapter yet Joyce's sustained engagement with women photographers renders her camerawork worthy of additional consideration, particularly since she is working in the same industry as Milly.

Joyce's choice of career for Milly was inspired by his youthful visits to Mullingar with his father and the emergence of the playful, female photographer in popular advertising and the press. In examining Milly in relation to the Triestine female photographers Marion and Wanda Wulz, who inherited their father's studio in 1928, new light is shed on Triestine photography and the relationship between this visual medium and familial duty. By *Finnegans Wake*, Joyce has transformed Milly into the dogged 'Tulloch-Turnbull girl with her coldblood kodak' (*FW* 171.31–32), in a move reflecting his continued interest in this subject. Through genetic analysis, Viviana Mirela Braslasu has revealed the multiplicity of ways in which Belle Moses's biography informs 'The Hen' episode in I.5 of the *Wake*.⁵⁰ She further acknowledges that Joyce may have taken the description of the 'national apostate' as 'camera shy' from Moses's account of Lewis Carroll.⁵¹ Joyce's use of Carroll as a photographic motif in I.3, I.5 and II.2 of the *Wake* allows him to imbue his portrayal of the paternal relationship with suggestions of impropriety. His turn towards Carroll's photography and position as an 'old old old gentleman' in relation to 'Alys' (*FW* 57.25) and 'Isa' (*FW* 226.4) sees him play with the double entendre of the photographic 'exposure' (*FW* 57.24) and build upon the eroticism he also associates with Milly and the Tulloch-Turnbull girl. Hemiplegia is the paralysis of one side of the body and is fundamental to Joyce's intention with *Dubliners* (1914) to 'betray the soul of that hemiplegia or paralysis which many consider a city' (*LI* 55). In *Ulysses* and the *Wake*, Joyce posits his 'Photo girl[s]' as hemiplegic, depicting them as engaging in new, technological work and of critical importance to their family units but still hyper-sexualized and mediated via men.

'I am getting on swimming in the photo business now'

In 1900 and 1901, Joyce assisted his father in updating Mullingar's electoral records, where he encountered Phil Shaw's photographic shop, in which 'he would put Milly Bloom to work' (*JJ* 78). In the 1901 Irish Census, Ethel Shaw aged seventeen years is recorded as working as a 'Photographic assistant' in Mullingar, likely inspiring Joyce's depiction of Milly.⁵² As well as taking photographs, Phil Shaw sold stationery and 'Rosary Beads, Prayer Books, Statues, Scapulars, Religious Pictures and Books'.⁵³ His studio was located on Earl Street, now known as Pearse Street, in the centre of Mullingar. Shaw engaged in traditional modes of photography and photographed clients outside. In a 1900's advertisement, he offers 'appointments for photographing out-door subjects […] at client's homes anywhere within 10 miles of Mullingar, or near Railway Station'.⁵⁴ This ten-mile radius is not insignificant and could have included appointments at 'Lough Owel', as well as travel to Mullingar's neighbouring villages (*U* 4.403). Had Milly worked at a similar shop, she would have been required to assist the principal photographer with the taking and development of photographs. She could have also carried out hand colouring or the 'artstouchups' of images (*FW* 171.27) and managed the shop with Mrs Coghlan whilst Mr Coghlan was elsewhere. Richard Ellmann describes Mullingar as 'much more provincial than Dublin and Cork, the only parts of the country that James so far knew' (*JJ* 77). This concept is apparent in *Stephen Hero* (1944), written roughly between 1904 and 1906 and published posthumously, where Joyce describes Nash telling Stephen, 'Mullingar was the last place God made, a God-forgotten hole' (*SH* 214).

Milly's earnings are revealed to be 'Twelve and six a week', which Bloom considers is 'Not much. Still, she might do worse' (*U* 4.425). Detailing women's photographic earnings in 1873, photographer Cornelius Jabez Hughes outlined the three types of women that typically found work; these were the 'maid-of-all-work' class, the 'shopwoman' class and the 'governess' class.[55] The earnings of the 'maid-of-all-work' typically stood at 'ten to fifteen shillings per week', whilst the salary of the 'shopwoman' varied between 'fifteen to thirty shillings per week'.[56] Given that Milly is in her first professional role with wages in the 'maid-of-all-work' category, it is reasonable to presume that she could have increased her earning potential given appropriate time and mentorship. In his analysis of the economy of *Ulysses*, Mark Osteen notes that Milly 'makes a bit more than £2 14s per month; by comparison, Stephen, a male seven years her senior with a college degree, earns just over 16s 6d per week'.[57] This is less than the 'eighteen bob a week' earnt by the barmaids of 'Sirens' (*U* 11.1076–77) but 'Twelve and six' is still a substantial amount, especially given that women's earnings often stood on par with children's or apprentices' wages.[58] Unlike Stephen, Milly is not expected to share her income with her family and would have been able to comfortably manage in Mullingar in the lodgings of her employer. Bloom has had the foresight to consider her financial situation in case of death or emergency, carefully stowing away 'an endowment assurance policy of £500 in the Scottish Widows' Assurance Society, intestated Millicent (Milly) Bloom, coming into force at 25 years' (*U* 17.1855–87). With no financial dependents, Milly's professional role would have allowed her to enjoy her earnings, after likely contributing to or having money deducted for rent.

Molly notes Bloom's paternal connections to photography but deems his choice of profession for their daughter to have been influenced by her 'flirting too with Tom Devans two sons' (*U* 18.1023–24). She also ascribes this decision to his growing awareness of her relationship with Blazes Boylan, acknowledging, 'only hed do a thing like that all the same on account of me and Boylan thats why he did it [...] I couldnt turn round with her in the place lately unless I bolted the door first' (*U* 18.1007–10). There is an irony to be found in Bloom having secured a position for Milly that grants her the ability to potentially capture images of her mother's indiscretions. Reflecting on Milly's departure, Molly thinks, 'Lord knows still its the feeling especially now with Milly such an idea for him to send the girl down there to learn to take photographs on account of his grandfather' (*U* 18.1003–05). Whilst she is sceptical of his choice to send her to Mullingar 'to learn to take photographs [...] instead of sending her to Skerrys academy where shed have to learn' (*U* 18.1005–06), her choice of verb in 'to learn to take photographs' indicates that Milly is acquiring the technical skills needed to capture photographic images, rather than only assisting in pre- or post-developmental stages. Molly considers that the move had been 'on account of his grandfather' but Bloom's 'daguerreotype' of his father and grandfather has actually been taken at the 'portrait atelier of their (respectively) 1st and 2nd cousin' (*U* 17.1875–77), suggesting either her inaccurate recall or an alternative family connection. The daguerreotype was an early form of photography using a silver-coated plate in the 1840s–60s, in which each image was unique and could only be reproduced by redaguerreotyping the original photograph.

At fifteen years old, Milly has surpassed the end of her schooling, as in 1892, education was only enforced for children aged six to fourteen years.[59] With Bloom having secured a position for her at Mr Coghlan's, Milly forges an alternative career pathway outside of the domestic stagnation that Joyce frequently associates with his Dublin protagonists. Despite the significance of her work and central place within her family unit, Milly never physically enters the text, bar her phantasmagoric appearance in 'Circe'. Instead, she is introduced via other characters and epistolary interludes. In the 'Calypso' episode, Bloom receives a letter from Milly. Her account of her time in Mullingar mimics the playful language used by Eastman in a 1921 advertisement for the Kodak Girl, in which the advertorial figure is pictured holding her camera above a typed letter to her father reading:

Dear old Dad,

Thanks ever so much for your long letter! Of course I can use the Kodak you gave me – anybody could! Here are some of my pictures – one of our cottage with tea ready in the garden and another of us all off for a bathe. The other two are of a picnic lunch we had at the foot of the cliffs – isn't the snapshot of mother jolly? Now do leave your stuffy old office and come down here!

Your loving daughter,
Betty.[60]

The advertisement appeared in *Punch*, *The Sphere*, *The Graphic*, *Tatler* and *The Belfast News-Letter* and is likely to have also featured in other publications.[61] Joyce had completed the 'Calypso' episode by 1918 and although Eastman's advertisement postdates this composition, they share a whimsical tone and focus on photographic activity attesting to the prevalence of the female photographer in visual culture. Skimming Milly's letter, Bloom reads, 'Thanks: new tam: Mr Coghlan: lough Owel picnic: young student: Blazes Boylan's seaside girls' (*U* 4.281–82). Rather than 'Dear old Dad', Milly addresses her correspondence to 'Dearest Papli' (*U* 4.397), a play on the Italian word for 'father'.

Milly and the Kodak Girl open their letters in conventional format by thanking their fathers for their gifts and letters, respectively. Just as Betty sends her father some of her 'pictures', so too does Milly reveal, 'Mr Coghlan took one of me and Mrs. Will send when developed' (*U* 4.401–02). In Eastman's advertisement, the Kodak Girl is depicted playfully raising her leg as she gazes out to sea at the forefront of the image.[62] The advertisement deliberately plays with multiple aspects of 'looking', the coy bend of her leg and the billowing of her dress designed to heighten her aesthetic appeal. In her account of the history of the Kodak Girl, Nancy Martha West argues that her 'amateur status rested in part on a traditional association between woman and child – on the presumed delicacy and tenderness of woman as the preservation of an infantile constitution'.[63] At the age of fifteen, Milly is similarly transitioning between childhood and womanhood, as recognized by Molly when she recalls telling her daughter 'not to cock her legs up like that on show on the windowsill before all the people passing' (*U* 18.1035–36). After reading Milly's letter, Bloom similarly thinks, 'A wild piece of goods. Her slim legs running up the staircase. Destiny. Ripening now' (*U* 4.430–31). Despite the advertisement's focus on her visual appeal, the Kodak Girl is shown using a sophisticated, high-end camera, holding what appears to be a No. 1A Autographic Kodak Special with a retractable folding shutter and speeds of 1/300 of a second. Joyce's 'Photo girl[s]' exist within this paradox of aesthetic allure and technological focus, as in his repeated play with the sexual innuendo of the photographic 'exposure' (*U* 1.686).

Milly would have performed a visual purpose in her work in marketing photography to others. She does this to apparent success, as she writes, 'We did great biz yesterday' (*U* 4.402). The 'Betty' of Eastman's advertisement enjoys a 'picnic lunch' at the 'foot of the cliffs', whilst Milly writes that they were 'going to lough Owel [...] with a few friends to make a scrap picnic' (*U* 4.403–04). With Milly travelling 'to lough Owel' (*U* 4.403) and the advertorial Kodak Girl occupying a space by the seaside, the women share in a sense of liberation associated with these waterside settings. As handheld cameras increased in popularity, seaside locations provided the public with new and dynamic photographic spaces. Amateur photographers capturing images could display these at home, send these as picture postcards from the early twentieth century or add their snapshots to photographic albums, as in the 1880-1890's 'World Tour' album taken using Kodak cameras shown in Figure 4.3. Reporting on the early-twentieth-century trend for capturing photographs at holiday locales, a Birmingham newspaper described how 'Thousands of Birmingham girls are scattered about the holiday resorts of Britain. [...] The girls snapshot their sweethearts, the young married women take their young hopefuls'.[64] Joyce was aware of the vogue for snapshot photography and depicts Bloom in 'Lestrygonians' as imagining that his fantasy world of 'Bloom of Flowerville' would contain a 'syllabus of intellectual pursuits' including 'Snapshot photography' (*U* 17.1588-89).

As Bloom thinks of Milly's childhood and that 'day round the Kish', he recalls 'Her pale blue scarf loose in the wind with her hair. *All dimpled cheeks and curls, | Your head it simply swirls*' (*U* 4.435-38). Bloom's italicized interjection is taken from Harry B. Norris's 1898 'Seaside Girls' song, a musical motif interspersed throughout *Ulysses*. In Norris's song, the girls are presented as objects of titillation, as 'The boys observe the latest thing in socks'.[65] Like Norris's 'Seaside

Figure 4.3 Herbert Bell, Amateur World Tour Album, Taken with Early Kodak Cameras, Plus Purchased Travel Photographs by Various Photographers, *c*. 1880-90. Digital image courtesy of the Getty's Open Content Program.

Girls', Eastman's Kodak Girls were designed to have a tantalizing effect on the observer. Public responses included poetry and in 1902, William E. S. Fables published 'Poem – The Kodak Girl', in which he writes, 'her dainty ankles make your senses whirl | [...] How I hope that in her glee | She has had a shot at me'.[66] Fables captures the contradictory expectation that the Kodak Girl appear both powerful and aggressive and 'delicate and sweet', retaining control of her camera whilst simultaneously avoiding the predatory nature of 'a man [...] | [Who] Would go far to clasp her waist'.[67] Like Veronica in 'The Passion Considered as an Uphill Bicycle Race' or Madame Lucien Gravé in *Jacob's Room*, the Kodak Girl of Fables' poem is engaged in the dogged pursuit of a photographic snapshot, yet as with Eastman's advertisement, her technological potential is inseparable from her visual appeal.

Milly, Alec Bannon and 'a locket that hung from a silk riband'

Milly associates Norris's 'Seaside Girls' song with romance and writes to her father:

> There is a young student comes here some evenings named Bannon his cousins or something are big swells and he sings Boylan's (I was on the pop of writing Blazes Boylan's) song about those seaside girls.
>
> (*U* 4.406–09)

Joyce uses the eroticism between Molly and Boylan to hint at the possibility of intimacy between Milly and Alec Bannon. The only image to have been printed of Milly exists in the 'Oxen of the Sun' episode, where in Joyce's play on English stylistic prose, Bannon wears 'a locket that hung from a silk riband, that very picture which he had cherished ever since her hand had wrote therein' (*U* 14.754–55). Joyce used Laurence Sterne's *A Sentimental Journey through France and Italy* (1766) as his inspiration for Bannon's locket.[68] With Sterne's text predating the 1839 public launch of photography, the image around Yorick's neck is inevitably not photographic but this possibility exists in *Ulysses* given Milly's professional role. Had the picture been a photograph, Margot Norris argues that there could have 'conceivably have been time for the photo to be developed, inserted into a locket, and brought by Bannon to Dublin from Mullingar'.[69]

The exchanging of miniature photographs proved a popular Victorian and Edwardian pastime, enhanced by Queen Victoria's decision to gift onyx pendant lockets and watches containing images of herself and her husband, Prince Albert to their relatives.[70] In 1907, readers of the *Irish Times* could call into the newspaper's 31 Westmoreland Street, Dublin office, 'to review their collection of photographic miniatures mounted as a brooch (3s. 1d. Postage 2d.) or pendant (1s. 6d. Postage 2d.)' which were finished 'in the highest style of water-colour art'.[71] Had Milly's picture been a photographic miniature, this use of her image is significant, since no other photographs exist of her elsewhere despite her occupation. Milly tells her father that 'Mr Coghlan took one of me and Mrs. Will send when developed' (*U* 4.401–02) but she has not yet been able to develop and send him the photograph. Instead, as Bloom tells Mrs Breen about her 'position down in Mullingar, you know' (*U* 8.206–07), he is reliant on her epistolary account, rather than a photographic portrait.

In *A Sentimental Journey*, Sterne's protagonist, Yorick reflects on his love life, 'It had ever, as I told the reader, been one of the singular blessings of my life, to be almost every hour of it miserably in love with some one'.[72] In turning to the locket, he thinks, 'I look'd at the picture she had tied in a black riband about my neck, – and blush'd as I look'd at it. – I would have given the world to have kiss'd it, – but was ashamed'.[73] Given that Yorick has already reproached himself for deciding to travel on to Brussels to meet Madame de L-, rather than the Eliza of his locket, his desire to have 'kiss'd' it is imbued with a sense of comedic shame, rather than revealing real depth of feeling. Joyce renders the power dynamics between Milly and Bannon similarly questionable. There is no mention of Milly reciprocating Bannon's actions and possessing his photograph and Joyce only briefly refers to her as having broken her 'amberoid necklace' as a child (*U* 4.285). Milly is unable to control the way in which her character is re-appropriated in *Ulysses*'s narrative but her decision to send Bannon her picture allows her to initially regulate the way in which she is viewed by others.

Joyce utilized photography in his pursuit of Nora Barnacle, writing to her in a letter dated 1 November 1909:

> You are a sad little person and I am a devilishly melancholy fellow myself so that ours is a rather mournful love I fancy. Do not cry about that tiresome young gentleman in the photograph [Joyce]. He is not worth it, dear.
>
> (*JJ* 305)

The couple were separated in Ireland and Trieste at the time, with Joyce's inclusion of a 'photograph' encouraging their courtship and flirtation. In Milly and Bannon's union, her 'picture' performs an equally intimate function. Reflecting on his daughter's relationship, Bloom considers, 'O, well: she knows how to mind herself. But if not? No, nothing has happened. Of course it might. Wait in any case till it does. A wild piece of goods' (*U* 4.428–29). Milly's sexual status is rendered ambiguous by the reference to her in conversation between Buck Mulligan and a young bather as ' – Snapshot, eh? Brief exposure' (*U* 1.686). Elsewhere, Joyce associates the photographic snapshot with erotically charged 'Mutoscope pictures' when Bloom asks, 'Do they snapshot those girls?' (*U* 13.794–96) and with Bloom's pornographic viewing of Molly and Boylan through the keyhole when he queries, 'May I bring two men chums to witness the deed and take a snapshot?' (*U* 15.3791–92). Bloom's decision to 'Wait' and see what happens between Milly and Bannon leaves scope for potential ramifications given the implications of a woman's loss of 'honour' evidenced in *Dubliners* (1914), where Mrs Mooney thinks in 'The Boarding House', 'It is all very well for the man: he can go his ways as if nothing had happened, having had his moment of pleasure, but the girl has to bear the brunt' (*D* 59–60).

'Photo's papli' and Trieste

Joyce's literary output was significant between 1904 and 1920, years he predominantly spent in Trieste. During his time in the port city, he 'published *Chamber Music*, finished *Dubliners*, revised *Stephen Hero* into *A Portrait of the Artist as a Young Man*', wrote *Exiles* and began *Ulysses* (*JJ* 389). Critics have addressed the relationship between Joyce's literature and Triestine cinematic culture, most notably in John McCourt's edited collection, *Roll Away the Reel World: James Joyce and Cinema* (2010).[74] The city's photographic history has received less attention, despite the fact that numerous photographers were operating in Trieste in the early to mid-twentieth century. This includes the professional practitioners, Franz Benque and Carlo Wulz and amateur photographers, Arturo Cuzzi and Giovanni Masutti. Kodak cameras could be purchased from Biagio Padovan's photographic studio, N. C. Films Emporio Fotografico in Via Sant'Antonio, 2, Trieste, with an advertisement for his business appearing in the 1 February 1911 edition of *L'Illustrazione Triestina*.[75] In 1905, Stanislaus Joyce had his photograph taken in Trieste and in 1913, Giorgio and Lucia were photographed at the window of their Triestine flat.[76] It is possible that Nora was also photographed in the city, as Vince Cosgrave wrote to Joyce *c.* 29 October 1905, 'I write to Nora tomorrow. Is that a tinted photograph of her on the card. If so compliment her for me. She looks much healthier than in

Brown Dublin' (*LII* 128). In 1914, Joyce visited Mario Circovich's photographic studio on Piazza della Borsa, 12, where he had an official photograph taken 'for the first time in twelve years' (*JJ* 353). He sent the image shown in Figure 4.4 to his publisher, Grant Richards, informing him, 'I went today to a photographer and he promised to have one ready by tomorrow so that it will be in your hands on Monday, I hope' (*LII* 334).

Figure 4.4 Mario Circovich, James Joyce, 1914. Courtesy of the Zürich James Joyce Foundation.

Joyce looks stoic in the photograph, the image intended as publicity for *Dubliners*.

Dublin's newspapers began to regularly feature photographs from the mid-teens.[77] The newspapers of Trieste followed a similar pattern. In 1911, *L'Illustrazione Triestina* printed photographs of the opera singer Carlo Wostry, football teams and a group of people sledging.[78] The appearance of photographic images would have been an exciting development, particularly for a newspaper advertising itself as an exception to other 'monotonous' presses.[79] As in Ireland, Trieste's professional photographers would have still been predominantly male but in 1924, a reporter for the feminist fortnightly paper, *Femmina, Quindicinale Femminile* acknowledged the quality of entries to their photographic competition designed specifically for women.[80] They thanked the Wulz photographic studio for acting as one of their three jury members and bemoaned the lack of entries from women compared to the number of amateur, female photographers operating in the city.[81] In the early twentieth century, the Wulz studio was owned by Carlo Wulz, one of the most well-known Triestine photographers.

Carlo's father, Giuseppe Wulz opened his 'daguerreotype atelier' (*U* 8.174–75) in Trieste's central Hirschl Palace in 1868 and entrusted his son with his studio in October 1912.[82] After Carlo's death in 1928, he bequeathed the studio to his daughters, Wanda and Marion. Wanda took predominant charge of running the atelier, whilst Marion provided skills in 'post-production retouching and printing'.[83] Wanda became a pioneer of futuristic photography and successfully maintained the studio until its closure in 1980. Joyce is likely to have been aware of the Wulz family, as Carlo was renowned for his photographic portraits and Wanda's work was displayed at the city's 1932 futurist exhibition. Wanda appeared in promotional content for her father's photographic studio shortly after her birth in 1903. At two years younger, Marion similarly featured in photographs adorning the studio's walls throughout her childhood and later life. For Silvia Valisa, the daughters are 'far from being the typical photographees' and are instead 'entirely free from the self-consciousness that often characterizes the photographed subject'.[84] This composure stemmed from the sisters' familiarity with the visual medium, the camera having always been present.

In the Ostend photographs likely to have been captured by Lucia in 1926, the Joyces display a similar ease with the camera, with one image showing Nora seated on a cart and another Joyce, Nora and Patrick J. Hoey reclining casually on a grass verge.[85] Lucia was not the only amateur photographer on the trip and there are numerous images in which she poses whilst Nora probably operated the camera. The women's engagement with photography demonstrates the increasing ease with which the general public could operate handheld cameras during Joyce's composition of the *Wake* and their ability to capture and develop images. As Bloom thinks of Milly's childhood, he recalls, 'Happier then. Snug little room that was with the red wallpaper. Dockrell's, one and ninepence a dozen. Milly's tubbing night. [...] Cosy smell of her bathwater. Funny she looked soaped all over' (*U* 8.170–73). His thought of Milly's 'tubbing night' immediately precludes his realization, 'Now photography' (*U* 8.173). In 1910, the Wulz sisters featured in a portrait of their 'tubbing night', in an image recalling the 'Cosy smell' and soap in Bloom's recollection of Milly (*U* 8.172).[86] The Wulz daughters often posed for images that were then displayed at their father's Triestine studio and the bathtub photograph is likely to have appeared on its walls or windows.

Joyce studied Italian since childhood and moves between languages in his letters to his daughter, Lucia and in his portrayal of Milly. During time spent in Trieste in 1910, Joyce sung to his daughter, 'Cera una volta, una bella bambina | Che si chiamava Lucia', roughly translating as 'Once upon a time a beautiful girl | Who was called Lucia' (*JJ* 309). Joyce's affectionate use of Italian is apparent in *Ulysses*, where Milly addresses her father as 'Dearest Papli' (*U* 4.397) and Bloom thinks, 'Soon be a woman. Mullingar. Dearest Papli' (*U* 6.88–89) and 'Photo's papli, by all that's gorgeous' (*U* 14.1535–36). The noun 'papli' suggests a play on 'paparino', the Italian word for 'daddy'. Joyce's description of Milly as 'Photo's papli' emphasizes the importance of the visual medium and 'Hereditary taste' on the bond between father and daughter (*U* 8.174). Shortly after considering the benefits of Stephen moving in with them as 'For the hostess: disintegration of obsession, acquisition of correct Italian pronunciation' (*U* 17.938–39), Bloom imagines that 'the way to daughter led through mother, the way to mother through daughter' (*U* 17.943–44). Photography and Italian are themes to be explored across the course of this newly imagined household, in which Bloom proposes that 'Bloom Cottage. Saint Leopold's. Flowerville' should include 'Snapshot photography' (*U* 17.1581–89).

Bloom's household drawers are rich with photographic content. His '2nd drawer' contains 'An indistinct daguerreotype of Rudolf Virag and his father Leopold Virag executed in the year 1852 in the portrait atelier of their (respectively) 1st and 2nd cousin' (*U* 17.1876–77) and 'a photocard of the Queen's Hotel' (*U* 17.1880–81). His '1st draw' contains '2 fading photographs of queen Alexandra of England and of Maud Branscombe' (*U* 17.178–79) and '2 erotic photocards' (*U* 17.1809). Luca Crispi notes that 'This very specific account of the photograph [the "indistinct daguerreotype"] first appears in "Ithaca" on the Rosenbach manuscript by the end of October 1921'.[87] The director of the

Hungarian National Museum, Endre Tóth, has uncovered evidence that the Hungarian photographer Sandor Virag worked 'in the heart' of Székesfehévár and proposes that Virag may have inspired Bloom's family lineage.[88] This is certainly possible but Joyce's depiction of the Virags may have also been influenced by the vibrancy of Trieste's photographic culture. The allusion to Bloom's father in 'Poor papa's daguerreotype atelier he told me of' (*U* 8.173–74) is lyrically similar to the 'Patatapapaveri's, fruiterers and musical florists with his '*Ciaho, chavi! Sar Shin, shillipen*', into which the Tulloch-Turnbull girl chases the 'national apostate' in *Finnegans Wake* (*FW* 171.31–32). In I.7, the italicized Italian approximately translates as 'Hey girl, how are you, are you feeling cold?' (*FW* 172.2).[89] John McCourt notes that 'Patatapapaveri' sounds 'to an English speaker, as Italian should sound but does not really mean anything; it translates as "potatopoppy" and sounds a little bit like a variation on Triestine words such as "patatin-patatun" (in an instant) or pataton (beautiful girl)'.[90]

Given the Tulloch-Turnbull girl's actions, Joyce's possible allusion to 'in an instant' in 'Patatapapaveri's' suggests a play on the instantaneous camera snapshot, with photographers able to capture images in a fraction of a second since the 1870s. Parisian photographers opened their fine art, photographic ateliers to the general public shortly after photography's 1839 public launch. Ateliers had previously been operated by artists or designers but Joyce's reference to Virag's 'portrait atelier' suggests an acknowledgement of photography's artistic potential and its ability to be 'disposed for an aesthetic end' (*OCPW* 104). Bloom thinks 'Poor papa's daguerreotype atelier' (*U* 8.173–74) but it is later revealed that the atelier belongs to his father's cousin, rather than Rudolph or Leopold Virag. Since Molly also thinks that Bloom has sent Milly 'to learn to take photographs on account of his grandfather' (*U* 18 1004–05), it is possible that Joyce may have at one point intended the 'papa' to refer to Bloom's grandfather, reinforcing the family's connection with this visual medium as a 'Hereditary taste' (*U* 8.173–74).

Filippo Tommaso Marinetti famously referred to Trieste as 'one of the three capitals of futurism' and the city hosted a futurist event on 12 January 1910.[91] Wanda Wulz began to experiment with the futuristic potential of photography in the 1920s, after Triestine artist and writer, Anita Pittoni introduced her to leading figures such as the painter, Marcello Claris and the founder of the *fotodinamismo* or Photodynamism movement, Anton Giulio Bragaglia.[92] Photodynamism was inspired by futurism and practitioners sought to progress modernism by capturing kineticism in photography. In a 1911 essay on '*Futurist Photodynamism*' Bragaglia declared, 'What interests me is movementism, which indeed might legitimately be termed Photo-movement-istics or

Photocinematics were it not for my intention to insist on the inner dynamics of Photodynamism'.[93] Photographic manipulation and proto-cinematic techniques would have arguably appealed to Joyce given his use of illusory, visual techniques throughout his literary works and his 1909–10 involvement in founding Dublin's first dedicated picture house, the Volta Cinematograph. The complexity of the Photodynamism movement is particularly striking in Wanda's photography and her images are far more experimental than the landscapes and historical scenes captured by her sister, Marion.

In a 1932 self-portrait, Wanda merges two photographic negatives, visually transforming herself into a half-human, half-cat figure.[94] Wanda contributed her photograph to the 1932 exhibition, 'Mostra Fotografica Futurista di Trieste', where it was praised by Marinetti and the Triestine press.[95] Her technical skills are evident in the soft, textured look of the photograph and the intricate mirroring of the cat's eye with her own. In *Ulysses*, Bloom draws a similar comparison between Milly and the family's cat, as he thinks of their resemblances and differences, 'Inasmuch as leaning she sustained her blond hair for him to ribbon it for her (cf neckarching cat)' (*U* 17.896–97). This anthropomorphism reveals his affection for his daughter and their pet but also hints at photography's futuristic potential, as suggested in the *Wake*'s 'futurist one-horse balletbattle pictures and the Pageant of Past History worked up with animal variations' (*FW* 221.18). In 1929, Berenice Abbott captured a Parisian image of Lucia dancing to Schubert's 'Marche Militaire'.[96] In *c.* 1930, Wanda photographed Marion in a similarly striking, metallic costume.[97] The photographs share a focus on capturing the female body in movement. In Abbot's static image, Lucia paradoxically comes to life, demonstrating her skills in dance training. Portraits of and by Marion, Wanda and Lucia attest to the dynamism made possible by the camera and to the '*verbivocovisual*' possibilities of modernist photography (*FW* 341.18).

The 'Tulloch-Turnbull girl' and the photographic snapshot

In I.7 of *Finnegans Wake*, the 'Tulloch-Turnbull girl with her coldblood kodak' aggressively shoots through the text as she snapshots the 'as yet unremuneranded national apostate' (*FW* 171.31–33). As with Milly, who only speaks in her hallucinatory appearance in 'Circe', the Tulloch-Turnbull girl is denied an active, narrative voice. Instead, her character initially appears as secondary in a chapter dedicated to Shem. Lorraine Weir has noted the voyeurism endemic in this chapter, arguing that the 'tompip peepestrella throug a threedraw eighteen hawkspower durdicky telescope [...] out of his westernmost keyhole' (*FW* 178.27) reminds us of 'Blazes Boylan's invitation to Bloom in the "Circe" chapter of *Ulysses* to watch through the keyhole (*U* 15.670)'.[98] Roland McHugh's annotations to I.7 reveal only that the 'unremuneranded national apostate' can be taken to be the 'National Apostle (St Patrick)' and he does not mention the Tulloch-Turnbull girl's origins.[99] This lack of critical attention is likely due to the sparsity of available information on her character but may also be attributed to the *Wake*'s interchanging of family members, where Shem manifests as Dolph, Jerry and Nick, and Issy as Alys, Izod and Iseult, amongst other variations. Despite this, there is only one obviously female photographer in the *Wake*, unlike the more passive and unidentifiable 'usual bilker's dozen of dowdy cameramen' (*FW* 435.9).

Having commenced work on I.7 in 1924, Joyce sent a photograph of himself to Sylvia Beach, writing, 'Here is the passport photo of Shem the Penman'.[100] Joyce was clearly contemplating visual media, sending a subsequent letter to Sylvia Beach on 25 April 1924 with a 'photograph of a portrait of my father, commissioned by me a year ago'.[101] Little is known of Joyce's use of 'Tulloch-Turnbull' but Major Douglas John Tulloch Turnbull R. H. A. was awarded the Distinguished Service Order for services in the Middle East in the British Army in 1941.[102] The Major's association with military warfare is apt given the aggressive and militaristic nature of the *Wake*'s photographic snapshotter, as is the etymology of her surname; Tulloch is a Scottish surname with Medieval origins and Turnbull is the name of a Scottish clan, who resided on the border between Scotland and England. The origins of the clan date back to the early fourteenth century, when the King of Scotland, Robert the Bruce was reportedly saved by William Rule 'turning' a charging bull from his direction. He subsequently gave Rule the surname Turnebull, later changed to Turnbull. In the *Wake*, the Tulloch-Turnbull girl is heavily associated with nationalistic pursuit and conflict, photographing the 'national apostate' during his 'short cut to Caer Fere' (*FW* 171.33–35), 'Caer' the Welsh for a fortress or stronghold in a town or castle.

In Joyce's January 1924 protodraft of I.7, the Tulloch-Turnbull girl originally appeared as the 'Thornton girl with her kodak'.[103] By his February 1924 to June 1925 draft of the 'Shem the Penman' episode, published in *This Quarter* magazine, Joyce had transformed her into the 'Kelly-Turnbull girl with her kodak', before her final appearance as the 'Tulloch-Turnbull girl' in a second typescript of June 1925.[104] Responding to these genetic changes, Luca Crispi and Sam Slote acknowledge that the '"Thornton" shop refers to that in *Ulysses*'.[105] Thornton's of 63 Grafton Street appears in an erotically charged scene in the 'Wandering Rocks' episode, where 'The blonde girl in Thornton's bedded the wicker basket with rustling fibre' (*U* 10.299–300) and Boylan peers into the 'shop assistant's blouse with more favour, the stalk of the red flower between his smiling teeth' (*U* 10.334–35). Joyce was familiar with the physical proximity of Thornton's and the Kodak store on 63 and 89 Grafton Street respectively, as revealed in his description of the 'Thornton girl with her kodak'.

George Eastman chose the brand name Kodak due to it being a 'mere arbitrary collection of sounds or letters', designed to have global appeal.[106] Kodak subsequently passed into general usage in photography. Joyce's copy of Otto Jespersen's *Growth and the Structure of the English Language* (1905), used as source material for the *Wake*, describes how popular trade names 'may live and even pass into common use outside the sphere for which they were originally invented; this is the case with *kodak*'.[107] Kodak was still synonymous with George Eastman's company and his advertorial Kodak Girls but Joyce's use of Jespersen's text suggests that branding in the *Wake* may be less important, a point reinforced by his deliberate notation of Kodak with a small 'k' as 'kodak'. In his first, second and third drafts of this chapter, Joyce recorded 'KodaK' with two capital K's; his typist changed this to 'Kodak' before Joyce altered the word to 'kodak' (lower-case) in his third typescript.[108]

By the 1890s, the word 'snapshot' was a popular photographic term variously referring to 'a photograph taken with a very brief exposure', 'a "candid" photograph taken without the subject's knowledge or permission' or 'a photograph taken by an unsophisticated amateur, using a simple camera'.[109] The term has its etymology in a gunshot taken at animals, quickly and without purposeful aim. Eastman played with the origins of the snapshot in his marketing, producing a hidden, detective camera in 1886 resembling a small travelling bag and announcing 'At short distances a gunner can kill without bringing his rifle or pistol to the eye. The Detective camera will be perfectly adapted to taking groups unobserved'.[110] Finn Fordham has highlighted the presence of the photographic snapshot in the text's Russian General motif, where 'The one with the "shutter" (the "shooter") is Butt, and yet the "shitter" is the Russian General. Butt and HCE, Buckley and the General, are indistinguishably combined'.[111] In I.7, it is Joyce's 'Photo girl' who commands the snapshot, revealing his sustained interest in women and photography.

Joyce alludes to 'artstouchups' in I.7 (*FW* 171.27), hinting at Milly's earlier involvement with the art of photographic retouching, yet only four lines later the Tulloch-Turnbull girl is independently operating a camera as she captures the 'fourth snap' (*FW* 171.31). Appearing as part of Shaun's critique of Shem, she demonstrates agency in snapshotting Shem's 'lowness' and the 'dog's quantity' of his drink, which 'visibly oozed out thickly from this dirty little blacking beetle' (*FW* 171.29-31). The Tulloch-Turnbull girl's ability to photograph Shem provides Shaun with leverage to put 'truth and untruth together a shot may be made at what this hybrid actually was like to look at' (*FW* 169.8-10), with Fordham recognizing the potential for photography to be used as blackmail.[112] The photographer is aware that 'the vice out of bridewell was a bad fast man by his walk on the spot' (*FW* 172.2-24), the references to 'vice' and 'bridewell', a prison in Dublin, reinforcing the possibility of a more salacious photograph having greater public interest and monetary worth.

Responding to the inclusion of the unusual 'snappograph' in III.3 of *Finnegans Wake* and the 'Souvenir of the Twenty-Fifth Anniversary of the Opening of the Gaiety Theatre' (1896), Pieter Bekker describes how the anniversary publication contains the lines, 'The snap-shot fiend now aims without remorse | And "click!" he's got you, at your worst, of course.'[113] Joyce owned this celebratory edition, which includes an opening address written by dramatist, Edwin Hamilton in which Old Father Time contrasts 'old photography and new' and remarks 'Thanks to X rays, the time will come no doubt | When he will snappograph you wrong side out'.[114] In III.3, the 'snappograph' occurs after 'the taller man, was accused of a certain offence or of a choice of two serious charges', as the assembled crowd question, 'What do you mean, sir, behind your hah! You don't hah to do thah, you know, snapograph' (*FW* 522.8-21). Joyce's portmanteau 'snapograph' merges 'snapshot' and 'photograph', evoking the furtive and aggressive nature of his earlier, female snapshotter.

For HCE, the man 'accused of a certain offence', the photographic 'snapograph' provides a potential, additional 'witness' to his rumoured indiscretions (*FW* 522.21-27), the crowd having previously only 'hear[d] things' with the 'bushes' having 'eyes' (*FW* 522.12-13). Despite the possibility of photographic evidence being produced, an exact account is never provided of HCE's Phoenix Park transgression and the camera fails to corroborate the frequent retelling of his actions. In his address in the *Souvenir*, Edwin Hamilton portrays photography as capable of enhancing estrangement and lacking the ability to 'link together all the human race', unlike 'drama'.[115] This hints at Joyce's own aesthetic tendencies, as in his 1900 lecture on 'Drama and Life' delivered to University College Dublin's Literary and Historical Society, in which he argued, 'In an art-loving and art-producing society the drama would naturally take up its position at the head of all artistic institutions' (*OCPW* 26). Despite Joyce's 'Photo girl[s]' lacking involvement with more highbrow culture, his interspersion of them throughout *Ulysses* and the *Wake* within the text's family units demonstrates the importance of their roles in relation to his literary paternal motifs and the significance of the medium as a 'Hereditary taste' (*U* 8.173–74).

'telltale stories' and 'tress clippings'

Reporting on the use of male and female photographic assistants in 1920, the *British Journal of Photography* argued that 'one cannot overlook the fact that a man [...] must get on or get out. He must advance or go to the wall: while a woman [...] has always the prospect of marriage to look forward to'.[116] The Tulloch-Turnbull girl is relegated to a single, explicit appearance in a chapter concerning Shem and Shaun's conflict but this is less surprising given the context in which Joyce was writing, where Britain's leading, weekly photographic periodical saw women's work as a precursor to wedding nuptials and women's work contracts in many industries were terminated after marriage.[117] Joyce had access to Irish newspapers during his time in Europe, asking Stanislaus on 18 October 1906, 'Is there nobody in Ireland who will think it worth his or her while to make a bundle of any old papers that are lying about his or her house and send them to me?' (*LII* 182). Reporters acknowledged the increasing prevalence of press photographers. In a 1910 article titled, 'Camera Fiends', Dublin's *Daily Express* reported on the case of a man who 'had been sent on an urgent errand by his employer' and had 'loitered on his way to witness the passage of a Royal procession'.[118] Upon returning to his office, the man 'stoutly denied the impeachment that he had lingered to watch the day's pageant', only to find himself fired when a newspaper featured 'an excellent portrait of himself as he stood in the front row of the crowd quietly smoking his pipe and waiting for the procession to pass'.[119]

Regulations were in place with regard to press photography and in 1911, the *Daily Express* wrote that official photographers intending to capture street images on Coronation Day must 'wear badges' and 'carry their own photograph upon them for the purpose of subsequent identification'.[120] This was deemed to be necessary 'after the manner in which some of the "camera fiends" behaved in the streets upon the occasion of the late King's funeral'.[121] Their article on Coronation Day photography appears on the same page as an advertisement for 'Skerry's School of Shorthand, Typewriting, and Commercial Training', to which Molly considers sending Milly in *Ulysses*.[122] In 1908, a press photographer managed to capture an image of Emmeline Pankhurst at court, having entered the building with his camera concealed within his top hat.[123] As one press photographer recalled of the early twentieth century, cameras 'were indeed so common on the press benches that those of us in the know used to watch the hats rise slightly when anything happened'.[124]

Writing on the changing nature of the press and the etymology of 'tabloid', Kevin J. H. Dettmar notes its use in 1901 to indicate the public's desire 'for a more concentrated, easier-to-swallow journalism'.[125] Joyce refers to the development of Irish tabloid presses in III.2, invoking A. C. W. Harmsworth, Viscount Northcliffe, the 'Irish newspaper magnate & founder of "tabloid" journalism' in 'I'll be so curiose to see in the Homesworth breakfast tablotts' (*FW* 458.22–23).[126] Photographers could capture surreptitious images using detective cameras. In 1905, British illustrated newspaper, *The Sketch* featured a photograph of the best-selling novelist Miss Marie Corelli with the caption, 'A photograph of a lady who will not be photographed [...] Miss Marie Corelli has a great aversion to photographers, and steadfastly refuses to sit to them – hence the particular interest of this snapshot'.[127] The press photographer's dogged determination and ability to see their image in print is apparent in I.7, where the Tulloch-Turnbull girl features alongside details of 'The house O'Shea or O'Shame' (*FW* 182.30). The house of Shem or 'Shame' contains 'telltale stories' and 'tress clippings' (*FW* 183.11) and whilst Shem purportedly seeks to keep 'the mystery of himsel' hidden (*FW* 184.9–10), his possession of stories and press 'clippings' suggests his vanity in accumulating this media, at least from Shaun's perspective. The use of 'O'Shea' suggests the presence of Charles Stewart Parnell's mistress, Katherine 'Kitty' O'Shea, who appears in photographic form in *Ulysses*'s 'Eumaeus' episode, where 'She loosened many a man's thighs. I seen her picture in a barber's' (*U* 16.1355–56).

Joyce was covertly photographed by Gisèle Freund, who describes the furtive nature of her actions during their 1939 Parisian meeting:

> I had positioned myself in the street, near the entrance to Adrienne's bookshop. Joyce did not notice that I was photographing him, but he sensed that someone was hovering nearby. [...] These photos were taken in the classic style of the *paparazzi* – twenty years before they came on the scene.[128]

As in Freund's '*paparazzi*' images, the Tulloch-Turnbull girl captures Shem seemingly unaware, 'taking what he fondly thought was a short cut' (*FW* 171.34). Since she has been 'told [...] to shade and shoot shy Shem', she could have been working in a professional capacity, either contributing to a feature designed for 'tress clippings' (*FW* 183.29) or paid by Shaun to capture the image as part of his critique of his brother. Joyce initially refused to be photographed by Freund citing 'eyesight' troubles and having 'too much work to do'.[129] Had the Tulloch-Turnbull girl's camera included the 'pandle of magnegnousioum' first used in flashlight photography in 1864 (*FW* 397.27), the national apostate's discomfort could have been further exacerbated. Technological improvements in flash lighting in the late 1880s led to a reduction in the amount of smoke produced by the camera flash but bulbs would have still been needed to produce images in darker settings. The photographic flash reoccurs in III.4, where the 'man in the street' witnesses the sexual encounter between HCE and Anna Livia Plurabelle (ALP) from the streetside; they are able to make it 'known through all Urania soon' by 'Photoflashing it far too wide' (*FW* 583.15–16).

Joyce was critical of the tabloid presses and wrote in a letter to F. V. Morley on 10 November 1932, 'I do not know where the British and American papers get their scare headlines about me. I have never given an interview in my life and do not receive journalists' (*LIII* 266). He was not immune to unwanted attention from press photographers. Prior to his 1931 marriage to Nora, he described their temporary residence in London as 'swarming with journalists' and 'the street outside the Registry Office [...] [as] occupied by a squad of cameramen'.[130] As the couple returned to their house after their wedding, a photographer captured an image of them with their solicitor, Fred Munro. The group's disdain for the cameraman or woman is apparent, as Nora and Munro are shown turning away from the camera whilst Joyce avoids direct eye contact. The image subsequently appeared 'on page three of the Evening Standard' with an article on their marriage.[131] With Joyce noting in I.8 that 'It was put in the newses what he did' (*FW* 196.20), Shem is right to fear the photographic actions of the 'unknown quarreller' (*FW* 179.4–5).

'many have paused before that exposure of him by old Tom Quad'

In I.3, Joyce uses his knowledge of Lewis Carroll to support the text's concerns with rumour and visual trickery. The chapter opens, 'Chest Cee! 'Sdense! Corpor di barragio! you spoof of visibility [...] The Blackfriars treacle plaster outrage be liddled!' (*FW* 48.1–4). Joyce took the 'Chest Cee' from the 'Souvenir of the Twenty-Fifth Anniversary of the Opening of the Gaiety Theatre', in which 'the operatic tenor of the old school [...] the gentleman who so strangely and wonderfully used to work himself up to the point of delivering his famous chest C'.[132] His reference to 'The blackfriars treacle plaster' invokes both the Black Friars Dominion Order and Blackfriars Road, London, where in 1912, a cashier at the Sennett Bros. firm of furriers was robbed [...] after being temporarily blinded with treacle-covered paper.[133] In a 1913 report on Old Bailey Proceedings, a witness described how 'I [...] saw Mr. Seyfang standing on the footway with his hat off and his face covered in treacle'.[134] The first case against the four, accused men was dismissed, before a retrial in which they were subsequently found guilty. The detective involved, Francis Carlin maintained that 'the verdict arrived at in this much-debated affair was a correct one'; he described the 'brain of the detective [...] [as] a kind of picture gallery' and argued he had reached 'that stage when a written description [...] becomes in an instant a mind's eye photograph'.[135] Joyce's allusion to 'treacle' also suggests his use of Carroll's *Alice's Adventures in Wonderland*, where in a made-up story about the 'treacle well', sisters Alice, Lorina and Edith are described by the Dormouse as living 'on treacle'.[136]

Questions of visual veracity abound in I.3, as when:

> Thus the unfacts, did we possess them, are too imprecisely few to warrant our certitude, the evidencegivers by legpoll too untrustworthily irreperible [...] And there many have paused before that exposure of him by old Tom Quad, a flashback in which he sits sated, gowndabout, in clericalease habit, watching bland sol slithe dodgsomely into the nethermore, a globule of maugdleness about to corrugitate his mild dewed cheek and the tata of a tiny victorienne, Alys, pressed by his limper looser.
>
> (*FW* 57.23–29)

Alongside its use as corroborating evidence, the 'flashback' in the 'exposure of him' suggests the 'filmic flashback' (*FW* 57.24–25).[137] The 'exposure' further hints at HCE's rumoured sexual transgression in Phoenix Park with a 'pair of dainty maidservants' (*FW* 34.19). The oxymoronic 'unfacts' are unable to provide 'certitude', the 'evidencegivers' deemed appropriately 'untrustworthily' given the chapter's opening 'spoof of visibility'. The 'dogsomely' and the 'old Tom Quad' refer to Charles Lutwidge Dodgson and the Great Quadrangle at Christ Church, Oxford, in which the author's flat and photographic studio was located.

In her biography, Belle Moses suggests that the colloquialism 'Tom Quad' was in popular usage but in Carroll's playful diary entry entitled 'Isa's Visit to Oxford', he writes 'You go in under a magnificent tower, called "Tom Tower", nearly four feet high [...] into the Great Quadrangle (which very vulgar people call "Tom Quad")'.¹³⁸ This vulgarity is apparent in Joyce's depiction of the 'him' in the photographic exposure, likely here merging HCE with Carroll, who 'sits stated, gowndabout, in clericalease habit, [...] a globule of maugdleness about to corrugitate his mild dewed cheek' (*FW* 57.25-27). The 'clericalease habit' indicates Joyce's awareness of the author's biography and his knowledge of Carroll's father's role as an Anglican parson. Carroll was ordained but chose not to enter the clergy, viewing his speech impediment and the 'puritanical strictness' required for this role as a hindrance.¹³⁹ The gender of the photographer is I.3 is not definitively confirmed but the 'exposure' hints at the 'Brief exposure' previously used with reference to Milly in *Ulysses* (*U* 1.686) and prefigures Shem's later exposure via photography by the Tulloch-Turnbull girl. The 'tata' in 'the tata of a tiny victorienne' translates as 'father' in Yiddish, with 'Alys' and 'alease' (*FW* 57.25) signifying both Alice Liddell and through the 'ease' sound, the presence of the text's daughter figure, Issy.¹⁴⁰

In I.5, Joyce combines photography with reference to the 'father' and 'alices', where:

Be who, farther potential? and so wider but we grisly old Sykos who have done our unsmiling bit on 'alices, when they were yung and easily freudened, in the penumbra of the procuring room and what oracular comepression we have had apply to them! could (did we care to sell our feebought silence *in camera*).

(*FW* 115.20-25)

He invokes psychologists Carl Jung and Sigmund Freud, to whom he referred to in a 14 June 1921 letter to Harriet Shaw Weaver as 'Doctor Jung (the Swiss Tweedledum who is not to be confused with the Viennese Tweedledee, Dr Freud' (*JJ* 510). Jung briefly treated Lucia in 1934, to initial but then limited success (*JJ* 678). The scene merges photography and psychoanalytic theory and is set during a trial 'in the procuring room'. The possibility of extortion via photography is suggested in the parenthesis '(did we care to sell our feebought silence *in camera*)' (*FW* 115.23-25). In his use of '*in camera*' and presence of the text's young girls in the 'alices' who were 'yung and easily freudened', Joyce plays with the duality of the photographic medium, using this to suggest impropriety. The reference to '*in camera*' invokes the photographic camera and the Latin legal terminology, where 'in camera' is a private jury session in which press and public are absent. The consulting room becomes both photographic darkroom and closed legal session, in which the actions of 'grisly old psychoes' towards 'alices' are revealed to those present.

In her account of Carroll's relationship with the young Liddell sisters, Belle Moses describes how 'the girls lived in the beautiful deanery in the northeast angle, and it was only a "puss-in-the-corner" game to get from one place to the other'.[141] In II.2, Joyce refers to the 'puss-in-the-corner' game alongside Dodgson and photography, where:

> It's time that all paid tribute to this massive mortality, the pink of punk perfection as photography in mud. Some may seek to dodge the gobbet for its quantity of quality but who wants to cheat the choker's got to learn to chew the cud. Allwhichhole scrubs on scroll Pitchcap and circuminiuminluminatedhave encuoniams here triangle, noose and improperies there.[1] With a pansy for the pussy in the corner.[2]
>
> (*FW* 277.18–278.5)

Dodgson is present in the 'dodge', with photography again associated with 'improperies', improper behaviour or improprieties. The 'gobbet' is lyrically similar to the 'globule of maugdleness', where HCE in proto-Carrollian form had sat back, 'flashback [...] his mild dewed cheek and the tata of a tiny victorienne, Alys, pressed by his limper looser' (*FW* 57.23–29). Appearing in II.2 in the 'Nightlessons' chapter, Joyce's 'tribute to this massive mortality', here HCE, fuses 'mortality' with 'martiality', suggesting the militaristic tendencies first evoked in the Tulloch-Turnbull girl. Shaun, Shem and Issy's account of how they 'drames our dreams tell Bappy returns' (*FW* 277.17–18) includes paternal reference, with 'bap' Hindu for 'father'.[142] The children's 'tribute to this massive mortiality' is infused with sexual connotation, as the 'pink of punk perfection' of their father contains 'punk', archaic slang for a prostitute. In Joyce's description of 'photography in mud' and 'THE MONGREL UNDER THE DUNG-MOUND', the visual medium is compared to the letter uncovered in the dung heap (*FW* 276.11–13). Just as the contents of the 'everydaylooking stamped addressed envelope' containing the letter are capable of being falsely 'stretched, filled out, if need or wish were' (*FW* 109.7–28), so too is the 'obliterated' photographic 'negative'. Image and letter are rendered malleable and unable to substantiate rumour (*FW* 111.34–35).

In *Ulysses*, photography passes via Bloom's family lineage to Milly, with her ability to 'learn to take photographs' suggesting her acquisition of technical skills (*U* 8.1005). Despite Bloom's decision that the photograph was not 'art in a word' (*U* 16.1451–55), Joyce depicts him as heavily invested in the professional and amateur opportunities offered to women by photography. Given that Joyce arranged for Lucia to obtain a camera, this was a hobby he deemed worthy of pursuing, albeit one lacking the intrinsic aestheticism he attributed to other art forms. Genevieve Sartor notes that in the 1930s, 'it is clear that Joyce initially tried to create a career for Lucia by using her talents as an illustrator', seeking to aid her 'increasingly splintered psychology and depression'.[143] Lucia did not pursue photography professionally, but this was another medium that Joyce encouraged to enhance her well-being. In *Finnegans Wake,* Joyce signals his transition from the statically framed women of *Dubliners* to the increasingly autonomous and militaristic camera woman. Milly and the Tulloch-Turnbull girl are largely mediated via male protagonists and subject to sexual innuendo and 'vice' (*FW* 172.3), yet they are also paradoxically positioned in photographic spaces increasingly tailored to and targeting young women. In his choice of professional roles, Joyce emphasizes the visual potential of what could be achieved by women using a 'pure and sensitive flash of light'.[144] In drawing upon knowledge of Lewis Carroll in relation to the 'him' of HCE and the text's young daughter figures, he further reinforces the hemiplegic nature of his engagement with photography and the importance of the paternal motif to his portrayal of his literary 'Photo girl[s]'.

Coda: 'A photograph [...] may be so disposed for an aesthetic end'

The period in which Joyce was writing marked a critical point in photography, as technological developments such as the introduction of handheld cameras increased the popularity and accessibility of this medium. Just as Leopold Bloom considers the gramophone to 'Remind you of the voice like the photograph reminds you of the face' (*U* 6.966–67), the photograph initially appears to contain the same suggestion of permanence. Yet Joyce interrogates photography's durability by presenting images as temporal, as in the photograph of Molly that is only 'Very like her then' (*U* 16.1438–39). Photography enables Joyce to expose Dublin's 'paralysis' (*LI* 55), with hemiplegia, the paralysis of one side of the body, proving key to his use of this visual medium. In Joyce's work, photographic portraits are able to inspire epiphany and kinesis whilst simultaneously reinforcing stasis. This project began by quoting from Joyce's critique of photography's aesthetic value. His view of the photograph as 'not a work of art' has been intrinsic to this study, which has used archival excavation to highlight the importance of the interrelationship between photography and paralysis in Joyce's literature. In his hemiplegic engagement with photography, he paradoxically recognizes the medium's ability to inspire animation and generate 'adventure'.[1]

In a 1907 lecture on 'Ireland: Island of Saints and Sages', Joyce argued that 'the Irishman, finding himself in another environment, outside Ireland, very often knows how to make his worth felt. The economic and intellectual conditions of his homeland do not permit the individual to develop' (*OPCW* 123). In combining close reading with historically informed research, this project highlights photography's role in enabling Joyce to expose the 'economic and intellectual conditions of his homeland' (*OPCW* 123). In Chapter 1 of this project, photographic portraits in *Dubliners* were presented as able to temporarily inspire change but unable to generate sustained progress and 'adventure'. A subsequent chapter revealed the importance of stereoscopic technology to Joyce's portrayal of Stephen Dedalus in his earlier works and to concerns with rumour and visual veracity in *Finnegans Wake*. Chapter 3 addressed the interrelationship between photography, art and eroticism in *Ulysses,* where Joyce posits Bloom's interaction with photography as underpinned by his preoccupation with women. For Bloom, photographs paradoxically signal lacking whilst acting as vehicles for enhancing his sexual fantasies. A final chapter showcased the professional opportunities offered to women during Joyce's composition of *Ulysses* and *Finnegans Wake* and their influence on Milly Bloom and the Tulloch-Turnbull girl. In then turning to Joyce's use of Lewis Carroll's biography in the *Wake,* this chapter reinforced the importance of impropriety and the paternal motif to his literary portrayal of his 'Photo girl[s]'.

What next for Joyce and visual culture? Whilst Chapter 4 considered Triestine photography, Joyce's continental position warrants exploration of the visual medium during time also spent in Pola, Rome, Zürich and Paris. In a letter to Stanislaus Joyce on 25 September 1906, sent from Rome, Joyce revealed that the area outside of 'the Forum' consisted of 'Carriages full of tourists, postcard sellers, medal sellers, photograph sellers' (*LII* 165). He sent countless photographic postcards to friends, family and colleagues. In *A Bloomsday Postcard* (2004), Niall Murphy publishes illustrative and photographic postcards sent in Dublin during 1904 but these are not those posted by Joyce.[2] Archival catalogues frequently reveal ownership of postcards by Joyce but rarely detail the image included on the opposing side. Joyce sent an undated photographic postcard to Sylvia Beach from Dijon, writing, 'Dear Miss Beach Solved Lewis Carroll [?] riddle in train.'[3] Thanks to contact with archivists at the University at Buffalo, the photograph on the postcard has been confirmed to show the Hôtel de la Cloche, Place Darcy and Statue de Rude. Images on photographic postcards are imbued with significance and whilst Joyce could have simply opted for convenience in purchasing the postcard at a hotel reception desk, his marrying of literature and photography in his work suggests that he would have given thought to the image accompanying his text.

As a book reliant upon archival excavation and largely completed between 2020 and 2021, this project has been affected by the impact of the Covid-19 global pandemic on international travel and, at times, the prolonged closure of museums and libraries. Joyce's photographic archives span Europe and the United States, with images held at the British Library's Harriet Shaw Weaver Collection, the Zürich James Joyce Foundation, the University at Buffalo's James Joyce Collection and the Harry Ransom Center, University of Texas. The

Zürich James Joyce Foundation holds the majority of Carola Giedion-Welcker's photographs of Joyce, and a visit proved possible during July to August 2020. Other international trips have had to be postponed. Despite the wealth of online, Joycean archival material and detailed catalogue notes, many discoveries will only be possible in person, such as finding an unlisted photographer's signature on a cabinet card or an unknown image in a document box. With this in mind, this project offers a starting point for Joyce and photography, looking forward to the resumption of in-person, archival visits. One need only look at Xavier Tricot's *James Joyce in Ostend* (2018) to recognize the impact of archival work, with Tricot's analysis of images at the University at Buffalo revealing Lucia Joyce's photographic practice.[4]

Archivally informed research is a process of detective work, where what is purported to be true is not necessarily the case. At a cursory glance, the British Library's Harriet Shaw Weaver Collection credits an image of 'James Joyce aged 6 – taken the day he went to Clongowes School' to the 'Photographer: Darby, Paul (1888)'.[5] This is true of the reproduction but not of the original image, which was taken at Lafayette's. The library's more detailed collection notes advise that the image is a 'Copy of original, made by the Paris photographer Paul Darby' but work is required to reach this conclusion.[6] The University at Buffalo's James Joyce Collection titles an image of Joyce in his elaborate ruff collar as 'James Joyce, age 3'.[7] Their listing also records Joyce's handwritten note on the rear of the photograph as '2 | Rathgar, Dublin'.[8] Since the Joyces lived at 41 Brighton Square, Rathgar and moved to 23 Castlewood Avenue, Rathmines before his third birthday, it is more likely that the photograph was taken when he was aged two.

In *James Joyce in Ostend*, Tricot's careful attributing of the photographer in the 1926 images to Joyce's family members reveals the changing dynamics between those operating the camera.[9] The University at Buffalo dates these images to 1924, despite Joyce only visiting Ostend two years later. This is not a criticism of archivists but instead a recognition of the need for continued conversation between subject-specific experts, archivists and those engaged in historicist and genetic research to aid and enhance understanding of Joyce and visual culture. Each archival listing requires interrogation, with face-to-face visits likely aiding greater, research cohesion. A comprehensive catalogue of all photographs by and of the Joyces is still needed and should be informed by images sold at auctions and housed in private collections where possible, as well as those in institutional holdings.

Joyce's relationship with women photographers did not culminate with Berenice Abbott and Gisèle Freund. Just as Freund worked with Man Ray, so too did American photographer, Lee Miller, who in 1946 was commissioned by *Vogue* magazine to capture images of Joyce's Dublin.[10] Terrence Killeen acknowledges that 'many of the photographs [...] credited to Man Ray were actually taken by Miller'.[11] As with Marion and Wanda Wulz, considered in Chapter 4 of this project, Miller provides an additional example of the strength of modernist photography conducted by women. Her photographs of Joyce's Dublin attest to the author's continued impact on visual culture, as is also apparent in the recent wealth of graphic responses to *Finnegans Wake*. These include Peter O'Brien's *The Echo Is Where: Pages 126–68 of Lots of Fun with Finnegans Wake* (2019), arranged to celebrate the eightieth anniversary of the publication of the *Wake*, in which contributors including Joycean scholars respond to O'Brien's illustrated annotations via media such as photography.

Within the '*verbivocovisual*' arena of Joyce and visual culture (*FW* 341.18), this project has situated his literary engagement with photography as hemiplegic, this visual medium imbued with technological potential and stasis. Joyce deemed the photograph 'not a work of art' but recognized that it could be disposed for 'aesthetic end' (*OCPW* 104). Instead of wholly negating photography's aesthetic worth, he acknowledges the value of the camera in showcasing art to others. Joyce's personal and professional interaction with photography spans the broad scope of visual technology, from the invention of the stereoscope, to more conventional cabinet portraits, to his literary 'Photo girl[s]'. Joyce playfully suggested of Carola Giedion-Welcker's 1937 photograph shown in this project's Figure 0.3, 'At last a view of myself I can look at with some pleasure' (*LII* 418). He posed for other images during their Zürich session, turning the opposite way so that she could capture him facing the camera, as in Figure 5.1. The multiple images captured by Giedion-Welcker showcase the dual possibilities of the camera and the importance of Joyce's personal and professional interaction with women photographers. In his most playful responses to photography, he positions the medium as hemiplegic, juxtaposing the image's sense of stasis with the technological promise of what could be achieved 'by a pure and sensitive flash of light'.[12]

Figure 5.1 Carola Giedion-Welcker, Joyce at Platzspitz, Zürich, 1938. Courtesy of the Zürich James Joyce Foundation.

Notes

Introduction

1   James Joyce, 'Paris and Pola Commonplace Book', 1903–04, *The National Library of Ireland*, MS 36,639/02/A, p. 22. Originally thought to be two copy books, 'The Paris Notebook' and 'The Pola Notebook', the National Library of Ireland's acquisition of this manuscript has shown that this was in fact one book, which Luca Crispi dates to 1903–12. The most comprehensive analysis of this notebook can be found in Luca Crispi, 'A Commentary on James Joyce's National Library of Ireland "Early Commonplace Book": 1903–1912 (MS 36,639/02/A)', *Genetic Joyce Studies*, 9 (2009), http://www.geneticjoycestudies.org [accessed 2 January 2021].
2   Joyce, 'Paris and Pola Commonplace Book', p. 26. For brevity in this project, and since it was the definitive version until 2002, further references to Joyce's aesthetic assessment of photography are abbreviated to *OCPW* and provided in-text using James Joyce, *Occasional, Critical and Political Writing*, ed. by Kevin Barry (Oxford: Oxford University Press, 2000), p. 104. For detailed context on Joyce's Paris notebook, see Catherine Flynn, *James Joyce and the Matter of Paris* (Cambridge: Cambridge University Press, 2019).
3   Roland Barthes, *Camera Lucida* (London: Vintage, 2000), p. 57.
4   Louis-Jacques-Mandé Daguerre, 'Daguerreotype (1839)', in *Classic Essays on Photography*, ed. by Alan Trachtenberg (New Haven: Leete's Island Books, 1980), pp. 11–14 (p. 13).
5   Ibid.
6   William Henry Fox Talbot, *The Pencil of Nature* (London: Longman, Brown Green and Longmans, 1844), p. 11.
7   Ibid., p. 19.
8   Anna Sparham, 'Introduction', in *Soldiers and Suffragettes: The Photography of Christina Broom*, ed. by Anna Sparham, Margaret Denny and Diane Atkinson (London: Philip Wilson, 2015), pp. 1–4 (p. 1).
9   'Photographic Society of Ireland's Exhibition', *British Journal of Photography*, 42.1816 (22 February 1895), 119.
10 Ibid.
11 'Meetings of Societies for Next Week', *British Journal of Photography*, 53.2428 (16 November 1906), 915–17 (pp. 916–17).
12 Justin Carville, *Photography and Ireland* (London: Reaktion Books, 2011), p. 24.

13 The National Archives of Ireland: Census of Ireland 1901/11, http://www.census.nationalarchives.ie [accessed 10 January 2021].
14 I am grateful to Rose Teanby for these observations on women's roles in photography, following her 27 October 2020 talk on 'The First Women of Photography 1839-1860' in collaboration with The Royal Photographic Society, Great Britain.
15 Justin Carville, 'Mr Lawrence's Great Photographic Bazaar', *Early Popular Visual Culture*, 5 (2007), 263-83 (p. 268).
16 See Figure 1.2 in Chapter 1 of this project for Lafayette's photograph of James Joyce and his mother, Mary Jane Murray Joyce. This was taken at an 1888 photographic session also attended by Joyce's father and maternal grandfather. The Curran Collection at University College Dublin contains a solo portrait of James Joyce from this studio sitting, where the photographer is listed as unknown: 'Photograph of James Joyce as a Boy', Constantine Curran Collection, University College Dublin Special Collections, http://digital.ucd.ie/view/ivrla:6937 [accessed 11 April 2021]. Through use of Lafayette's archives, I have been able to identify the photograph as having been taken at Lafayette's. See Lafayette, 'Photograph of James Joyce as a Boy with His Mother, Mary Jane Murray Joyce', 1888, Lafayette Photography (Historical Photographs), https://ireland.lafayettephotography.com (showing 505 to 516 of 725 items) [accessed 11 April 2021].
17 'Commercial News', *Freeman's Journal*, 7 February 1898, p. 3.
18 'The Opening and Back Page of a Lafayette Publicity Brochure *circa* 1902', The Lafayette Negative Archive, http://lafayette.org.uk/lafhist.html [accessed 10 April 2021].
19 Ibid.
20 Ibid.
21 'Photographers (Dublin and Suburbs Trades' Directory)', in *Thom's Official Directory of the United Kingdom of Great Britain and Ireland* (Dublin: Alexander Thom and Co., 1904), p. 2077. Lafayette is incorrectly recorded as LaFayette in *Thom's Official Directory* under Dublin photographers but corrected in a second entry.
22 Ibid.
23 Otto Jespersen, *Growth and Structure of the English Language*, 2nd edn (Leipzig: B. G. Teubner, 1912), pp. 157-8.
24 'Charivaria', *Punch*, 5 October 1904, p. 243.
25 John A. Randall, 'Photography as an Occupation for Women', *British Journal of Photography*, 47.2099 (27 July 1900), 473-4 (p. 473).
26 Ibid.
27 Rune Hasser, 'Photography and the Press', in *A History of Photography*, ed. by Jean-Claude Lemagny and André Rouillé, trans. by Janet Lloyd (Cambridge: Cambridge University Press, 1987), pp. 76-9 (p. 78).

28 See 'Death of Mr. Dan Leno, The Famous Comedian', *Daily Mirror,* 1 November 1904, p. 1 and 'Mr. Bradley, the Ex-footman Who Received £60,000', *Daily Mirror,* 10 February 1910, p. 115.
29 Eloise Knowlton, 'Showings Forth: *Dubliners*, Photography, and the Rejection of Realism', *Mosaic: A Journal for the Interdisciplinary Study of Literature,* 38.1 (2005), 133–50 (p. 140).
30 Ibid.
31 See *Camera Work* (New York), ed. by Alfred Stieglitz, 1 January 1913, *Modernist Journals Project*, https://modjourn.org [accessed 16 April 2021].
32 Quoted in Douglas R. Nickel, *Dreaming in Pictures: The Photography of Lewis Carroll* (London: Yale University Press, 2002), p. 15.
33 Diane Waggoner, *Lewis Carroll's Photography and Modern Childhood* (Princeton, NJ: Princeton University Press, 2020), p. XV.
34 Lewis Carroll, 'Photography Extraordinary', 1855, *The Morgan Library & Museum*, https://www.themorgan.org [accessed 10 June 2021].
35 See *Shakespeare and Company Project*, version 1.5.0, Center for Digital Humanities, Princeton University, 2021, https://shakespeareandco.princeton.edu/members/joyce-james/cards/ [accessed 19 April 2021].
36 Alfred Siteglitz (ed.), 'An Apology', *Camera Work* (New York), 1 January 1903, pp. 15–16 (p. 15).
37 André Breton, 'Surrealist Situation of the Object (1935)', in *Manifestoes of Surrealism*, trans. by Richard Seaver and Helen R. Lane (Ann Arbor: University of Michigan Press, 1972), pp. 255–78 (p. 275).
38 Brian Winkenweder, 'Dada' in *Encyclopedia of Twentieth-Century Photography*, 3 vols, ed. by Lynne Warren (New York: Routledge, 2006), I, pp. 353–5 (p. 353–54).
39 Ibid.
40 Unknown Photographer, 'James Joyce, age 3'. This age is provided by the University at Buffalo but Joyce's handwriting on the rear of the photograph reads '2 | Rathgar, Du'. The family left their address in Rathgar when he was aged two, in the year before he turned three.
41 See Lafayette's, 'James Joyce in sailor suit, aged 6', 1888, James Joyce Collection, University at Buffalo.
42 Ibid.
43 'The opening and back page of a Lafayette publicity brochure *circa* 1902'.
44 Carville, 'Mr Lawrence's Great Photographic Bazaar', p. 264.
45 Stanislaus Joyce, *My Brother's Keeper: James Joyce's Early Years*, ed. by Richard Ellmann (Cambridge, MA: Da Capo Press, 2003), p. 39.
46 Ibid.
47 Unknown Photographer, 'James Joyce's graduation from Royal University (later University College Dublin)', 1902, James Joyce Collection, University at Buffalo.

48 See Paul Darby, 'James Joyce standing beside greenhouse, Dublin', 1904, copy of the original photograph by Constantine Curran, x, Vol. XXI A, B. Photographs, mostly of James Joyce; 1888–1938, British Library, https://www.bl.uk/collection-items [accessed 10 February 2021]. Details of Paul Darby's photography can be found at Hervé Lestang, 'Paul Darby', *Portrait Sépia*, http://www.portraitsepia.fr/photographes/darby [accessed 10 February 2021].

49 Harriet Shaw Weaver Papers, British Library.

50 See Lucia Joyce, 'Mr and Mrs Joyce and Giorgio, taken by Lucia?', 1924, Harriet Shaw Weaver Papers, British Library for the photographs taken in Saint Malo and Xavier Tricot, *James Joyce in Ostend* (Devriendt: Belgium, 2018) for those taken in Ostend in 1926.

51 Brenda Maddox, *Nora: A Biography of Nora Joyce* (London: Hamish Hamilton, 1988), pp. 416–17.

52 Gordon Bowker, *James Joyce: A New Biography* (New York: Farrar, Straus and Giroux, 2012), p. 299.

53 Julia Van Haaften, *Berenice Abbott: A Life in Photography* (New York: W. W. Norton & Company, 2018), p. 84.

54 Ibid.

55 Ibid.

56 Dean R. Leroy, 'A Tribute to Gisèle Freund (1908–2000)', *James Joyce Quarterly*, 36.2 (1999), 32–6 (p. 33).

57 Geoffrey Grigson, 'James Joyce', *Picture Post*, 13 May 1939, pp. 54–5.

58 Gisèle Freund and V. B. Carleton, *James Joyce in Paris: His Final Years* (London: Cassell, 1965), p. 5.

59 Ibid.

60 Ibid.

61 Freund, 'Joyce, Sylvia and Adrienne in Sylvia's Bookshop', 1938, in *James Joyce in Paris,* pp. 60–1.

62 Van Haaften, *Berenice Abbott*, p. 84.

63 Thomas E. Connolly, 'Home Is Where the Art Is: The Joyce Family Gallery', *James Joyce Quarterly*, 20.1 (1982), 11–31.

64 See Connolly for reproductions of these images. These are now housed at the Lockwood Memorial Library's Poetry Collection at the University at Buffalo.

65 'Picture postcard of painted portrait by Jacques Émile Blanche, titled "James Augustine Aloysius Joyce"', 1935, Sylvia Beach Papers, Box 169, Folder 17, Princeton University Library.

66 Sean Latham, 'Twenty-First-Century Critical Contexts', in *James Joyce in Context*, ed. by John McCourt (Cambridge: Cambridge University Press, 2009), pp. 148–60 (p. 152).

67 R. Brandon Kershner, 'Framing Rudy and Photography', *Journal of Modern Literature*, 22.2 (1998–9), 265–92 (pp. 265–6).

68 Kershner, *The Culture of Joyce's 'Ulysses'* (New York: Palgrave Macmillan, 2010).
69 Garry Leonard, *Advertising and Commodity Culture in Joyce* (Gainesville: University Press of Florida, 1998).
70 Ibid., p. 21.
71 Ibid., p. 73.
72 Jennifer Wicke, 'Joyce and Consumer Culture', in *The Cambridge Companion to James Joyce*, ed. by Derek Attridge, 2nd edn (Cambridge: Cambridge University Press, 2004), pp. 234–53 (p. 237).
73 Ibid., p. 236.
74 Knowlton, p. 134.
75 Ibid., p. 145.
76 Louise E. J. Hornby, 'Visual Clockwork: Photographic Time and the Instant in "Proteus"', *James Joyce Quarterly*, 42–3.1–4 (2004), 49–68 (pp. 49–50).
77 Ibid., p. 59.
78 Graham Smith, *'Light That Dances in the Mind': Photographs and Memory in the Writings of E. M. Forster and His Contemporaries* (Bern, Switzerland: Peter Lang, 2007), pp. 155–76.
79 Ibid., pp. 156, 174.
80 Philip Sicker, *'Ulysses', Film and Visual Culture* (Cambridge: Cambridge University Press, 2018).
81 Ibid., p. 7
82 Ibid.
83 John McCourt (ed.), *Roll away the Reel World: James Joyce and Cinema* (Cork: Cork University Press, 2010).
84 Cleo Hanaway-Oakley, *James Joyce and the Phenomenology of Film* (Oxford: Oxford University Press, 2017) and Keith Williams, *James Joyce and Cinematicity: Before and After Film* (Edinburgh: Edinburgh University Press, 2020).
85 Ibid., p. 3.
86 Ibid., p. 4.
87 Williams, p. 250.
88 Ibid., p. 126.
89 John A. Rea, 'A Bit of Lewis Carroll in *Ulysses*', *James Joyce Quarterly*, 15.1 (1977), 86–9.
90 James S. Atherton, 'Lewis Carroll and *Finnegans Wake*', *English Studies*, 33.1–6 (1952), 1–15 (p. 127).
91 Atherton, *The Books at the 'Wake': A Study of Literary Allusions in James Joyce's 'Finnegans Wake'* (Illinois: Southern Illinois University Press, 2009), p. 129.
92 Hugh Kenner, *Dublin's Joyce* (New York: Columbia University Press, 1956), p. 288.
93 Ibid.
94 Viviana Mirela Braslasu, '"Why, Mr J. and His God Alone Know!": Joyce and Lewis Carroll', *Dublin James Joyce Journal*, 8 (2015), 114–21.

95 Ibid., p. 115.
96 Genevieve Sartor, 'Genetic Connections in *Finnegans Wake*: Lucia Joyce and Issy Earwicker', *Journal of Modern Literature*, 41.1 (2018), 18–30 (p. 24).
97 Ciara Breathnach and Catherine Lawless (eds), 'Introduction', in *Visual, Material and Print Culture in Nineteenth-Century Ireland* (Dublin: Four Courts Press, 2010), pp. 15–19 (p. 15). https://www.fourcourtspress.ie/books/archives/visual-material-and-print-culture-in-nineteenth-century-ireland/contents.
98 Justin Carville, 'Introduction: Popular Visual Culture in Ireland', *Early Popular Visual Culture*, 5 (2007), 229–30 (p. 229).
99 Carville, 'With His "Mind-Guided Camera": J. M. Synge, J. J. Clarke, and the Visual Politics of Edwardian Street Photography', in *Synge and Edwardian Ireland*, ed. by Brian Cliff and Nicholas Grene (Oxford: Oxford University Press, 2012), pp. 186–207 (p. 186).
100 Kevin Rockett and Emer Rockett, *Magic Lantern, Panorama and Moving Picture Shows in Ireland, 1786–1909* (Dublin: Four Courts Press, 2011), p. 161.
101 Katherine Mullin, *James Joyce, Sexuality and Social Purity* (Cambridge: Cambridge University Press, 2003).
102 Latham, p. 152.
103 Stephen Watt, 'Brief Exposures: Commodification, Exchange Value, and the Figure of Woman in "Eumaeus"', *James Joyce Quarterly*, 30.4–31.1 (1993), 757–82.
104 Flynn, pp. 19–34.
105 Ibid.
106 Ibid.
107 Tristan Tzara, 'La photographie à l'envers' (Photography from the Verso), 1922, in Walter Benjamin, *Selected Writings: Volume 2, Part 2, 1931–1934*, trans. by Rodney Livingstone and et al., ed. by Michael W. Jennings and et al. (Cambridge, MA: Harvard University Press, 2005), p. 55.
108 'Fine Arts', *The Cork Examiner*, 1851, n. p.
109 Alison Smith, *The Victorian Nude: Sexuality, Morality, and Art* (Manchester: Manchester University Press, 1996), p. 59.

Chapter 1

1 'Photographic Convention of the United Kingdom: Dublin Meeting', *British Journal of Photography*, 41.1784 (13 July 1894), 437–40 (p. 438).
2 Tristan Tzara, 'Dada Manifesto 1918', in *Modernism: An Anthology*, ed. by Lawrence Rainey (Oxford: Wiley-Blackwell, 2005), pp. 479–83 (p. 481).
3 John B. Tabb, 'From a Photograph', in *Camera Work* (New York), ed. by Alfred Stieglitz, 1 January 1903, *Modernist Journals Project*, https://modjourn.org/issue/bdr566054 [accessed 16 April 2021] (pp. 16).

4   Tristan Tzara, '"La photographie à l'envers" (Photography from the Verso)', 1922, in Walter Benjamin, *Selected Writings: Volume 2, Part 2, 1931–1934*, trans. by Rodney Livingstone and et al., ed. by Michael W. Jennings and et al. (Cambridge, MA: Harvard University Press, 2005), p. 55.
5   Ibid.
6   Ibid.
7   'Photographic Convention of the United Kingdom', pp. 437–40 (p. 440).
8   Jacques Lafayette, 'Photograph of James Joyce as a Boy with His Mother, Mary Jane Murray Joyce', 1888, Lafayette Photography (Historical Photographs), https://ireland.lafayettephotography.com (showing 505 to 516 of 725 items) [accessed 11 April 2021]. Whilst this image is credited to Lafayette's, it would not have necessarily been taken by the store's owner.
9   'The Opening and Back Page of a Lafayette Publicity Brochure *circa* 1902', The Lafayette Negative Archive, http://lafayette.org.uk/lafhist.html [accessed 10 April 2021].
10 Edward Chandler, *Photography in Ireland: The Nineteenth Century* (Dublin: Edmund Burke, 2001), p. 97.
11 See Roland Barthes, *Camera Lucida* (London: Vintage, 2000).
12 Ibid., p. 26.
13 Ibid., pp. 43–5.
14 Tzara, 'Dada Manifesto 1918', p. 481.
15 Peadar Slattery, 'Lauder, James Stack ("Jacques Lafayette")', Dictionary of Irish Biography, https://www.dib.ie/biography [accessed 1 August 2021].
16 'Exhibitions: Photography at the Dublin Exhibition', *British Journal of Photography*, 12.263 (2 June 1865), 1–2 (p. 2).
17 Donald Torchiana, 'Joyce's "Eveline" and the Blessed Margaret Mary Alacoque', *James Joyce Quarterly*, 6.1 (1968), 22–8 (p. 25).
18 'James Joyce at age 6 ½, with his parents John and Mary Jane, and his maternal grandfather, John Murray', 1888, in Bob Cato and Greg Vitiello, *Joyce Images* (London: W. W. Norton & Company, 1994), p. 18. Though the photographer is unlisted, this image was taken at Lafayette's.
19 Barthes, pp. 26–7.
20 Ibid., p. 42.
21 Susan Sontag, *On Photography* (London: Penguin Modern Classics, 2008), p. 89.
22 Constantine Curran, 'James Joyce Standing beside Greenhouse, Dublin, 1904', James Joyce Collection, University at Buffalo, https://library.buffalo.edu/jamesjoyce/catalog/xvii [accessed 14 January 2021].
23 Ibid.
24 'The Gaiety Theatre', *Freeman's Journal*, 26 August 1898, p. 5.
25 'Pictures and Opera', *The Irish Times*, 10 January 1906, p. 7.

26 'Living Pictures and Scottish Meistersingers at the Rotunda', *The Irish Times*, 6 April 1901, p. 6.
27 'Pictures and Opera'.
28 Stanislaus Joyce, *My Brother's Keeper: James Joyce's Early Years*, ed. by Richard Ellmann (Cambridge, MA: Da Capo Press, 2003), p. 114.
29 Steve Edwards, *The Making of English Photography: Allegories* (University Park, PA: Penn State University Press, 2006), p. 83.
30 Ibid.
31 Katherine Mullin, *James Joyce, Sexuality and Social Purity* (Cambridge: Cambridge University Press, 2003), pp. 62–3.
32 Ibid.
33 Sontag, p. 4.
34 Ibid.
35 Barthes, p. 26.
36 Clarence F. Ray, 'Making Women Look Pretty in Their Photographs', *British Journal of Photography*, 57.2626 (2 September 1910), 663.
37 Garry Leonard, *Advertising and Commodity Culture in Joyce* (Gainesville: University Press of Florida, 1998), p. 94.
38 Sandra S. Phillips, 'Exposed: Voyeurism, Surveillance and the Camera', *Tate Exhibition Guide*, www.tate.org.uk/whats-on/tate-modern/exhibition [accessed 14 June 2021].
39 Deirdre Flynn, 'An Uncomfortable Fit: Joyce's Women in Dublin and Trieste', in *Joyce and the City: The Significance of Place*, ed. by Michael Begnal (Syracuse, NY: Syracuse University Press, 2002), pp. 51–64 (p. 55).
40 *The House That Jack Built* (London and Otley: William Walker and Sons, 1807).
41 Suzette A. Henke, *James Joyce and the Politics of Desire* (New York: Routledge, 1990), p. 30.
42 George Gordon, Lord, Byron, 'On the Death of a Young Lady, Cousin to the Author, and Very Dear to Him', in *The Works of Lord Byron: Complete in One Volume* (Frankfurt: H.L. Broenner, 1837), p. 376.
43 'Poole and Young's Panorama', *The Irish Times*, 9 October 1877, p. 5 and 'New Views of the World', *Quiver*, 30 January 1910, p. 30.
44 'The Great American Panorama', *The Irish Times*, 26 July 1875, p. 6.
45 Ibid.
46 Joseph V. O'Brien, *Dear, Dirty Dublin: A City in Distress, 1899–1916* (Berkeley: University of California Press, 1982), p. 173.
47 Ibid.
48 Kevin Rockett and Emer Rockett, *Magic Lantern, Panorama and Moving Picture Shows in Ireland, 1786–1909* (Dublin: Four Courts Press, 2011), pp. 71–2.
49 Ibid.

50 Keith Williams, '*Dubliners*, "the Magic-Lantern Business" and Pre-Cinema', in *James Joyce in the Nineteenth Century*, ed. by John Nash (Cambridge: Cambridge University Press, 2013), pp. 215–33 (p. 222).
51 Tzara, 'La photographie à l'envers', p. 55.
52 Richard Ellmann, *The Consciousness of Joyce* (London: Faber, 1977), p. 116.
53 Pope Leo XIII, 'Ars Photographica' in *Poem, Charades, Inscriptions of Pope Leo XIII: Including the Revised Compositions of His Early Life in Chronological Order*, trans. by H. T. Henry (New York and Philadelphia: American Ecclesiastical Review, 1902), p. 44.
54 Rev. E. Husband, '"The Photographers" Church Parade – Sermon', *Folkstone Express*, 49.2195 (24 May 1902), quoted in the *British Journal of Photography*, 30 May 1902, pp. 428–9.
55 Heinz K. Henisch and Bridget Ann Henisch, *The Photographic Experience, 1839–1914: Images and Attitudes* (University Park, PA: Penn State University Press, 1994), p. 433.
56 'The Biograph in the Vatican', *British Journal of Photography*, 46.2022 (3 February 1899), 15.
57 Ibid.
58 Rockett and Rockett, p. 73.
59 Ibid., p. 60.
60 'Coloured Cartes', *Freeman's Journal*, 2 March 1866, p. 2.
61 Tzara, 'La photographie à l'envers', p. 55.
62 Quoted in Stanislaus Joyce, p. 90.
63 Terence Brown, 'Notes', in James Joyce, *Dubliners* (London: Penguin Books, 2000), pp. 237–317 (p. 239).
64 Williams, p. 49.
65 Keith Williams, *James Joyce and Cinematicity: Before and After Film* (Edinburgh: Edinburgh University Press, 2020), p. 38.
66 Sontag, p. 97.
67 See 'St. Peter's College, Wexford', 1955 in Lafayette Photography (Historical Photographs) <https://ireland.lafayettephotography.com/photoselection/selectphotos?albumId=8> (showing 85 to 96 of 725 items) [accessed 11 April 2021] for an example of Lafayette's college photographs of priests.
68 Brown, pp. 237–317 (p. 309).
69 Justin Carville, *Photography and Ireland* (London: Reaktion Books, 2011), p. 39.
70 Brown, p. 310.
71 Anne Fogarty, 'Ghostly Intertexts: James Joyce and the Legacy of Synge', in *Synge and Edwardian Ireland*, ed. by Brian Cliff and Nicholas Grene (Oxford: Oxford University Press, 2012), pp. 225–44 (p. 242).
72 Ibid.

73 Carville, p. 106.
74 Ibid.
75 See John Millington Synge, 'Currach Collecting Turf from a Galway Hooker', c.1900, in Synge, *The Aran Islands* (Oxford: Oxford University Press, 1979), p. 146.
76 Ibid., pp. 75–6.
77 Sontag, p. 15.
78 *The Dead*, dir. by John Huston (Vestron Pictures, 1987) [on DVD].
79 Sontag, p. 15.
80 R. Brandon Kershner, 'Framing Rudy and Photography', *Journal of Modern Literature*, 22.2 (1998–99), 265–92 (p. 267).
81 Kershner, p. 273.
82 John Archer, *The Nature of Grief: The Evolution and Psychology of Reactions to Loss* (London: Routledge, 1999), p. 191.
83 C. Brangwin Barnes, 'Post-Mortem Photography', *British Journal of Photography*, 30.1213 (3 August 1883), 449–50 (p. 449).
84 Beth Ann Guynn, 'Postmortem Photography', in *Encyclopedia of Nineteenth-Century Photography*, ed. by John Hannavy, 2 vols (New York: Routledge, 2007), I, pp. 1164–7 (p. 1167).
85 Martson Moore, 'Memento Mori', *British Journal of Photography*, 34.1443 (30 December 1887), 826–27 (p. 827).
86 Barthes, p. 97.
87 Fritz Senn, 'Retrosemantics: How Understanding Trails Behind', *Papers on Joyce*, 7–8 (2001–02), 1–27 (p. 8).
88 Barthes, pp. 14–20.
89 Ibid.
90 Tzara, p. 55.

Chapter 2

1 David Allison, 'Photography and the Mass Market', in *The Kodak Museum: The Story of Popular Photography*, ed. by Colin Ford (London: Century Hutchinson, 1989), pp. 42–59 (p. 58).
2 Brian Coe, *Cameras: From Daguerreotypes to Instant Pictures* (Gothenburg: Nordbok, 1978), p. 165.
3 David Brewster, *The Stereoscope: Its History, Theory, and Construction, with Its Application to the Fine and Useful Arts and to Education* (London: John Murray, 1856), p. 1.
4 'Our Anaglyph Mask Coupon', *The Illustrated London News*, 29 March 1924, p. IV.
5 'Fine Arts', *The Cork Examiner*, 19 December 1851, n. p.

6   Sir Charles Wheatstone, 'Contributions to the Physiology of Vision – Part the First. On Some Remarkable, and Hitherto Unobserved, Phenomena of Binocular Vision', *Philosophical Transactions of the Royal Society*, 128 (1838), pp. 371–94 (p. 375).
7   Brian Liddy, 'Sir David Brewster', in *Encyclopedia of Nineteenth-Century Photography: A-I*, ed. by John Hannavy, 2 vols (New York: Routledge, 2008), I, pp. 209–11.
8   Ibid.
9   Brewster, p. 36.
10 André Rouillé, '*The Rise of Photography (1851–70)*', in *A History of Photography*, ed. by Jean-Claude Lemagny and André Rouillé, trans. by Janet Lloyd (Cambridge: Cambridge University Press, 1987), pp. 29–52 (p. 41).
11 'Great Depot, 11 Upper Sackville Street', *Freeman's Journal*, 17 August 1865, p. 1.
12 'Charles Dickens, ESQ – Splendid Photographic Portraits', *Freeman's Journal*, 28 August 1858, p. 1.
13 Ibid.
14 Kathleen Davidson, 'Connecting the Senses: Natural History and the British Museum in the *Stereoscopic Magazine*', *Interdisciplinary Studies in the Long Nineteenth Century*, 19 (2014), 11–14 (p. 12).
15 *The Contents of 'The Stereoscopic Magazine'*, ed. by Julian Holland (London: Lovell Reeve, 1858–1865), http://members.optusnet.com.au/jph8524/JHstereoscopic_mag.htm [accessed 2 November 2021].
16 Davidson, p. 6.
17 Fintan Cullen, *Ireland on Show: Art, Union, and Nationhood* (Farnham, Surrey: Ashgate, 2012), p. 34.
18 Oliver Wendell Holmes, 'The Stereoscope and the Stereograph', *The Atlantic Monthly*, 3 (1859), http://www.theatlantic.com [accessed 1 June 2021].
19 Luca Crispi, 'Manuscript Timeline, 1905–1922', *Genetic Joyce Studies*, 4 (2004), http://www.geneticjoycestudies.org [accessed 1 May 2021].
20 Charles Baudelaire, 'The Salon of 1859', in *The Mirror of Art: Critical Studies by Charles Baudelaire*, trans. and ed. by Jonathan Mayne (New York: Doubleday Anchor Books, 1956), pp. 220–305 (pp. 232).
21 Baudelaire, p. 296.
22 Ray Zone, *Stereoscopic Cinema and the Origins of 3-D Film, 1838–1952* (Lexington: University Press of Kentucky, 2007), p. 94.
23 Kevin and Emer Rockett, *Magic Lantern, Panorama and Moving Picture Shows in Ireland, 1786–1909* (Dublin: Four Courts Press, 2011), p. 161.
24 Lisa Z. Sigel, *Governing Pleasures: Pornography and Social Change in England, 1815–1914* (New Brunswick: Rutgers University Press, 2002), pp. 85–6.
25 James Joyce, *A First-Draft Version of 'Finnegans Wake'*, ed. by David Hayman (Austin: University of Texas Press, 1963), p. 70.

26 Kentwood D. Wells, 'The Stereopticon Men: On the Road with John Fallon's Stereopticon, 1860–1870', *The Magic Lantern Gazette*, 23.3 (2011), 3–34 (p. 3).
27 'The Passion Play', *The Kerry Sentinel*, 23 November 1910, p. 2.
28 Ibid.
29 'Solid Cinematography: Alleged Important New Discovery', *Weekly Irish Times*, 7 November 1903, p. 14.
30 David Weir, 'Stephen Dedalus: Rimbaud or Baudelaire?' *James Joyce Quarterly*, 18.1 (1980), 87–91 (p. 88).
31 Ibid.
32 Ibid.
33 Clive Hart, *Structure and Motif in 'Finnegans Wake'* (Evanston: Northwestern University Press, 1962), p. 159.
34 David Trotter, 'Stereoscopy: Modernism and the "Haptic"', *Critical Quarterly*, 46 (2004), 38–58 (p. 54).
35 Ibid.
36 Cleo Hanaway-Oakley, *James Joyce and the Phenomenology of Film* (Oxford: Oxford University Press, 2017), pp. 86–7.
37 Ibid., p. 91.
38 Joseph Duncan, 'The Modality of the Audible in Joyce's *Ulysses*', *PMLA*, 72 (1957), 286–95 and Fritz Senn, 'Esthetic Theories', *James Joyce Quarterly*, 2.2 (1965), 134–6.
39 Philip Sicker, 'Ulysses,' in *Film and Visual Culture* (Cambridge: Cambridge University Press, 2018), p. 56.
40 Ibid., p. 61.
41 Keith Williams, *James Joyce and Cinematicity: Before and After Film* (Edinburgh: Edinburgh University Press, 2020), p. 160.
42 Ibid., p. 160.
43 Alison Smith, *The Victorian Nude: Sexuality, Morality, and Art* (Manchester: Manchester University Press, 1996), p. 59.
44 Susan Sontag, *On Photography* (London: Penguin Modern Classics, 2008), p. 97.
45 Laura Burd Schiavo, 'From Phantom Image to Perfect Vision: Physiological Optics, Commercial Photography, and the Popularization of the Stereoscope', in *New Media, 1740–1915*, ed. by Lisa Gitelman and Geoffrey B. Pingree (Cambridge, MA: MIT Press, 2003), pp. 113–38 (p. 116).
46 Holmes.
47 Walter Benjamin, *The Work of Art in the Age of Mechanical Reproduction*, trans. by J. A. Underwood (London: Penguin, 2008), p. 8.
48 Juliana Bruno, *Atlas of Emotion: Journeys in Art, Architecture, and Film* (London: Verso, 2002), p. 6.

49 Katherine Mullin, *James Joyce, Sexuality and Social Purity* (Cambridge: Cambridge University Press, 2003), p. 145.
50 John Plunkett, 'Selling Stereoscopy, 1890–1915: Penny Arcades, Automatic Machines and American Salesmen', *Early Popular Visual Media*, 6 (2008), 239–55 (p. 250).
51 Ibid.
52 Ibid.
53 Tim Conley, 'Marcella the Midget Queen', *James Joyce Quarterly*, 48.1 (2010), 149–53.
54 'The Burglary in Henry Street', *Freeman's Journal*, 14 July 1899, p. 2.
55 'Cyclopia', *Freeman's Journal*, 23 May 1896, n. p.
56 'Advertisements and Notices', *The Era*, 12 August 1899, p. 27.
57 Ibid.
58 Nic Costa, *Automatic Pleasures: The History of the Coin Machine* (London: Kevin Francis, 1988), p. 193.
59 Plunkett, p. 247.
60 'Lotteries and Advertisements', *The Spectator*, 19 September 1908, p. 8.
61 Plunkett, p. 250.
62 Ibid.
63 Linda Williams, 'Corporealized Observers: Visual Pornographics and the "Carnal Density of Vision"', in *Fugitive Images: From Photography to Video*, ed. by Patrice Petro (Bloomington: Indiana University Press, 1995), pp. 3–41 (p. 34).
64 Keith Williams, 'Time and Motion Studies: Joycean Cinematicity in *A Portrait of the Artist as a Young Man*', in *Cinematicity in Media History*, ed. by Jeffrey Geiger and Karin Littau (Edinburgh: Edinburgh University Press, 2013), pp. 88–106 (p. 91).
65 See Darcy O'Brien, *The Conscience of James Joyce* (Princeton: Princeton University Press, 1968), p. 160.
66 Smith, p. 59.
67 G. R. Baker, 'The Stereoscope and "Art"', *The British Journal of Photography*, 41.1808 (28 December 1894), p. 822.
68 Radiant, 'The Search Light', *The British Journal of Photography*, 42.1835 (4 January 1895), 3–4 (pp. 3–4).
69 E. Agelou, 'Stereoscopic Image on Paper', c. 1900, in Serge Nazarieff, *The Stereoscopic Nude 1850–1930* (Köln: Benedikt Taschen Verlag GmbH, 1993), p. 132.
70 George du Maurier, *Trilby* (Oxford: Oxford University Press, 1995), p. 15.
71 Ibid.
72 Smith, p. 59.
73 Ibid., p. 8.
74 Ibid., p. 59.

75 Trotter, p. 41.
76 'Lotteries and Advertisements'.
77 'In Bloemfontein: Collapse of the Free Staters – How the Boers Were Deceived Entry of the Sixth Division', *The Irish Times*, 19 March 1900, p. 5.
78 Williams, *James Joyce and Cinematicity*, p. 160.
79 Simeon Headsman, 'Letters to a Photographic Friend', *The British Journal of Photography*, 8.148 (15 August 1860, 241–3 (p. 242).
80 Brewster, p. 205.
81 Ibid., p. 206
82 Colin Harding, 'G is for Ghosts … the Birth and Rise of Spirit Photography', *National Media Museum Blog*, https://nationalmediamuseumblog.wordpress.com [accessed 20 February 2021].
83 Rockett and Rockett, p. 48.
84 Williams, *James Joyce and Cinematicity*, p. 87.
85 'Advertisements & Notices', *Freeman's Journal*, 11 May 1874, n. p.
86 Edmund H. Wilkie, 'Optical Illusions', in *The Optical Lantern and Cinematograph Journal* (London: E. T. Heron, 1904), pp. 41–3 (p. 42).
87 Maria DiBattista, 'The Ghost Walks: Joyce and the Spectres of Silent Cinema', in *Roll Away the Reel World: James Joyce and Cinema*, ed. by John McCourt (Cork: Cork University Press, 2010), pp. 57–68 (p. 60).
88 Rockett and Rockett, p.62.
89 Underwood & Underwood, '(3)-7907- And in trying to please both, this is the result', 1906.
90 Heinz K. Henisch, *Positive Pleasures: Early Photography and Humor* (University Park, PA: Penn State University Press, 1998), p. 139.
91 Strohmeyer & Wyman, New York, '"Be the Howly St. Patrick! – there's Mickie's Ghost"', 1894.
92 Mary Lowe-Evans, *Catholic Nostalgia in Joyce and Company* (Gainesville: University of Florida Press, 2008), p. 1.
93 Roland McHugh, *Annotations to 'Finnegans Wake'*, 4th edn (Baltimore: Johns Hopkins University Press, 2016), p. 107.
94 Joyce, *A First-Draft Version of 'Finnegans Wake'*, p. 70.
95 Williams, p. 57.
96 Ibid.
97 T. H. McAllister, *Catalogue of Stereopticons, Dissolving View Apparatus, Magic Lanterns: A List of Over 3000 Carefully Selected Views for the Illustration of Subjects of Popular Interest – Primary Source Edition* (New York: Nabu Press, 2011), pp.11–12.
98 'General Mulholland at the Rotunda', *Freeman's Journal*, 19 April 1892, p. 5.

99 *Philadelphia Press,* 1 October 1862, quoted in Kentwood D. Wells, 'The Stereopticon Photographic Illustrations', *The Magic Lantern Gazette*, 20.3 (2008), 2 (p. 2).
100 Rockett and Rockett, p. 51.
101 Hayman, p. 175.
102 Ibid.
103 Eric McLuhan, *The Role of Thunder in 'Finnegans Wake'* (Toronto: University of Toronto Press, 1997), p. 123.
104 Ibid.
105 Holmes.
106 Joyce, 'Protodrafts 2nd draft', December 1923, I.4§2 draft level 1, MS 47471b 12, 16, British Library, *James Joyce Digital Archive,* ed. by Danis Rose and John O'Hanlon, https://jjda.ie [accessed 2 February 2021]. Hereafter referred to as *JJDA*.
107 Joyce, 'Protodrafts 1st typescript', January 1924–early 1927, I.4§2 draft level 3, MS 47472 161–2, British Library, *JJDA*.
108 Finn Fordham, *Lots of Fun at 'Finnegans Wake'* (Oxford: Oxford University Press, 2007), p. 99.
109 William York Tindall, *A Reader's Guide to 'Finnegans Wake'* (Syracuse, NY: Syracuse University Press, 1969), p. 197.
110 'The Opening and Back Page of a Lafayette Publicity Brochure *circa* 1902', The Lafayette Negative Archive, http://lafayette.org.uk/lafhist.html [accessed 10 April 2021].
111 Louis-Jacques-Mandé Daguerre, 'Daguerreotype (1839)', in *Classic Essays on Photography*, ed. by Alan Trachtenberg (New Haven: Leete's Island Books, 1980), pp. 11–14 (p. 13).
112 '*The Times* Correspondent in the East', *Irish Examiner,* 1 November 1854, p. 4.
113 William Howard Russell, *The British Expedition to the Crimea* (London: George Routledge and Sons, 1877), p. 2.
114 Roger Fenton to Grace Fenton, Letter, 8 March 1855, Joseph Fenton letter-book, Gernsheim Collection, Harry Ransom Humanities Research Centre, Austin, http://rogerfenton.dmu.ac.uk/showLetter.php?letterNo=3 [accessed 10 February 2021].
115 Ibid.
116 Hirst Milhollen, 'Roger Fenton, Photographer of the Crimean War', *Quarterly Journal of Current Acquisitions*, 3.4 (1946), pp. 10–12 (p. 12).
117 Roger Fenton to Grace Fenton, 'Letter Number 11', 29 April 1855, Annie Grace Fenton letter-book, Royal Photographic Society Collection, National Museum of Photography, Film & Television, Bradford.
118 'Advertisements and Notices', *Freeman's Journal,* 6 February 1856, n. p.
119 'Boys of the Old Brigade: Belfast and the Veteran Soldiers', *Weekly Irish Times,* 14 November 1908, p. 7.
120 'Mr Fenton's Crimean Photographs', *Freeman's Journal,* 24 January 1856, p. 3

121 Robert Hunt, 'On the Applications of Science to the Fine and Useful Arts. Improvements in Photography – Hyalotype, & C.', *The Art-Journal*, XIII (1851), 106–7 (p. 106).
122 Quoted in Zone, p. 57.
123 Zone, p. 103.
124 Unknown Photographer, 'Seen in Stereoscopic Relief if Viewed through Red and Green Films: Occupants of the New "Zoo" Aquarium', *The Illustrated London News*, 29 March 1924, pp. 548–9.
125 'Our Anaglyph Mask Coupon'.
126 Hanaway-Oakley, p. 236.
127 McHugh, p. 423.

Chapter 3

1   See Sophie Chmura, 'Cartes-Postales de Rennes ou D'Ailleurs', http://cartes-postales35.monsite-orange.fr [accessed 10 February 2021].
2   The contents of James Joyce's Paris and Pola notebooks, initially thought to be separate entities, form part of his wider commonplace book composed between 1903 and 1912. See Luca Crispi, 'A Commentary on James Joyce's National Library of Ireland "Early Commonplace Book": 1903–1912 (MS 36,639/02/A)', *Genetic Joyce Studies*, 9 (2009), 1–25.
3   See Richard F. Peterson, 'More Aristotelian Grist for the Joycean Mill', *James Joyce Quarterly*, 17.2 (1980), 213–16 and Catherine Flynn, *James Joyce and the Matter of Paris* (Cambridge: Cambridge University Press, 2019), pp. 48–9.
4   Frank Budgen, *James Joyce and the Making of 'Ulysses'* (Oxford: Oxford University Press, 1989), p. 327.
5   Bernard Marbot, 'The New Image Takes Its First Steps (1839–50)', in *A History of Photography*, ed. by Jean-Claude Lemagny and André Rouillé, trans. by Janet Lloyd (Cambridge: Cambridge University Press, 1987), pp. 19–29 (p. 20).
6   Dominique de Font-réaulx, 'France', in *Encyclopedia of Nineteenth-Century Photography: A-I*, ed. by John Hannavy, 2 vols (New York: Routledge, 2008), I, pp. 544–51 (p. 546).
7   Charles Baudelaire, 'The Salon of 1859', in *The Mirror of Art: Critical Studies by Charles Baudelaire*, trans. and ed. by Jonathan Mayne (New York: Doubleday Anchor Books, 1956), pp. 220–305 (pp. 230–1).
8   Ibid., p. 232.
9   'Opening of the Dublin International Exhibition', *The Irish Times*, 10 May 1865, p. 5.
10 Ibid.
11 'Private Correspondence', *The Irish Times*, 7 June 1866, p. 3.

12 'Article 3 – No Title', *The Irish Times*, 12 March 1873, p. 2.
13 'Honours in Art Photography', *The Irish Times*, 3 December 1895, p. 6.
14 'Art Photography', *The Irish Times*, 13 July 1876, p. 3.
15 Rev. Henry W. Dick, 'The Relation of Photography to Art', *The American Amateur Photographer*, 1 March 1906, pp. 125–8 (pp. 126–7).
16 'L'envoi. Photography – Not Art', *The Photographic Times*, 1 March 1899, pp. 125–8 (p. 126).
17 Ibid.
18 'Photographers (Dublin and Suburbs Trades' Directory)', in *Thom's Official Directory of the United Kingdom of Great Britain and Ireland* (Dublin: Thom's, 1904), p. 2077.
19 Edward Chandler, *Photography in Ireland: The Nineteenth Century* (Dublin: Edmund Burke, 2001), p. 88.
20 Russell Harris, 'Lafayette, James (James Stack Lauder) (1853–1923)', in *Encyclopedia of Nineteenth-Century Photography: J-Z*, ed. by John Hannavy, 2 vols (New York: Routledge, 2008), II, pp. 813–14 (p. 813).
21 Ibid.
22 Ibid., p. 814.
23 Ibid.
24 'Irish Portraits for the Chicago Exhibition', *The Irish Times*, 29 March 1893, p. 8.
25 Ibid.
26 Ibid.
27 Helmut Gernsheim, *A Concise History of Photography*, 3rd edn (New York: Dover Publications, 1986), p. 26.
28 'Irish Portraits for the Chicago Exhibition'.
29 'Lafayette's Photographic Studio', *The Irish Times*, 16 August 1888, p. 4.
30 'Fashionable Intelligence', *The Irish Times*, 18 March 1902, p. 6.
31 'New Portraits in Ivory', *Weekly Irish Times*, 16 April 1904, p. 24.
32 'Oil Paintings at Lafayette's', *The Irish Times*, 28 February 1907, p. 6.
33 'The Lady's Pictorial', *The Irish Times*, 23 June 1900, p. 9.
34 Walter Kendrick, 'The Corruption of Gerty MacDowell', *James Joyce Quarterly*, 37.3–4 (2000), 413–23 (p. 415).
35 'Queen Victoria: In Memoriam', *Lady's Pictorial*, 2 February 1901.
36 'Photo-Mechanical Notes: Half-Tones in Newspaper Illustrations', *British Journal of Photography*, p. 727.
37 'Weddings', *Lady's Pictorial*, 23 February 1907, p. 545.
38 'Supplement', *Lady's Pictorial*, 23 November 1907, p. 32.
39 Luca Crispi, 'Manuscript Timeline, 1905–1922', *Genetic Joyce Studies*, 4 (2004), http://www.geneticjoycestudies.org [accessed 1 May 2021].

40 'Princess Alexander of Teck', *Lady's Pictorial*, 2 November 1907, http://www.torontopubliclibrary.ca [accessed 26 April 2021] (p. 1).

41 'Illustrated Sources: Women's Interest', *Cardiff University Library Special Collections*, http://www.cardiff.ac.uk [accessed 2 December 2020].

42 Don Gifford and Robert J. Seidman, *'Ulysses' Annotated: Notes for James Joyce's 'Ulysses'*, 2nd edn (Berkeley: University of California Press, 1989), p. 392.

43 Margaret Beetham, 'Periodicals and the New Media: Women and Imagined Communities', *Women's Studies International Forum*, 29 (2006), 231–40 (p. 237).

44 Mark Osteen, *The Economy of Ulysses: Making Both Ends Meet* (Syracuse, NY: Syracuse University Press, 1995), p. 298.

45 'Special Number: Matisse, Picasso, and Stein', *Camera Work* (New York), ed. by Alfred Stieglitz, 1 August 1912, *Modernist Journals Project*, https://modjourn.org/journal/camera-work [accessed 10 February 2021].

46 Ibid.

47 Sylvia Beach, *Shakespeare and Company* (London: Faber and Faber, 1956), p. 40.

48 'P. & S. Semi-Achromatic Lenses', *Camera Work*, 1 August 1912, Modernist Journal Project, p. 83.

49 Joseph T. Keiley, 'The Salon: Its Purpose, Character and Lesson', *Camera Notes*, 3.3 (1900), n. p.

50 'L'envoi. Photography – Not Art'.

51 Ibid.

52 Joseph Gleeson White, 'On Photographing the Nude IV', *The Photogram*, 1.6, June 1894, in *A Carnal Medium: fin-de-siècle Essays on the Photographic Nude*, ed. by James Downs (Portsmouth: Callum James Books, 2012), pp. 81–106 (p. 96).

53 Ibid.

54 *British Journal of Photography*, 1898, quoted in Colin Harding, 'Snapshot', in *Encyclopedia of Nineteenth-Century Photography: J-Z*, ed. by John Hannavy, 2 vols (New York: Routledge, 2008), I, pp. 1277–9 (p. 1279).

55 Gleeson White, 'The Nude in Photography. With Some Studies Taken in the Open Air. The Studio', 15 June 1893, in *A Carnal Medium*, pp. 35–44 (pp. 37–8).

56 Gleeson White, 'On Photographing the Nude II', *The Photogram*, April 1894, in *A Carnal Medium*, pp. 53–60 (p. 54).

57 'News and Notes of the Week: Artists' Model, and Postcard', *British Journal of Photography*, 78.3701 (17 April 1931), 234.

58 Ibid.

59 Alison Smith, *The Victorian Nude: Sexuality, Morality, and Art* (Manchester: Manchester University Press, 1996), p. 62.

60 George Du Maurier, *Trilby* (Oxford: Oxford University Press, 1995), p. 233.

61 Ibid.

62 George du Maurier, 'Things One Would Rather Have Left Unsaid', *Punch*, 5 May 1888, http://punch.photoshelter.com [accessed 10 January 2021].
63 Reena Suleman, 'Still Lives: The Art of Edward Linley Sambourne', in *Model and Supermodel: The Artists' Model in British Art and Culture*, ed. by Jane Desmarais, Martin Postle and Martin Vaughan (Manchester: Manchester University Press, 2006), pp. 75–88 (p. 78).
64 Ibid., p. 81.
65 *Punch*, c. 1887, quoted in Tom Gunning, 'Embarrassing Evidence: The Detective Camera and the Documentary Impulse', in *Collecting Visible Evidence*, ed. by Jane M. Gaines and Michael Renov (Minneapolis: University of Minnesota Press, 1999), pp. 46–64 (p. 46).
66 Mary Ann Roberts, 'Edward Linley Sambourne', *History of Photography*, 17 (1993), 207–13 (p. 212).
67 'Commercial and Legal Intelligence', *British Journal of Photography*, 19 November 1909, p. 904.
68 Ibid.
69 Ibid.
70 'The Opening and Back Page of a Lafayette Publicity Brochure *circa* 1902', The Lafayette Negative Archive, http://lafayette.org.uk/lafhist.html [10 April 2021].
71 See Figure 1.2 in Chapter 1 of this project for further details on Lafayette's 1888 photographs of the Joyces.
72 See Mark Osteen, *The Economy of 'Ulysses': Making Both Ends Meet* for a detailed discussion of their respective earnings.
73 Jacques Henri Lartigue, '*Mon livre de photographie*', 1925, in *Hidden Depths*, trans. and ed. by William Hibbert (London: Design for Life, 2004), p. 95.
74 Lartigue, 'Young Woman Walking in the Bois', 1912, in *Hidden Depths*, p. 17.
75 Sandra S. Phillips (ed.), 'Looking Out, Looking In: Voyeurism and Its Affinities from the Beginning of Photography', in *Exposed: Voyeurism, Surveillance and the Camera* (London: Tate Publishing, 2010), pp. 11–18 (p. 14).
76 *L'Amateur Photographe*, 1887, quoted in Gunning, p. 50.
77 Justin Carville, 'With His "Mind-Guided Camera": J. M. Synge, J. J. Clarke, and the Visual Politics of Edwardian Street Photography', in *Synge and Edwardian Ireland*, ed. by Brian Cliff and Nicholas Grene (Oxford: Oxford University Press, 2012), pp. 186–207 (p. 199).
78 'Lafayette's Photographic Studios. By Royal Warrant to the Queen and Prince and Princess of Wales', *The Irish Times*, 16 September 1895, p. 4.
79 Ibid.
80 'Advertisements', *Photo Bits*, 11 March 1911, p. 2.
81 Harding, 'Snapshot', pp. 1277–9 (p. 1279).
82 Fritz Senn, 'Retrosemantics: How Understanding Trails Behind', *Papers on Joyce*, 7–8 (2001–02), pp. 1–27 (p. 8).

83 'The Living Complexions of Living Beauties for Sale, and The Identical Complexion of Your Girlhood', *Lady's Pictorial*, 23 November 1907, p. 891.
84 H. H. Snelling, 'American National Photographic Association', *British Journal of Photography*, 20.686 (27 June 1873), 308–9 (p. 308).
85 Ibid.
86 Peadar Slattery, 'Lauder, James Stack ("Jacques Lafayette")', Dictionary of Irish Biography, https://www.dib.ie/biography [accessed 1 August 2021].
87 'London "Punch" and Its Makers: I – The Writers', *The Book Buyer*, 1 July 1899, 18, pp. 451–8 (p. 458).
88 'Oil Paintings at Lafayette's', p. 6.
89 Ibid.
90 Nicholas Fargnoli and Michael Patrick Gillespie, *James Joyce A to Z: The Essential Reference to the Life and Work* (Oxford: Oxford University Press, 1995), p. 110.
91 'Classified Ad 302 – No Title', *The Irish Times*, 8 July 1903, p. 6.
92 'The Animated Pictures at the Star Theatre: Action by the Edison Manufacturing Company', *The Irish Times*, 29 July 1903, p. 3.
93 Sue E. Atkinson, 'Cigarette Advertising: A History', *The British Journal of Photography*, 20 November 1981, 1190–9.
94 See Gifford and Seidman, p. 283.
95 Tess Marsh, 'Is There More to "Photo Bits" than Meets the Eye?', *James Joyce Quarterly*, 30.4–31.1 (1993), 877–93 (pp. 878–2).
96 Baudelaire, pp. 230–1.
97 Gleeson White, 'The Nude in Photography. With Some Studies Taken in the Open Air'.
98 Bob Nicholson, 'Nineteenth-Century Nuts: The Anatomy of a Victorian Lad's Mag', *The Digital Victorianist*, http://www.digitalvictorianist.com [accessed 15 July 2021].
99 'Front Cover' and 'Some Great Actresses', *The National Police Gazette*, 28 December 1912, p. 1 and p. 11.
100 Joseph Valente, 'The Novel and the Police (Gazette)', *Novel: A Forum on Fiction*, 29 (1995), 8–18 (p. 14).
101 Richard K. Bass, 'Additional Allusions in "Eumaeus"', *James Joyce Quarterly*, 10.3 (1973), 321–9 (p. 327).
102 Marco Camerani, 'Joyce and Early Cinema: Peeping Bloom through the Keyhole', in *Joyce in Progress: Proceedings of the 2008 James Joyce Graduate Conference in Rome*, ed. by Franca Ruggieri, John McCourt and Enrico Terrinoni (Newcastle: Cambridge Scholars Press, 2009), pp. 114–28 (p. 115).
103 Katherine Mullin, *James Joyce, Sexuality and Social Purity* (Cambridge: Cambridge University Press, 2003).
104 'Lafayette's Photographic Studios. By Royal Warrant to the Queen and Prince and Princess of Wales'.

105 Kimberly J. Devlin, '"See Ourselves as Others See Us": Joyce's Look at the Eye of the Other', *PMLA*, 104 (1989), 882–93 (p. 883).

106 Nicholas Hiley, 'Candid Camera Edwardian Tabloids', *History Today*, 43 (1993), http://www.historytoday.com [accessed 10 October 2020], n. p.

107 'Photography', *Encyclopædia Britannica*, 11th edn (New York: The Encyclopædia Britannica Company, 1910), pp. 485–522 (pp. 501–2).

108 Ibid.

109 Ibid.

110 'Real Evidence', *Citizens Information Board*, 6 January 2014, http://www.citizensinformation.ie [accessed 13 April 2021].

111 Ibid.

112 'One of our Most Enthusiastic Admirers', *Photo Bits*, 11 March 1911, p. 4.

113 Ibid.

114 Asa Briggs, *Victorian Things* (Chicago: University of Chicago Press, 1988), p. 135.

115 Steve Edwards, *The Making of English Photography: Allegories* (University Park, PA: Penn State University Press, 2006), p. 32.

116 Andreas Kitzmann, *Saved from Oblivion: Documenting the Daily from Diaries to Web Cams* (New York: Peter Lang, 2004), p. 42.

117 Gleeson White, 'On Photographing the Nude IV', p. 91.

118 'Mary Murray', The National Archives of Ireland: Census of Ireland, 1911, http://www.census.nationalarchives.ie [accessed 1 July 2021].

119 'John and Nealie Deegan', The National Archives of Ireland: Census of Ireland, 1911.

120 Roberts, p. 209.

121 Ibid.

122 'Phyllis Sutcliffe and Frances Sutcliffe', 95 Melrose Street, Windsor, Antrim, The National Archives of Ireland: Census of Ireland 1901, http://www.census.nationalarchives.ie [accessed 1 July 2021].

123 Jane Desmarais, Martin Postle and William Vaughan (eds), 'Introduction', in *Model and Supermodel: The Artists' Model in British Art and Culture*, pp. 1–8 (p. 2).

124 James Joyce, 'Ibsen's New Drama', *The Fortnightly Review*, 1 April 1900, https://fortnightlyreview.co.uk [accessed 23 December 2020].

125 Roberts, p. 208.

126 Ibid.

127 'Croydon Camera Club', *British Journal of Photography*, 11 November 1932, p. 690.

128 Luca Crispi, *Joyce's Creative Process and the Construction of Characters in 'Ulysses': Becoming the Blooms* (Oxford: Oxford University Press, 2015), p. 249.

129 For a detailed exploration of Frank's request to Eveline that they travel to 'Buenos Ayres', see Mullin, pp. 56–82.

Chapter 4

1. Susan Sontag, *On Photography* (London: Penguin, 2008), p. 23.
2. See Xavier Tricot, *James Joyce in Ostend* (Devriendt: Belgium, 2018) for images captured in Ostend in 1926 and now housed in the University at Buffalo's James Joyce Collection. The Buffalo archives incorrectly date these photographs to 1924, two years prior to their visit to Ostend. For photographs taken in Saint Malo, France, see Lucia Joyce, 'Mr and Mrs Joyce and Giorgio, taken by Lucia?', 1924, Harriet Shaw Weaver Papers, Vol. XXI A, B. Photographs, mostly of James Joyce; 1888–1938, British Library, https://www.bl.uk/collection-items [accessed 10 June 2021].
3. Tricot, p. 33.
4. Ibid., p. 33.
5. Nora Joyce, 'Lucia Joyce on the pier at Ostend', dated between 6 and 26 August 1926, in *James Joyce in Ostend,* p. iv.
6. See Lucia Joyce, 'Nora Joyce sitting in her room of the Hôtel de l'Océan at Ostend', dated between 9 and 26 August 1926, p. v and 'James Joyce, Nora and Giorgio Joyce at a dining table in the park at Ostend, dated between 5 and 12 September 1926', in *James Joyce in Ostend,* p. xiv.
7. 'News and Notes', *British Journal of Photography,* 73.3472 (19 November 1926), 683.
8. 'New Apparatus and Materials: The Baby "Brownie", Sold by Kodak, Limited, Kingsway, London, W.C.1.', *British Journal of Photography,* 28 June 1935, p. 412.
9. H. J. Falk and M. G. Spencer, 'The Occupations of Women in London', *The Speaker: The Liberal Review,* 16 January 1904, pp. 380–1.
10. Ibid.
11. 'Women Photographers', *Irish Society and Social Review,* 17 September 1921, p. 634.
12. Ibid.
13. Ibid.
14. Christiaan Corlett, *Jane W. Shackleton's Ireland* (Wilton, Cork: The Collins Press, 2012), p. 5.
15. Ibid.
16. The National Archives of Ireland: Census of Ireland 1901/11, http://www.census.nationalarchives.ie/ [accessed 20 April 2021].
17. Ibid.
18. Ibid.
19. I am grateful to Rose Teanby for providing this information on women photographers' census records, following her 27 October 2020 on 'The First Women of Photography 1839–1860' in collaboration with The Royal Photographic Society, Great Britain.

20 Maggie Humm, *Modernist Women and Visual Cultures* (Edinburgh: Edinburgh University Press, 2002), p. 19.
21 Frances Dimond, *Developing the Picture: Queen Alexandra and the Art of Photography* (London: Royal Collection Publications, 2004), p. 61.
22 Justin Carville, *Photography and Ireland* (London: Reaktion Books, 2011), p. 112.
23 'Catherine Brennan' and 'Margaret Mary Leonard', The National Archives of Ireland: Census of Ireland 1911, http://www.census.nationalarchives.ie [accessed 3 April 2021].
24 'Advertisements and Notices', *Freeman's Journal*, 28 October 1899, n. p.
25 'Kodak Photographic Apparatus & Materials', 1910, The Kodak Heritage Collection, Museums Victoria Collections, https://collections.museumsvictoria.com.au/items/2181129 [accessed 20 April 2021].
26 'Display Ad 9 – No Title', *The Irish Times*, 17 April 1903, p. 3.
27 'Kodak, Limited, Staff Dance', *The Irish Times*, 28 January 1910, p. 3.
28 James Joyce, *A First-Draft Version of 'Finnegans Wake'*, ed. by David Hayman (Austin: University of Texas Press, 1963), p. 111.
29 Michael R. Peres (ed.), 'Profiles of Selected Photographic Film and Digital Companies', in *The Focal Encyclopedia of Photography*, 4th edn (Waltham, MA: Focal Press, 2007), pp. 301–20 (p. 311).
30 George Eastman quoted in Elizabeth Brayer, *George Eastman: A Biography* (Rochester, NY: University of Rochester Press, 2006), p. 135.
31 'Avery's car at Brighton Carnival', 1922, in Colin Harding, 'The Kodak Girl', *Photographica World*, 78 (1996), 10–15 (p. 13).
32 *The Photographic News*, 1891, quoted in Alison Nordström, 'Lovely, Smart, Modern: Women with Cameras in a Changing World', in *Kodak Girl: From the Martha Cooper Collection*, ed. by John P. Jacob (Göttingen: Steidl, 2011), pp. 64–71 (p. 69).
33 Ibid.
34 Alfred Jarry, 'The Passion Considered as an Uphill Bicycle Race', in *Anthology of Black Humor*, ed. by Andre Bréton, trans. by Mark Polizzotti (San Francisco: City Lights Books, 1997), pp. 223–5 (p. 225).
35 'London Letter', *The Western Daily Press, Bristol*, 17 May 1899, p. 8.
36 'Bicycle Kodaks', *The Illustrated Sporting and Dramatic News*, 26 June 1897, p. 699.
37 Virginia Woolf, *Jacob's Room* (London: The Hogarth Press, 1960), p. 150. Just as Woolf removes the company's capital 'K', so too does Joyce in his depiction of the 'Tulloch-Turnbull girl with her coldblood kodak' (*FW* 171.31–32).
38 Viviana Mirela Braslasu, '"Why, Mr J. and His God alone Know!": Joyce and Lewis Carroll', *Dublin James Joyce Journal*, 8 (2015), 114–21.
39 James Joyce, *James Joyce's Letters to Sylvia Beach, 1921–1940*, ed. by Melissa Banta and Oscar A, Silverman (Oxford: Plantain Publishers, 1990), p. 167.
40 James Joyce, 'Borrowing Activities', *Shakespeare and Company Project*.

41 Ibid.
42 Joyce, 'Continuation of a Work in Progress (II.2§8)', *transition*, 11 (1928), pp. 7–18, https://gallica.bnf.fr/ark:/12148/bpt6k6448050n/f9.image [21 September 2021] (p. 10).
43 Isa Bowman, *The Story of Lewis Carroll, Told for Young People by the Real Alice in Wonderland* (New York: E. P. Dutton & Company, 1900), p. 5.
44 Diane Waggoner, *Lewis Carroll's Photography and Modern Childhood* (Princeton, NJ: Princeton University Press, 2020), p. 19.
45 Ibid., p. 194.
46 Joseph Valente, 'Joyce and Sexuality', in *The Cambridge Companion to James Joyce*, ed. by Derek Attridge (Cambridge: Cambridge University Press, 2004), pp. 213–33 (pp. 217–18).
47 Jennifer Wicke, 'Joyce and Consumer Culture', in *The Cambridge Companion to James Joyce*, ed. by Derek Attridge (2004), pp. 234–53 (p. 244).
48 Katherine Mullin, 'Joyce, Early Cinema and the Erotics of Everyday Life', in *Roll Away the Reel World: James Joyce and Cinema*, ed. by John McCourt (Cork: Cork University Press, 2010), pp. 43–56 (pp. 50–1).
49 See William Anastasi with Michael Seidel, 'Jarry in Joyce: A Conversation', in *Joyce Studies Annual*, ed. by Thomas F. Staley (Austin: University of Texas Press, 1995), pp. 39–58 and Susan Brienza, 'Murphy, Shem, Morpheus, and Murphies: Eumaeus Meets the *Wake*', in *Joycean Occasions: Essays from the Milwaukee James Joyce Conference*, ed. by Janet Egleson Dunleavy, Melvin J. Friedman and Michael Patrick Gillespie (Newark: University of Delaware Press, 1991), pp. 80–94 (p. 88).
50 Braslasu, p. 115.
51 Ibid.
52 'Ethel Shaw', The National Archives of Ireland: Census of Ireland 1901, http://www.census.nationalarchives.ie/ [accessed 20 April 2021].
53 Ibid.
54 'Philip Shaw, Clonkill, Mullingar', *c.* 1900, in '"Milly Bloom", Apprentice Photographer, Mullingar, 1904', JACOLETTE: A Gallery of Irish Snapshots and Vernacular Photography, https://jacolette.wordpress.com [accessed 1 January 2021].
55 Jabez Hughes, 'Photography as Industrial Occupation for Women: 1873', in *Camera Fiends & Kodak Girls: 50 Selections By and About Women in Photography, 1840–1930*, ed. by Peter E. Palmquist (New York: Midmarch Arts, 1989), pp. 29–37 (p. 33).
56 Ibid., p. 34.
57 Mark Osteen, *The Economy of Ulysses: Making Both Ends Meet* (Syracuse, NY: Syracuse University Press, 1995), p. 80.
58 Myrtle Hill and Vivienne Pollock, *Images and Experiences: Photographs of Irishwomen c. 1880–1920* (Belfast: Blackstaff Press, 1993), p. 40.

59 'Education: Ireland in the Early 20th Century', The National Archives of Ireland, http://www.census.nationalarchives.ie/exhibition/dublin/education.html [accessed 2 September 2021].

60 'Tell the Story of Your Happy Days – with a Kodak', *Punch*, 3 August 1921, in John Taylor, *A Dream of England: Landscape, Photography, and the Tourist's Imagination* (Manchester: Manchester University Press, 1994), p. 140.

61 'Tell the Story of Your Happy Days – with a Kodak', in *The Sphere*, 20 August 1921, p. 33, *The Graphic*, 13 August 1921, p. 25, *The Tatler*, 10 August 1921, p. 55 and *The Belfast News-Letter*, 24 August 1921, p. 7.

62 Ibid.

63 Nancy Martha West, *Kodak and the Lens of Nostalgia* (Charlottesville: University Press of Virginia, 2000), p. 75.

64 Quoted in Brian Coe, 'The Rollfilm Revolution', in *The Kodak Museum: The Story of Popular Photography*, ed. by Colin Ford (London: Century Hutchinson, 1989), pp. 60–89 (p. 65).

65 Margot Norris, *Virgin and Veteran Readings of 'Ulysses'* (New York: Palgrave, 2011), p. 275.

66 William E. S. Fables, 'Poem – The Kodak Girl (1902)', in *Camera Fiends & Kodak Girls: 50 Selections By and About Women in Photography, 1840–1930*, ed. by Peter E. Palmquist (New York: Midmarch Arts Press, 1989), p. 127. Previously published in *Photo-Beacon* (1902), p. 38.

67 Ibid.

68 Robert Janusko, 'From Seymour to Amby to Bannon and Out: A Metamorphosis in Draft', *James Joyce Quarterly*, 29.2 (1992), 393–7 (p. 395).

69 Norris, p. 275.

70 'Royal Gifts Auctioned', *Yorkshire Post and Leeds Intelligencer*, 1 May 1942, p. 2.

71 'Display Ad 6 – No Title', *The Irish Times*, 2 November 1907, p. 16.

72 Laurence Sterne, *A Sentimental Journey through France and Italy* (New York: Dover Publications, 2004), pp. 36–7.

73 Ibid., p. 37.

74 See John McCourt (ed.), *Roll Away the Reel World: James Joyce and Cinema* (Cork: Cork University Press, 2010).

75 'Kodak', *L'Illustrazione Triestina*, 1 February 1911, p. 11.

76 See 'Stanislaus Joyce in Trieste', *c.* 1905, in Stanislaus Joyce, *My Brother's Keeper: James Joyce's Early Years*, ed. by Richard Ellmann (Cambridge, MA: Da Capo Press, 1958), p. xxiii and Unknown Photographer, 'Giorgio and Lucia Joyce at the window of their flat in Trieste', *c.* 1913, James Joyce Collection, University at Buffalo, https://library.buffalo.edu/jamesjoyce/catalog/xvii [accessed 14 January 2021].

77 Eloise Knowlton, 'Showings Forth: *Dubliners*, Photography, and the Rejection of Realism', *Mosaic: A Journal for the Interdisciplinary Study of Literature*, 38.1 (2005), 133–50 (p. 140).

78 'Carlo Wostry', 'Squadra della, Venezia F.C.' and 'Alla Primavera d'Italia', *L'Illustrazione Triestina*, 1 February 1911, pp. 13–16.
79 'Front Cover', *L'Illustrazione Triestina*, 1 February 1911, p. 1.
80 'L'esito del nostro Concorso fotografico', *Femmina, Quindicinale Femminile*, 1 March 1924, p. 1.
81 Ibid.
82 Silvia Valisa, 'An Imaged Life: Wanda Wulz and the Familiar Archive', in *A Window on the Italian Female Modernist Subjectivity: From Neera to Laura Curino*, ed. by Rossella Maria Riccobono (Newcastle upon Tyne: Cambridge Scholars Publishing, 2013), pp. 45–77 (p. 47).
83 Ibid., p. 55.
84 Ibid., p. 54.
85 Unknown Photographer (Likely Lucia Joyce), 'Nora Joyce seated on steps of cart, Ostend', 1926 and 'James Joyce, Nora Joyce, and P.J. Hoey seated on grass', 1926, James Joyce Collection, University at Buffalo, https://library.buffalo.edu/jamesjoyce/catalog/xvii [accessed 14 January 2021].
86 Carlo Wulz, 'Wanda e Marion Wulz durante il bagno', 1905, AIM Alinari Image Museum, Trieste.
87 Luca Crispi, 'The Genesis of Leopold Bloom: Writing the Lives of Rudolph Virag and Ellen Higgins in "Ulysses"', *Journal of Modern Literature*, 35.4 (2012), 13–31 (p. 25).
88 Endre Tóth quoted in R. Brandon Kershner, *The Culture of Joyce's 'Ulysses'* (New York: Palgrave Macmillan, 2010), p. 237.
89 I am grateful to this project's anonymous reviewer for clarifying this meaning and for their suggestions regarding research on the Tulloch-Turnbull girl and Scottish clans.
90 John McCourt, 'Joyce, *il Bel Paese* and the Italian Language', in *Joycean Unions: Post-Millennial Essays from East to West,* European Joyce Studies, 22, ed. by R. Brandon Kershner and Tekla Mecsnóber (Amsterdam: Rodopi, 2013), pp. 61–80 (p. 66).
91 John McCourt (ed.), 'Trieste', in *James Joyce in Context* (Cambridge: Cambridge University Press, 2009), pp. 228–38 (p. 235).
92 Valisa, p. 61.
93 Anton Giulio Bragaglia, *Futurist Photodynamism* (1911), trans. and ed. by Lawrence Rainey, *Modernism/modernity*, 15.2 (2008), 363–79 (p. 364).
94 Wanda Wulz, 'Io + gatto', 1932, courtesy of Ford Motor Company Collection, The Metropolitan Museum of Art, http://www.metmuseum.org/ [accessed 25 November 2021].
95 Valisa, p. 64.
96 Berenice Abbott, 'Lucia Joyce dancing to Schubert's "Marche Militaire"', 1929, in Carol Loeb Shloss, *Lucia Joyce: To Dance in the Wake* (London: Bloomsbury Publishing, 2005), p. 164.

97 Wanda Wulz, 'Ritratto di Marion Wulz in costume egiziano', *c.* 1930 in Valisa, pp. 45–77 (p. 47).
98 Lorainne Weir, 'Joyce, Myth and Memory', *Irish University Review*, 2.2 (1972), 172–88 (p. 180).
99 McHugh, p. 171.
100 Crispi and Slote, p. 144.
101 James Joyce, 'Letter to Sylvia Beach', 16 April 1924, in Peter Spielberg, *James Joyce's Manuscripts and Letters at the University at Buffalo: A Catalogue* (Buffalo: University at Buffalo, 1962), p. 188.
102 'Awards to O.C. s', *Gloucestershire Echo,* 8 April 1941, p. 3.
103 Joyce, 'Protodrafts,1st draft', January 1924, I.7§1 draft level 0, MS 47471b 33v-25v, British Library, *James Joyce Digital Archive* <https://jjda.ie> [accessed 10 June 2021]. Hereafter referred to as *JJDA*.
104 Joyce, '1st typescript', February 1924 and June 1925, I.7 draft level 3, MS 47474 38–58, British Library, *JJDA*.
105 Luca Crispi and Sam Slote, *How Joyce Wrote 'Finnegans Wake': A Chapter-by-Chapter Genetic Guide* (Madison: University of Wisconsin Press, 2007), p. 145.
106 Otto Jespersen, *Growth and Structure of the English Language*, 2nd edn (Leipzig: B. G. Teubner, 1912), pp. 157–8.
107 Ibid.
108 Thanks are due to John O'Hanlon for providing this note on Joyce's *Finnegans Wake* drafts and typescripts following correspondence regarding Danis Rose and John O'Hanlon (eds), *JJDA*, https://jjda.ie [accessed 10 June 2021].
109 Colin Harding, 'Snapshot', in *Encyclopedia of Nineteenth-Century Photography: J-Z*, ed. by John Hannavy, 2 vols (New York: Routledge, 2007), II, pp. 1277–9 (p. 1279).
110 Brayer, p. 60.
111 Ibid.
112 Finn Fordham, *Lots of Fun at 'Finnegans Wake'* (Oxford: Oxford University Press, 2007), p. 99.
113 Pieter Bekker, 'The Gaiety', *James Joyce Broadsheet*, 23 (1987), 2.
114 'Souvenir of the Twenty-Fifth Anniversary of the Opening of the Gaiety Theatre' (Dublin: s.n., 1896), p. 6.
115 Ibid.
116 Henry J. Comley, Correspondence: 'Men v. Women Assistants', *British Journal of Photography*, 67.3160 (26 November 1920), 629.
117 See Irene Mosca and Robert E. Wright, 'The Long-Term Consequences of the Irish Marriage Bar', *IZA Discussion Papers*, 12301, Institute of Labor Economics (IZA), Bonn, 1–39.
118 'The Camera Fiend', *Daily Express* (Dublin), 9 March 1910, p. 4.
119 Ibid.
120 'Photography in the Abbey', *Daily Express* (Dublin), 20 June 1911, p. 4.

121 Ibid.
122 'Skerry's School of Shorthand, Typewriting, and Commercial Training', *Daily Express* (Dublin), 20 June 1911, p. 4.
123 Hiley.
124 Ibid.
125 Kevin J. H. Dettmar, *The Illicit Joyce of Postmodernism: Reading Against the Grain* (Madison: University of Wisconsin Press, 1996), p. 251.
126 McHugh, p. 458.
127 Annette R. Federico, *Idol of Suburbia: Marie Corelli and Late-Victorian Literary Culture* (Charlottesville: University Press of Virginia, 2000), p. 28.
128 Gisèle Freund, *Three Days with Joyce: Photographs by Gisèle Freund* (New York: Persea Books, 1985), p. 17.
129 Ibid., p. 2.
130 Gordon Bowker, *James Joyce: A New Biography* (New York: Farrar, Straus and Giroux, 2012), p. 420.
131 Ibid.
132 'Souvenir of the Twenty-Fifth Anniversary of the Opening of the Gaiety Theatre', p. 31.
133 Francis Carlin, *Reminisces of an Ex-Detective* (London: Hutchinson & Co., 1925). This text is referenced in Jerry White, *London in the Twentieth Century: A City and Its People* (London: Vintage, 2008), p. 454.
134 'Proceedings of the Central Criminal Court, 7 January 1913', *Old Bailey Proceedings Online*, https://www.oldbaileyonline.org [accessed 10 June 2021] (p. 107).
135 Carlin, p. 454.
136 Lewis Carroll, *Alice's Adventures in Wonderland: 150th Anniversary Edition* (Princeton: Princeton University Press, 2015), p. 60.
137 For the influence of filmic flashbacks on *Dubliners*, see Keith Williams, *James Joyce and Cinematicity: Before and After Film* (Edinburgh: Edinburgh University Press, 2020), pp. 76–7.
138 Carroll, 'Isa's Visit to Oxford, 1888', in Bowman, p. 40.
139 Stuart Dodgson Collingwood, *The Life and Letters of Lewis Carroll (Rev. C. L. Dodgson)* (London: T. Fisher Unwin, 1898), p. 74.
140 Roland McHugh, *Annotations to 'Finnegans Wake'*, 4th edn (Baltimore: Johns Hopkins University Press, 2016), p. 57.
141 Belle Moses (ed), *Lewis Carroll in Wonderland and at Home: The Story of His Life* (New York: D. Appleton and Company, 1910), p. 109.
142 McHugh, p. 277.
143 Genevieve Sartor, 'Genetic Connections in *Finnegans Wake*: Lucia Joyce and Issy Earwicker', *Journal of Modern Literature*, 41.4 (2018), 18–30 (p. 28).
144 Tristan Tzara, '"La photographie à l'envers" (Photography from the Verso)' in Walter Benjamin, *Selected Writings: Volume 2, Part 2, 1931–1934*, trans. by Rodney Livingstone and et al., ed. by Michael W. Jennings and et al. (Cambridge, MA: Harvard University Press, 2005), p. 55.

Coda

1. Roland Barthes, *Camera Lucida* (London: Vintage, 2000), p. 20.
2. See Niall Murphy, *A Bloomsday Postcard* (Dublin: Lilliput Press, 2004).
3. James Joyce, '*X. B. 178. § Autograph Picture Postcard to Sylvia Beach: "Dear Miss Beach Solved Lewis Carroll [?] riddle in train"', n.d., James Joyce Collection, University at Buffalo, https://library.buffalo.edu/jamesjoyce/catalog/xvii [accessed 14 January 2021].
4. Xavier Tricot, *James Joyce in Ostend* (Devriendt: Belgium, 2018).
5. See Harriet Shaw Weaver Papers, 'Vol. XXI A, B. Photographs, mostly of James Joyce; 1888–1938', British Library, https://www.bl.uk/collection-items [accessed 10 February 2021].
6. Ibid.
7. Unknown Photographer, 'James Joyce, age 3', 1885, James Joyce Collection, University at Buffalo.
8. Ibid.
9. Tricot.
10. See Terrence Killeen, 'Lee Miller: Photographing Joycean Dublin (1946)', in *Voices on Joyce*, ed. by Anne Fogarty and Fran O'Rourke (Dublin: University College Dublin Press, 2015), pp. 133–8 for extensive commentary on Miller's photography.
11. Ibid.
12. Tristan Tzara, '"La photographie à l'envers" (Photography from the Verso)' in Walter Benjamin, *Selected Writings: Volume 2, Part 2, 1931–1934*, trans. by Rodney Livingstone and et al., ed. by Michael W. Jennings and et al. (Cambridge, MA: Harvard University Press, 2005), p. 55.

Works Cited

'Advertisements and Notices', *The Era*, 12 August 1899, p. 27

'Advertisements and Notices', *Freeman's Journal*, 6 February 1856, n. p.

'Advertisements and Notices', *Freeman's Journal*, 28 October 1899, n. p.

'Advertisements', *Photo Bits*, 11 March 1911, p. 2

Allison, David, 'Photography and the Mass Market', in *The Kodak Museum: The Story of Popular Photography*, ed. by Colin Ford (London: Century Hutchinson, 1989), pp. 42–59

Anastasi, William with Michael Seidel, 'Jarry in Joyce: A Conversation', in *Joyce Studies Annual*, ed. by Thomas F. Staley (Austin: University of Texas Press, 1995), pp. 39–58

'The Animated Pictures at the Star Theatre: Action by the Edison Manufacturing Company', *The Irish Times*, 29 July 1903, p. 3

Archer, John, *The Nature of Grief: The Evolution and Psychology of Reactions to Loss* (London: Routledge, 1999)

'Art Photography', *The Irish Times*, 13 July 1876, p. 3

'Article 3 – No Title', *The Irish Times*, 12 March 1873, p. 2

Atherton, James S., *The Books at the 'Wake': A Study of Literary Allusions in James Joyce's 'Finnegans Wake'* (Illinois: Southern Illinois University Press, 2009)

Atherton, James S., 'Lewis Carroll and *Finnegans Wake*', *English Studies*, 33.1–6 (1952), 1–15

Atkinson, Sue E., 'Cigarette Advertising: A History', *The British Journal of Photography*, 20 November 1981, 1190–9

'Awards to O.C. s', *Gloucestershire Echo*, 8 April 1941, p. 3

Baker, G. R., 'The Stereoscope and "Art"', *The British Journal of Photography*, 41.1808 (28 December 1894), 822

Barnes, C. Brangwin, 'Post-Mortem Photography', *British Journal of Photography*, 30.1213 (3 August 1883), 449–50

Barthes, Roland, *Camera Lucida* (London: Vintage, 2000)

Bass, Richard K., 'Additional Allusions in "Eumaeus"', *James Joyce Quarterly*, 10.3 (1973), 321–9

Baudelaire, Charles, 'The Salon of 1859', in *The Mirror of Art: Critical Studies by Charles Baudelaire*, trans. and ed. by Jonathan Mayne (New York: Doubleday Anchor Books, 1956), pp. 220–305

Beach, Sylvia, *Shakespeare and Company* (London: Faber and Faber, 1956)

Beetham, Margaret, 'Periodicals and the New Media: Women and Imagined Communities', *Women's Studies International Forum*, 29 (2006), 231–40

Bekker, Pieter, 'The Gaiety', *James Joyce Broadsheet*, 23 (1987), 2

Benjamin, Walter, *The Work of Art in the Age of Mechanical Reproduction*, trans. by J. A. Underwood (London: Penguin, 2008)

'Bicycle Kodaks', *The Illustrated Sporting and Dramatic News*, 26 June 1897, p. 699

'The Biograph in the Vatican', *British Journal of Photography*, 3 February 1899, p. 15

Bowman, Isa, *The Story of Lewis Carroll, Told for Young People by the Real Alice in Wonderland* (New York: E. P. Dutton & Company, 1900)

Bowker, Gordon, *James Joyce: A New Biography* (New York: Farrar, Straus and Giroux, 2012)

Bragaglia, Anton Giulio, *Futurist Photodynamism* (1911), trans. and ed. by Lawrence Rainey, *Modernism/modernity*, 15.2 (2008), 363–79

Braslasu, Viviana Mirela, '"Why, Mr J. and His God alone Know!": Joyce and Lewis Carroll', *Dublin James Joyce Journal*, 8 (2015), 114–21

Brayer, Elizabeth, *George Eastman: A Biography* (Rochester, NY: University of Rochester Press, 2006)

Breathnach, Ciara, and Catherine Lawless (eds), 'Introduction', in *Visual, Material and Print Culture in Nineteenth-Century Ireland* (Dublin: Four Courts Press, 2010), pp. 15–19

Breton, André, 'Surrealist Situation of the Object (1935)', in *Manifestoes of Surrealism*, trans. by Richard Seaver and Helen R. Lane (Ann Arbor: University of Michigan Press, 1972), pp. 255–78

Brewster, David, *The Stereoscope: Its History, Theory, and Construction, with Its Application to the Fine and Useful Arts and to Education* (London: John Murray, 1856), p. 1

Brienza, Susan, 'Murphy, Shem, Morpheus, and Murphies: Eumaeus Meets the *Wake*', in *Joycean Occasions: Essays from the Milwaukee James Joyce Conference*, ed. by Janet Egleson Dunleavy, Melvin J. Friedman and Michael Patrick Gillespie (Newark: University of Delaware Press, 1991), pp. 80–94

Briggs, Asa, *Victorian Things* (Chicago: University of Chicago Press, 1988)

Brown, Terence, 'Notes', in James Joyce, *Dubliners* (London: Penguin Books, 2000), pp. 237–317

Bruno, Juliana, *Atlas of Emotion: Journeys in Art, Architecture, and Film* (London: Verso, 2002)

Budgen, Frank, *James Joyce and the Making of 'Ulysses'* (Oxford: Oxford University Press, 1989)

Burd Schiavo, Laura, 'From Phantom Image to Perfect Vision: Physiological Optics, Commercial Photography, and the Popularization of the Stereoscope', in *New Media, 1740–1915*, ed. by Lisa Gitelman and Geoffrey B. Pingree (Cambridge, MA: MIT Press, 2003), pp. 113–38

Byron, George Gordon, Lord, 'On The Death of a Young Lady, Cousin to the Author, and Very Dear to Him', in *The Works of Lord Byron: Complete in One Volume* (Frankfurt: H.L. Broenner, 1837), p. 376

'The Burglary in Henry Street', *Freeman's Journal*, 14 July 1899, p. 2

'The Camera Fiend', *Daily Express* (Dublin), 9 March 1910, p. 4

Camerani, Marco, 'Joyce and Early Cinema: Peeping Bloom through the Keyhole', in *Joyce in Progress: Proceedings of the 2008 James Joyce Graduate Conference in Rome*, ed. by Franca Ruggieri, John McCourt and Enrico Terrinoni (Newcastle: Cambridge Scholars Press, 2009), pp. 114–28

Carlin, Francis, *Reminisces of an Ex-Detective* (London: Hutchinson & Co., 1925)

'Carlo Wostry', 'Squadra della, Venezia F.C.' and 'Alla Primavera d'Italia', *L'Illustrazione Triestina*, 1 February 1911, pp. 13–16

Carroll, Lewis, *Alice's Adventures in Wonderland: 150th Anniversary Edition* (Princeton: Princeton University Press, 2015)

Carroll, Lewis, '"Isa's Visit to Oxford, 1888"', in Belle Moses, *Lewis Carroll in Wonderland and at Home: The Story of His Life*, ed. by Belle Moses (New York: D. Appleton and Company, 1910), p. 37

Carroll, Lewis, 'Photography Extraordinary', 1855, *The Morgan Library & Museum*, https://www.themorgan.org [accessed 10 June 2021]

Carville, Justin, 'Introduction: Popular Visual Culture in Ireland', *Early Popular Visual Culture*, 5 (2007), 229–30

Carville, Justin, 'Mr Lawrence's Great Photographic Bazaar', *Early Popular Visual Culture*, 5 (2007), 263–83

Carville, Justin, *Photography and Ireland* (London: Reaktion Books, 2011)

Carville, Justin, 'With His "Mind-Guided Camera": J. M. Synge, J. J. Clarke, and the Visual Politics of Edwardian Street Photography', in *Synge and Edwardian Ireland*, ed. by Brian Cliff and Nicholas Grene (Oxford: Oxford University Press, 2012), pp. 186–207

Cato, Bob and Greg Vitiello, *Joyce Images* (London: W. W. Norton & Company, 1994)

Chandler, Edward, *Photography in Ireland: The Nineteenth Century* (Dublin: Edmund Burke, 2001)

'Charivaria', *Punch*, 5 October 1904, p. 243

'Charles Dickens, ESQ – Splendid Photographic Portraits', *Freeman's Journal*, 28 August 1858, p. 1

Chmura, Sophie, 'Cartes-Postales de Rennes ou D'Ailleurs', http://cartes-postales35.monsite-orange.fr [accessed 10 February 2021]

'Classified Ad 302 – No Title', *The Irish Times*, 8 July 1903, p. 6

Coe, Brian, *Cameras: From Daguerreotypes to Instant Pictures* (Gothenburg: Nordbok, 1978)

Coe, Brian, 'The Rollfilm Revolution', in *The Kodak Museum: The Story of Popular Photography*, ed. by Colin Ford (London: Century Hutchinson, 1989), pp. 60–89

Collingwood, Stuart Dodgson, *The Life and Letters of Lewis Carroll (Rev. C. L. Dodgson)* (London: T. Fisher Unwin, 1898)

'Commercial and Legal Intelligence', *British Journal of Photography*, 55.2494 (19 November 1909), 904

'Coloured Cartes', *Freeman's Journal*, 2 March 1866, p. 2

Comley, Henry J., 'Correspondence: Men v. Women Assistants', *British Journal of Photography*, 67.3160 (26 November 1920), 629

'Commercial News', *Freeman's Journal*, 7 February 1898, p. 3

'Concert Room, Rotundo, Dublin', *Freeman's Journal*, 25 May 1874, p. 1

Conley, Tim, 'Marcella the Midget Queen', *James Joyce Quarterly*, 48.1 (2010), 149–53

Connolly, Thomas E., 'Home Is Where the Art Is: The Joyce Family Gallery', *James Joyce Quarterly*, 20.1 (1982), 11–31

The Contents of 'The Stereoscopic Magazine' (London: Lovell Reeve, 1858–1865), ed. by Julian Holland, http://members.optusnet.com.au/jph8524/JHstereoscopic_mag.htm [accessed 2 November 2021]

Corlett, Christiaan, *Jane W. Shackleton's Ireland* (Wilton, Cork: The Collins Press, 2012)

Costa, Nic, *Automatic Pleasures: The History of the Coin Machine* (London: Kevin Francis, 1988)

Crispi, Luca, 'A Commentary on James Joyce's National Library of Ireland "Early Commonplace Book": 1903–1912 (MS 36,639/02/A)', *Genetic Joyce Studies*, 9 (2009), http://www.geneticjoycestudies.org [accessed 2 January 2021]

Crispi, Luca, 'The Genesis of Leopold Bloom: Writing the Lives of Rudolph Virag and Ellen Higgins in "Ulysses"', *Journal of Modern Literature*, 35.4 (2012), 13–31

Crispi, Luca, *Joyce's Creative Process and the Construction of Characters in 'Ulysses': Becoming the Blooms* (Oxford: Oxford University Press, 2015)

Crispi, Luca, 'Manuscript Timeline, 1905–1922', *Genetic Joyce Studies*, 4 (2004), http://www.geneticjoycestudies.org [accessed 1 May 2021]

Crispi, Luca and Sam Slote, *How Joyce Wrote 'Finnegans Wake': A Chapter-by-Chapter Genetic Guide* (Madison: University of Wisconsin Press, 2007), p. 145

'Croydon Camera Club', *British Journal of Photography*, 79.3784 (11 November 1932), 690

Cullen, Fintan, *Ireland on Show: Art, Union, and Nationhood* (Farnham, Surrey: Ashgate, 2012)

Curran, Constantine, 'James Joyce Standing Beside Greenhouse, Dublin, 1904', *James Joyce Collection, University at Buffalo,* https://library.buffalo.edu/jamesjoyce/catalog/xvii [accessed 14 January 2021]

'Cyclopia', *Freeman's Journal*, 23 May 1896, n. p.

Daguerre, Louis-Jacques-Mandé, 'Daguerreotype (1839)', in *Classic Essays on Photography*, ed. by Alan Trachtenberg (New Haven: Leete's Island Books, 1980), pp. 11–14

Darby, Paul, 'James Joyce Standing beside Greenhouse, Dublin', 1904, copy of the original photograph by Constantine Curran, Harriet Shaw Weaver Papers, Vol. XXI A, B. Photographs, mostly of James Joyce; 1888–1938, British Library, https://www.bl.uk/collection-items [accessed 10 February 2021]

Davidson, Kathleen, 'Connecting the Senses: Natural History and the British Museum in the *Stereoscopic Magazine*', *Interdisciplinary Studies in the Long Nineteenth Century*, 19 (2014), 11–14

The Dead, dir. by John Huston (Vestron Pictures, 1987) [on DVD]

'Death of Mr. Dan Leno, The Famous Comedian', *Daily Mirror*, 1 November 1904, p. 1

Desmarais, Jane, Martin Postle and William Vaughan (eds), 'Introduction', in *Model and Supermodel: The Artists' Model in British Art and Culture* (Manchester: Manchester University Press, 2006), pp. 1–8

Dettmar, Kevin J. H., *The Illicit Joyce of Postmodernism: Reading against the Grain* (Madison: University of Wisconsin Press, 1996)

Devlin, Kimberly J., '"See Ourselves as Others See Us": Joyce's Look at the Eye of the Other', *PMLA*, 104 (1989), 882–93

DiBattista, Maria, 'The Ghost Walks: Joyce and the Spectres of Silent Cinema', in *Roll Away the Reel World: James Joyce and Cinema*, ed. by John McCourt (Cork: Cork University Press, 2010), pp. 57–68

Dick, Rev. Henry W., 'The Relation of Photography to Art', *The American Amateur Photographer*, 1 March 1906, pp. 125–8

Dimond, Frances, *Developing the Picture: Queen Alexandra and the Art of Photography* (London: Royal Collection Publications, 2004)

'Display Ad 6 – No Title', *The Irish Times*, 2 November 1907, p. 16

'Display Ad 9 – No Title', *The Irish Times*, 17 April 1903, p. 3

Du Maurier, George, 'Things One Would Rather Have Left Unsaid', *Punch*, 5 May 1888, http://punch.photoshelter.com [accessed 10 January 2021]

Du Maurier, George, *Trilby* (Oxford: Oxford University Press, 1995)

Duncan, Joseph, 'The Modality of the Audible in Joyce's *Ulysses*', *PMLA*, 72 (1957), 286–95

Edwards, Steve, *The Making of English Photography: Allegories* (University Park, PA: Penn State University Press, 2006)

Ellman, Richard, *The Consciousness of Joyce* (London: Faber, 1977)

Ellman, Richard, *James Joyce*, revised edn (New York: Oxford University Press, 1982)

'Education: Ireland in the Early 20th Century', The National Archives of Ireland, http://www.census.nationalarchives.ie/exhibition/dublin/education.html [accessed 2 September 2021]

'L'envoi. Photography – Not Art', *The Photographic Times*, 1 March 1899, pp. 125–8

'L'esito del nostro Concorso fotografico', *Femmina, Quindicinale Femminile*, 1 March 1924, p. 1

'Exhibitions: Photography at the Dublin Exhibition', *British Journal of Photography*, 12.263 (2 June 1865), 1–2

Fables, William E. S., 'Poem – The Kodak Girl (1902)', in *Camera Fiends & Kodak Girls: 50 Selections By and About Women in Photography, 1840–1930*, ed. by Peter E. Palmquist (New York: Midmarch Arts Press, 1989), p. 127

Falk, H. J. and M. G. Spencer, 'The Occupations of Women in London', *The Speaker: The Liberal Review*, 16 January 1904, pp. 380–1

Fargnoli, Nicholas and Michael Patrick Gillespie, *James Joyce A to Z: The Essential Reference to the Life and Work* (Oxford: Oxford University Press, 1995)

'Fashionable Intelligence', *The Irish Times*, 18 March 1902, p. 6

Federico, Annette R., *Idol of Suburbia: Marie Corelli and Late-Victorian Literary Culture* (Charlottesville: University Press of Virginia, 2000)

Fenton, Roger to Grace Fenton, 'Letter, 8 March 1855', Joseph Fenton letter-book, Gernsheim Collection, Harry Ransom Humanities Research Centre, Austin, http://rogerfenton.dmu.ac.uk/showLetter.php?letterNo=3 [accessed 10 February 2021]

Fenton, Roger to Grace Fenton, 'Letter Number 11', 29 April 1855, Annie Grace Fenton letter-book, Royal Photographic Society Collection, National Museum of Photography, Film & Television, Bradford

'Fine Arts', *The Cork Examiner*, 1851, n. p.

Fogarty, Anne, 'Ghostly Intertexts: James Joyce and the Legacy of Synge', in *Synge and Edwardian Ireland*, ed. by Brian Cliff and Nicholas Grene (Oxford: Oxford University Press, 2012), pp. 225–44

Fordham, Finn, *Lots of Fun at 'Finnegans Wake'* (Oxford: Oxford University Press, 2007)

Flynn, Catherine, *James Joyce and the Matter of Paris* (Cambridge: Cambridge University Press, 2019)

Flynn, Deirdre, 'An Uncomfortable Fit: Joyce's Women in Dublin and Trieste', in *Joyce and the City: The Significance of Place*, ed. by Michael Begnal (Syracuse, NY: Syracuse University Press, 2002), pp. 51–64

Font-Réaulx, Dominique, 'France', in *Encyclopedia of Nineteenth-Century Photography: A-I*, ed. by John Hannavy, 2 vols (New York: Routledge, 2008), I, pp. 544–51

Freund, Gisèle, *Three Days with Joyce: Photographs by Gisèle Freund* (New York: Persea Books, 1985)

Freund, Gisèle and V. B. Carleton, *James Joyce in Paris: His Final Years* (London: Cassell, 1965)

'Front Cover', *L'Illustrazione Triestina*, 1 February 1911, p. 1

'Front Cover', *The National Police Gazette*, 28 December 1912, p. 1

'The Gaiety Theatre', *Freeman's Journal*, 26 August 1898, p. 5

'General Mulholland at the Rotunda', *Freeman's Journal*, 19 April 1892, p. 5

Gernsheim, Helmut, *A Concise History of Photography*, 3rd edn (New York: Dover Publications, 1986), p. 26

Gifford, Don and Robert J. Seidman, *'Ulysses' Annotated: Notes for James Joyce's 'Ulysses'*, 2nd edn (Berkeley: University of California Press, 1989)

Gleeson White, Joseph, 'The Nude in Photography. With Some Studies Taken in the Open Air. The Studio', 15 June 1893, in *A Carnal Medium: fin-de-siècle Essays on the Photographic Nude*, ed. by James Downs (Portsmouth: Callum James Books, 2012), pp. 35–44

Gleeson White, Joseph, 'On Photographing the Nude II', *The Photogram*, April 1894, in *A Carnal Medium*, pp. 53–60

Gleeson White, Joseph, 'On Photographing the Nude IV', *The Photogram*, 1.6 (June 1894), in *A Carnal Medium*, 81–106

'The Great American Panorama', *The Irish Times*, 26 July 1875, p. 6

'Great Depot, 11 Upper Sackville Street', *Freeman's Journal*, 17 August 1865, p. 1

Grigson, Geoffrey, 'James Joyce', *Picture Post*, 13 May 1939, pp. 54–5

Gunning, Tom, 'Embarrassing Evidence: The Detective Camera and the Documentary Impulse', in *Collecting Visible Evidence*, ed. by Jane M. Gaines and Michael Renov (Minneapolis: University of Minnesota Press, 1999), pp. 46–64

Guynn, Beth Ann, 'Postmortem Photography', in *Encyclopedia of Nineteenth-Century Photography*, ed. by John Hannavy, 2 vols (New York: Routledge, 2007), I, pp. 1164–7

Hanaway-Oakley, Cleo, *James Joyce and the Phenomenology of Film* (Oxford: Oxford University Press, 2017)

Harding, Colin, 'G is for Ghosts… the Birth and Rise of Spirit Photography', *National Media Museum Blog*, https://nationalmediamuseumblog.wordpress.com [accessed 20 February 2021]

Harding, Colin, 'The Kodak Girl', *Photographica World*, 78 (1996), 10–15

Harding, Colin, 'Snapshot', in *Encyclopedia of Nineteenth-Century Photography: J-Z*, ed. by John Hannavy, 2 vols (New York: Routledge, 2008), I, pp. 1277–9

Harriet Shaw Weaver Papers, Vol. XXI A, B. Photographs, mostly of James Joyce; 1888–1938, British Library, https://www.bl.uk/collection-items [accessed 10 February 2021]

Harris, Russell, 'Lafayette, James (James Stack Lauder) (1853–1923)', in *Encyclopedia of Nineteenth-Century Photography: J-Z*, ed. by John Hannavy, 2 vols (New York: Routledge, 2008), II, pp. 813–14

Hart, Clive, *Structure and Motif in 'Finnegans Wake'* (Evanston: Northwestern University Press, 1962)

Headsman, Simone, 'Letters to a Photographic Friend', *The British Journal of Photography*, 15 August 1860, pp. 241–3

Henisch, Heinz K., and Bridget Ann Henisch, *The Photographic Experience, 1839–1914: Images and Attitudes* (University Park, PA: Penn State University Press, 1994)

Henisch, Heinz K., *Positive Pleasures: Early Photography and Humor* (University Park, PA: Penn State University Press, 1998)

Henke, Suzette A., *James Joyce and the Politics of Desire* (New York: Routledge, 1990)

Hiley, Nicholas, 'Candid Camera Edwardian Tabloids', *History Today*, 43 (1993), http://www.historytoday.com [accessed 10 October 2020], n. p.

Hill, Myrtle, and Vivienne Pollock, *Images and Experiences: Photographs of Irishwomen c. 1880–1920* (Belfast: Blackstaff Press, 1993)

Holmes, Oliver Wendell, 'The Stereoscope and the Stereograph', *The Atlantic Monthly*, 3 (1859), http://www.theatlantic.com [accessed 1 June 2021]

'Honours in Art Photography', *The Irish Times*, 3 December 1895, p. 6

Hornby, Louise E. J., 'Visual Clockwork: Photographic Time and the Instant in "Proteus"', *James Joyce Quarterly*, 42–3.1–4 (2004), 49–68

The House That Jack Built (London and Otley: William Walker and Sons, 1807)

Hughes, Jabez, 'Photography as Industrial Occupation for Women: 1873', in *Camera Fiends & Kodak Girls: 50 Selections By and About Women in Photography, 1840–1930*, ed. by Peter E. Palmquist (New York: Midmarch Arts, 1989), pp. 29–37

Humm, Maggie, *Modernist Women and Visual Cultures* (Edinburgh: Edinburgh University Press, 2002)

Hunt, Robert, 'On the Applications of Science to the Fine and Useful Arts. Improvements in Photography – Hyalotype, & C.', *The Art-Journal*, XIII (1851), 106–7

Husband, Rev. E., 'The Photographers' Church Parade – Sermon', *Folkstone Express*, 24 May 1902, quoted in *British Journal of Photography*, 49.2195 (30 May 1902), 428–9

'Illustrated Sources: Women's Interest', *Cardiff University Library Special Collections*, http://www.cardiff.ac.uk [accessed 2 December 2020]

'In Bloemfontein: Collapse of the Free Staters – How the Boers Were Deceived Entry of the Sixth Division', *The Irish Times*, 19 March 1900, p. 5

'Irish Portraits for the Chicago Exhibition', *The Irish Times*, 29 March 1893, p. 8

Janusko, Robert, 'From Seymour to Amby to Bannon and Out: A Metamorphosis in Draft', *James Joyce Quarterly*, 29.2 (1992), 393–7

Jarry, Alfred, 'The Passion Considered as an Uphill Bicycle Race', in *Anthology of Black Humor*, ed. by Andre Bréton, trans. by Mark Polizzotti (San Francisco: City Lights Books, 1997), pp. 223–5

Jespersen, Otto, *Growth and Structure of the English Language*, 2nd edn (Leipzig: B. G. Teubner, 1912), pp. 157–8

Joyce, James, '*X. B. 178. § Autograph Picture Postcard to Sylvia Beach: "Dear Miss Beach Solved Lewis Carroll [?] riddle in train"', n.d., *James Joyce Collection, University at Buffalo*, https://library.buffalo.edu/jamesjoyce/catalog/xvii [accessed 14 January 2021]

Joyce, James, '1st typescript', February 1924 and June 1925, I.7 draft level 3, MS 47474 38–58, British Library, *James Joyce Digital Archive*, ed. by Danis Rose and John O'Hanlon, https://jjda.ie [accessed 2 February 2021]

Joyce, James, 'Continuation of a Work in Progress (II.2§8)', *Transition*, 11 (1928), 7–18, https://gallica.bnf.fr/ark:/12148/bpt6k6448050n/f9.image [21 September 2021]

Joyce, James, *Dubliners*, ed. by Terence Brown (London: Penguin, 1992)

Joyce, James, *Finnegans Wake*, ed. by John Bishop (London: Penguin, 1999)

Joyce, James, *A First-Draft Version of 'Finnegans Wake'*, ed. by David Hayman (Austin: University of Texas Press, 1963)

Joyce, James, 'Ibsen's New Drama', *The Fortnightly Review*, 1 April 1900, https://fortnightlyreview.co.uk [accessed 23 December 2020]

Joyce, James, *James Joyce's Letters to Sylvia Beach, 1921–1940*, ed. by Melissa Banta and Oscar A, Silverman (Oxford: Plantain Publishers, 1990)

Joyce, James, *Letters of James Joyce, Vol. I*, ed. by Stuart Gilbert (New York: Viking Press, 1966)

Joyce, James, *Letters of James Joyce, Vol. II*, ed. by Richard Ellmann (New York: Viking Press, 1966)

Joyce, James, *Letters of James Joyce, Vol. III*, ed. by Richard Ellmann (New York: Viking Press, 1966)

Joyce, James, 'Letter to Sylvia Beach', 16 April 1924, in *James Joyce's Manuscripts and Letters at the University at Buffalo: A Catalogue*, edited by Peter Spielberg (Buffalo: University at Buffalo, 1962), p. 188

Joyce, James, *Occasional, Critical and Political Writing*, ed. by Kevin Barry (Oxford: Oxford University Press, 2000)

Joyce, James, 'Paris and Pola Commonplace Book', 1903-04, *The National Library of Ireland*, MS 36,639/02/A

Joyce, James, *A Portrait of the Artist as a Young Man*, ed. by Jeri Johnson (Oxford: Oxford University Press, 2000)

Joyce, James, 'Protodrafts,1st Draft', January 1924, I.7§1 draft level 0, MS 47471b 33v-25v, British Library, *James Joyce Digital Archive*

Joyce, James, 'Protodrafts, 2nd Draft', December 1923, I.4§2 draft level 1, MS 47471b 12, 16, British Library, *James Joyce Digital Archive*

Joyce, James, 'Protodrafts 1st Typescript', January 1924–early 1927, I.4§2 draft level 3, MS 47472 161–162, British Library, *James Joyce Digital Archive*

Joyce, James, *Selected Letters of James Joyce*, ed. by Richard Ellmann (New York: Viking, 1975)

Joyce, James, *Stephen Hero*, ed. by Theodor Spencer, John Slocum and Herbert Cahoon (New York: New Directions Publications, 1963)

Joyce, James, *Ulysses: The Corrected Texts*, ed. by Hans Walter Gabler, Wolfhard Steppe and Clause Melchor (New York: Random House, 1986)

Joyce, Lucia, 'Mr and Mrs Joyce and Giorgio, Taken by Lucia?', 1924, Harriet Shaw Weaver Papers, Vol. XXI A, B. Photographs, mostly of James Joyce; 1888–1938, British Library, https://www.bl.uk/collection-items [accessed 10 June 2021]

Joyce, Stanislaus, *My Brother's Keeper: James Joyce's Early Years*, ed. by Richard Ellmann (Cambridge, MA: Da Capo Press, 2003)

Keiley, Joseph T., 'The Salon: Its Purpose, Character and Lesson', *Camera Notes*, 3.3 (1900), n. p.

Kendrick, Walter, 'The Corruption of Gerty MacDowell', *James Joyce Quarterly*, 37.3-4 (2000), 413-23

Kenner, Hugh, *Dublin's Joyce* (New York: Columbia University Press, 1956)

Kershner, R. Brandon, *The Culture of Joyce's 'Ulysses'* (New York: Palgrave Macmillan, 2010)

Kershner, R. Brandon, 'Framing Rudy and Photography', *Journal of Modern Literature*, 22.2 (1998-99), 265-92

Killeen, Terrence, 'Lee Miller: Photographing Joycean Dublin (1946)', in *Voices on Joyce*, ed. by Anne Fogarty and Fran O'Rourke (Dublin: University College Dublin Press, 2015), pp. 133-8

Kitzmann, Andreas, *Saved from Oblivion: Documenting the Daily from Diaries to Web Cams* (New York: Peter Lang, 2004)

Knowlton, Eloise, 'Showings Forth: *Dubliners*, Photography, and the Rejection of Realism', *Mosaic: A Journal for the Interdisciplinary Study of Literature*, 38.1 (2005), 133–50

'Kodak', *L'Illustrazione Triestina*, 1 February 1911, p. 11

'Kodak, Limited, Staff Dance', *The Irish Times*, 28 January 1910, p. 3

'Kodak Photographic Apparatus & Materials', 1910, The Kodak Heritage Collection, Museums Victoria Collections, https://collections.museumsvictoria.com.au/items/2181129 [accessed 20 April 2021]

'The Lady's Pictorial', *The Irish Times*, 23 June 1900, p. 9

'Lafayette's Photographic Studio', *The Irish Times*, 16 August 1888, p. 4

'Lafayette's Photographic Studios. By Royal Warrant to the Queen and Prince and Princess of Wales', *The Irish Times*, 16 September 1895, p. 4

Lafayette's, 'James Joyce in Sailor Suit, Aged 6', 1888, James Joyce Collection, University at Buffalo, https://library.buffalo.edu/jamesjoyce/catalog/xvii [accessed 14 January 2021]

Lafayette's, 'St. Peter's College, Wexford', 1955, Lafayette Photography (Historical Photographs), https://ireland.lafayettephotography.com/photoselection/selectphotos?albumId=8 (showing 85 to 96 of 725 items) [accessed 11 April 2021]

'St. Peter's College, Wexford', 1955, Lafayette Photography (Historical Photographs), https://ireland.lafayettephotography.com/photoselection/selectphotos?albumId=8 (showing 85 to 96 of 725 items) [accessed 11 April 2021]

Lartigue, Jacques Henri, '*Mon livre de photographie*', 1925, in *Hidden Depths*, trans. and ed. by William Hibbert (London: Design for Life, 2004), p. 95

Lartigue, Jacques Henri, 'Young Woman Walking in the Bois', 1912, in *Hidden Depths*, p. 17

Latham, Sean, 'Twenty-First-Century Critical Contexts', in *James Joyce in Context*, ed. by John McCourt (Cambridge: Cambridge University Press, 2009), pp. 148–60

Leonard, Garry, *Advertising and Commodity Culture in Joyce* (Gainesville: University Press of Florida, 1998)

Leo XIII, Pope, 'Ars Photographica', in *Poem, Charades, Inscriptions of Pope Leo XIII: Including the Revised Compositions of His Early Life in Chronological Order*, trans. by H. T. Henry (New York and Philadelphia: American Ecclesiastical Review, 1902), p. 44

Leroy, Dean R., 'A Tribute to Gisèle Freund (1908–2000)', *James Joyce Quarterly*, 36.2 (1999), 32–6

Lestang, Hervé, 'Paul Darby', *Portrait Sépia*, http://www.portraitsepia.fr/photographes/darby [accessed 10 February 2021]

Liddy, Brian, 'Sir David Brewster', in *Encyclopedia of Nineteenth-Century Photography: A-I*, ed. by John Hannavy, 2 vols (New York: Routledge, 2008), I, pp. 209–11

'The Living Complexions of Living Beauties for Sale, and The Identical Complexion of Your Girlhood', *Lady's Pictorial*, 23 November 1907, p. 891

'Living Pictures and Scottish Meistersingers at the Rotunda', *The Irish Times*, 6 April 1901, p. 6

'London Letter', *The Western Daily Press*, Bristol, 17 May 1899, p. 8

'London "Punch" and Its Makers: I – The Writers', *The Book Buyer*, 1 July 1899, 18, pp. 451–8

'Lotteries and Advertisements', *The Spectator*, 19 September 1908, p. 8

Lowe-Evans, Mary, *Catholic Nostalgia in Joyce and Company* (Gainesville: University of Florida Press, 2008)

Maddox, Brenda, *Nora: A Biography of Nora Joyce* (London: Hamish Hamilton, 1988)

Marbot, Bernard, 'The New Image Takes Its First Steps (1839–50)', in *A History of Photography*, ed. by Jean-Claude Lemagny and André Rouillé, trans. by Janet Lloyd (Cambridge: Cambridge University Press, 1987), pp. 19–29

Marsh, Tess, 'Is There More to "Photo Bits" than Meets the Eye?', *James Joyce Quarterly*, 30.4–31.1 (1993), 877–93

McAllister, T. H., *Catalogue of Stereopticons, Dissolving View Apparatus, Magic Lanterns: A List of Over 3000 Carefully Selected Views for the Illustration of Subjects of Popular Interest – Primary Source Edition* (New York: Nabu Press, 2011)

McCourt, John, 'Joyce, *il Bel Paese* and the Italian Language', in *Joycean Unions: Post-Millennial Essays from East to West*, European Joyce Studies, 22, ed. by R. Brandon Kershner and Tekla Mecsnóber (Amsterdam: Rodopi, 2013), pp. 61–80

McCourt, John (ed.), *Roll Away the Reel World: James Joyce and Cinema* (Cork: Cork University Press, 2010)

McCourt, John (ed.), 'Trieste', in *James Joyce in Context* (Cambridge: Cambridge University Press, 2009), pp. 228–38

McHugh, Roland, *Annotations to 'Finnegans Wake'*, 4th edn (Baltimore: Johns Hopkins University Press, 2016)

McLuhan, Eric, *The Role of Thunder in 'Finnegans Wake'* (Toronto: University of Toronto Press, 1997)

'Meetings of Societies: Meetings of Societies for Next Week', *British Journal of Photography*, 53.2428 (16 November 1906), 915–17

Milhollen, Hirst, 'Roger Fenton, Photographer of the Crimean War', *Quarterly Journal of Current Acquisitions*, 3.4 (1946), 10–12

Moore, Martson, 'Memento Mori', *British Journal of Photography*, 30 December 1887, pp. 826–27

Mosca Irene and Robert E. Wright, 'The Long-Term Consequences of the Irish Marriage Bar', *IZA Discussion Papers*, 12301, Institute of Labor Economics (IZA), Bonn, 1–39

'Mr. Bradley, the Ex-footman Who Received £60,000', *Daily Mirror*, 10 February 1910, p. 115

'Mr Fenton's Crimean Photographs', *Freeman's Journal*, 24 January 1856, p. 3

Mullin, Katherine, *James Joyce, Sexuality and Social Purity* (Cambridge: Cambridge University Press, 2003)

Mullin, Katherine, 'Joyce, Early Cinema and the Erotics of Everyday Life', in *Roll Away the Reel World: James Joyce and Cinema*, ed. by John McCourt (Cork: Cork University Press, 2010), pp. 43–56

Murphy, Niall, *A Bloomsday Postcard* (Dublin: Lilliput Press, 2004)

The National Archives of Ireland: Census of Ireland 1901/11, http://www.census.nationalarchives.ie [accessed 10 January 2021]

Nazarieff, Serge, *The Stereoscopic Nude 1850–1930* (Köln: Benedikt Taschen Verlag GmbH, 1993)

'New Apparatus and Materials: The Baby "Brownie", Sold by Kodak, Limited, Kingsway, London, W.C.1', *British Journal of Photography*, 28 June 1935, p. 412

'New Portraits in Ivory', *Weekly Irish Times*, 16 April 1904, p. 24

'News and Notes', *British Journal of Photography*, 73.3472 (19 November 1926), 683

'News and Notes of the Week: Artists' Model, and Postcard', *British Journal of Photography*, 78.3701 (17 April 1931), 234

'New Views of the World', *Quiver*, 30 January 1910, p. 30

Nicholson, Bob, 'Nineteenth-Century Nuts: The Anatomy of a Victorian Lad's Mag', *The Digital Victorianist*, http://www.digitalvictorianist.com [accessed 15 July 2021]

Nickel, Douglas R., *Dreaming in Pictures: The Photography of Lewis Carroll* (London: Yale University Press, 2002)

Nordström, Alison, 'Lovely, Smart, Modern: Women with Cameras in a Changing World', in *Kodak Girl: From the Martha Cooper Collection*, ed. by John P. Jacob (Göttingen: Steidl, 2011), pp. 64–71

Norris, Margot, *Virgin and Veteran Readings of 'Ulysses'* (New York: Palgrave, 2011)

O'Brien, Darcy, *The Conscience of James Joyce* (Princeton: Princeton University Press, 1968)

O'Brien, Joseph V., *Dear, Dirty Dublin: A City in Distress, 1899–1916* (Berkeley: University of California Press, 1982)

'Oil Paintings at Lafayette's', *The Irish Times*, 28 February 1907, p. 6

'One of Our Most Enthusiastic Admirers', *Photo Bits*, 11 March 1911, p. 4

'The Opening and Back Page of a Lafayette Publicity Brochure circa 1902', The Lafayette Negative Archive, http://lafayette.org.uk/lafhist.html [accessed 10 April 2021]

'Opening of the Dublin International Exhibition', *The Irish Times*, 10 May 1865, p. 5

Osteen, Mark, *The Economy of Ulysses: Making Both Ends Meet* (Syracuse, NY: Syracuse University Press, 1995)

'Our Anaglyph Mask Coupon', *The Illustrated London News*, 29 March 1924, p. IV

'P. & S. Semi-Achromatic Lenses', *Camera Work*, ed. by Alfred Stieglitz, 1 August 1912, Modernist Journals Project, https://modjourn.org/journal/camera-work [accessed 10 February 2021] (p. 83)

'The Passion Play', *The Kerry Sentinel*, 23 November 1910, p. 2

Peres, Michael R. (ed.), 'Profiles of Selected Photographic Film and Digital Companies', in *The Focal Encyclopedia of Photography*, 4th edn (Waltham, MA: Focal Press, 2007), pp. 301–20

Peterson, Richard F., 'More Aristotelian Grist for the Joycean Mill', *James Joyce Quarterly*, 17.2 (1980), 213–16

Philadelphia Press, 1 October 1862, quoted in Kentwood D. Wells, 'The Stereopticon Photographic Illustrations', *The Magic Lantern Gazette*, 20.3 (2008), 2 (p. 2)

'Philip Shaw, Clonkill, Mullingar', c. 1900, in '"Milly Bloom", Apprentice Photographer, Mullingar, 1904', JACOLETTE: A Gallery of Irish Snapshots and Vernacular Photography, https://jacolette.wordpress.com [accessed 1 January 2021]

Phillips, Sandra S., 'Exposed: Voyeurism, Surveillance and the Camera', *Tate Exhibition Guide*, www.tate.org.uk/whats-on/tate-modern/exhibition [accessed 14 June 2021]

Phillips, Sandra S. (ed.), 'Looking Out, Looking In: Voyeurism and Its Affinities from the Beginning of Photography', in *Exposed: Voyeurism, Surveillance and the Camera* (London: Tate Publishing, 2010), pp. 11–18

'Photo-Mechanical Notes: Half-Tones in Newspaper Illustrations', *British Journal of Photography*, 66.3110, 727

'Photographers (Dublin and Suburbs Trades' Directory)', in *Thom's Official Directory of the United Kingdom of Great Britain and Ireland* (Dublin: Alexander Thom and Co., 1904), p. 2077

'Photographic Convention of the United Kingdom: Dublin Meeting', *British Journal of Photography*, 41.1784 (13 July 1894), 437–40

'Photographic Society of Ireland's Exhibition', *British Journal of Photography*, 42.1816 (22 February 1895), 119

'Photography', in *Encyclopædia Britannica*, 11th edn (New York: The Encyclopædia Britannica Company, 1910), pp. 485–522

'Photography as an Occupation for Women', *British Journal of Photography*, 47.2099 (27 July 1900), 473–4

'Photography in the Abbey', *Daily Express* (Dublin), 20 June 1911, p. 4

'Picture Postcard of Painted Portrait by Jacques Émile Blanche, Titled "James Augustine Aloysius Joyce"', 1935, Sylvia Beach Papers, Box 169, Folder 17, Princeton University Library

'Pictures and Opera', *The Irish Times*, 10 January 1906, p. 7

'Princess Alexander of Teck', *Lady's Pictorial; A Weekly Illustrated Journal of Fashion, Society, Art, Literature, Music and the Drama*, 2 November 1907, http://www.torontopubliclibrary.ca [accessed 26 April 2021] (p. 1)

Plunkett, John, 'Selling Stereoscopy, 1890–1915: Penny Arcades, Automatic Machines and American Salesmen', *Early Popular Visual Media*, 6 (2008), 239–55

'Poole and Young's Panorama', *The Irish Times*, 9 October 1877, p. 5

'Private Correspondence', *The Irish Times*, 7 June 1866, p. 3

'Proceedings of the Central Criminal Court, 7th January 1913', *Old Bailey Proceedings Online*, https://www.oldbaileyonline.org [accessed 10 June 2021]

'Queen Victoria: In Memoriam', *Lady's Pictorial*, 2 February 1901

Ray, Clarence F., 'Making Women Look Pretty in Their Photographs', *British Journal of Photography*, 57.2626 (2 September 1910), 663

Rea, John A., 'A Bit of Lewis Carroll in *Ulysses*', *James Joyce Quarterly*, 15.1 (1977), 86–9

'Real Evidence', *Citizens Information Board*, 6 January 2014, http://www.citizensinformation.ie [accessed 13 April 2021]

Roberts, Mary Ann, 'Edward Linley Sambourne', *History of Photography*, 17 (1993), 207–13

Rockett, Kevin, and Emer Rockett, *Magic Lantern, Panorama and Moving Picture Shows in Ireland, 1786–1909* (Dublin: Four Courts Press, 2011)

Rose, Danis, and John O'Hanlon (eds), *JJDA*, https://jjda.ie [accessed 10 June 2021]
André

Rouillé, André, 'The Rise of Photography (1851–70)', in *A History of Photography*, ed. by Jean-Claude Lemagny and André Rouillé, trans. by Janet Lloyd (Cambridge: Cambridge University Press, 1987), pp. 29–52

'Royal Gifts Auctioned', *Yorkshire Post and Leeds Intelligencer*, 1 May 1942, p. 2

Russell, William Howard, *The British Expedition to the Crimea* (London: George Routledge and Sons, 1877)

Sartor, Genevieve, 'Genetic Connections in *Finnegans Wake*: Lucia Joyce and Issy Earwicker', *Journal of Modern Literature*, 41.1 (2018), 18–30

'The Search Light', *The British Journal of Photography*, 4 January 1895, pp. 3–4

Senn, Fritz, 'Esthetic Theories', *James Joyce Quarterly*, 2.2 (1965), 134–6

Senn, Fritz, 'Retrosemantics: How Understanding Trails Behind', *Papers on Joyce*, 7–8 (2001–02), 1–27

Shakespeare and Company Project, version 1.5.0, Center for Digital Humanities, Princeton University, 2021, https://shakespeareandco.princeton.edu/members/joyce-james/cards/ [accessed 19 April 2021]

Shloss, Carol Loeb, *Lucia Joyce: To Dance in the Wake* (London: Bloomsbury Publishing, 2005)

Sicker, Philip, *'Ulysses', Film and Visual Culture* (Cambridge: Cambridge University Press, 2018)

Sigel, Lisa Z., *Governing Pleasures: Pornography and Social Change in England, 1815–1914* (New Brunswick: Rutgers University Press, 2002), pp. 85–6

'Skerry's School of Shorthand, Typewriting, and Commercial Training', *Daily Express* (Dublin), 20 June 1911, p. 4

Slattery, Peadar, 'Lauder, James Stack ("Jacques Lafayette")', *Dictionary of Irish Biography*, https://www.dib.ie/biography [accessed 1 August 2021]

Smith, Alison, *The Victorian Nude: Sexuality, Morality, and Art* (Manchester: Manchester University Press, 1996)

Smith, Graham, *'Light That Dances in the Mind': Photographs and Memory in the Writings of E. M. Forster and His Contemporaries* (Bern, Switzerland: Peter Lang, 2007)

Snelling, H. H., 'American National Photographic Association', *British Journal of Photography*, 20.686 (27 June 1873), 308–9

'Solid Cinematography: Alleged Important New Discovery', *Weekly Irish Times*, 7 November 1903, p. 14

'Some Great Actresses', *The National Police Gazette*, 28 December 1912, p. 11

Sontag, Susan, *On Photography* (London: Penguin Modern Classics, 2008)

'Souvenir of the Twenty-Fifth Anniversary of the Opening of the Gaiety Theatre' (Dublin: s.n., 1896)

Sparham, Anna, 'Introduction', in *Soldiers and Suffragettes: The Photography of Christina Broom*, ed. by Anna Sparham, Margaret Denny and Diane Atkinson (London: Philip Wilson, 2015), pp. 1–4

Siteglitz, Alfred (ed.), 'An Apology', *Camera Work*, 1 January 1903, Modernist Journals Project, https://modjourn.org/journal/camera-work [accessed 10 February 2021] (pp. 15–16)

Siteglitz, Alfred (ed.), *Camera Work*, 1 January 1913 Modernist Journals Project

Siteglitz, Alfred (ed.), 'Special Number: Matisse, Picasso, and Stein', *Camera Work*, 1 August 1912, Modernist Journals Project

Sterne, Laurence, *A Sentimental Journey through France and Italy* (New York: Dover Publications, 2004), pp. 36–7

Suleman, Reena, 'Still Lives: The Art of Edward Linley Sambourne', in *Model and Supermodel: The Artists' Model in British Art and Culture*, ed. by Jane Desmarais, Martin Postle and Martin Vaughan (Manchester: Manchester University Press, 2006), pp. 75–88

'Supplement', *Lady's Pictorial*, 23 November 1907, p. 32

Surman, Phil, Klaus Hopf and et al., 'Solving the 3D Problem – The History and Development of Viable Domestic 3DTV Displays', in *Three-Dimensional Television: Capture, Transmission, Display*, ed. by H.M. Ozaktas and Levent Onural (New York: Springer, 2008), pp. 471–504

Tabb, John B., 'From a Photograph', in *Camera Work*, ed. by Alfred Stieglitz, 1 January 1903, Modernist Journals Project, https://modjourn.org/issue/bdr566054 [accessed 16 April 2021] (p. 16)

Talbot, William Henry Fox, *The Pencil of Nature* (London: Longman, Brown Green and Longmans, 1844)

'Tell the Story of Your Happy Days – With a Kodak', *Punch*, 3 August 1921, in John Taylor, *A Dream of England: Landscape, Photography, and the Tourist's Imagination* (Manchester: Manchester University Press, 1994), p. 140

'Tell the Story of Your Happy Days – With a Kodak', in *The Sphere*, 20 August 1921, p. 33, *The Graphic*, 13 August 1921, p. 25, *The Tatler*, 10 August 1921, p. 55 and *The Belfast News-Letter*, 24 August 1921, p. 7

Thom's Official Directory of the United Kingdom of Great Britain and Ireland (Dublin: Alexander Thom and Co., 1904)

'*The Times* Correspondent in the East', *Irish Examiner*, 1 November 1854, p. 4

Tindall, William York, *A Reader's Guide to 'Finnegans Wake'* (Syracuse, NY: Syracuse University Press, 1969)

Torchiana, Donald, 'Joyce's "Eveline" and the Blessed Margaret Mary Alacoque', *James Joyce Quarterly*, 6.1 (1968), 22–8

Tricot, Xavier, *James Joyce in Ostend* (Devriendt: Belgium, 2018) for those taken in Ostend in 1926

Trotter, David, 'Stereoscopy: Modernism and the "Haptic"', *Critical Quarterly*, 46 (2004), 38–58

Tzara, Tristan, 'La photographie à l'envers' (Photography from the Verso)', 1922, in *Selected Writings: Volume 2, Part 2, 1931–1934*, ed. By Walter Benjamin, trans. by Rodney Livingstone and et al., ed. by Michael W. Jennings and et al. (Cambridge, MA: Harvard University Press, 2005), p. 55

Underwood & Underwood, '(3)-7907- And in Trying to Please Both, This Is the Result', 1906

Unknown Photographer, 'Giorgio and Lucia Joyce at the window of their flat in Trieste', c. 1913, James Joyce Collection, University at Buffalo

Unknown Photographer, 'James Joyce, Age 3', 1885, James Joyce Collection, University at Buffalo, https://library.buffalo.edu/jamesjoyce/catalog/xvii [accessed 14 January 2021]

Unknown Photographer, 'James Joyce's Graduation from Royal University (later University College Dublin)', 1902, James Joyce Collection, University at Buffalo

Unknown Photographer (Likely Lucia Joyce), 'Nora Joyce Seated on Steps of Cart, Ostend', 1926 and 'James Joyce, Nora Joyce, and P.J. Hoey seated on grass', 1926, James Joyce Collection, University at Buffalo

Unknown Photographer (Taken at Lafayette's), 'Photograph of James Joyce as a Boy', Constantine Curran Collection, University College Dublin Special Collections, http://digital.ucd.ie/view/ivrla:6937 [accessed 11 April 2021]

Unknown Photographer, 'Seen in Stereoscopic Relief if Viewed through Red and Green Films: Occupants of the New "Zoo" Aquarium', *The Illustrated London News*, 29 March 1924, pp. 548–9

Valisa, Silvia, 'An Imaged Life: Wanda Wulz and the Familiar Archive', in *A Window on the Italian Female Modernist Subjectivity: From Neera to Laura Curino*, ed. by

Rossella Maria Riccobono (Newcastle upon Tyne: Cambridge Scholars Publishing, 2013), pp. 45–77

Valente, Joseph, 'Joyce and Sexuality', in *The Cambridge Companion to James Joyce*, ed. by Derek Attridge (Cambridge: Cambridge University Press, 2004), pp. 213–33

Valente, Joseph, 'The Novel and the Police (Gazette)', *Novel: A Forum on Fiction*, 29 (1995), 8–18

Van Haaften, Julia, *Berenice Abbott: A Life in Photography* (New York: W. W. Norton & Company, 2018)

Waggoner, Diane, *Lewis Carroll's Photography and Modern Childhood* (Princeton, NJ: Princeton University Press, 2020)

Watt, Stephen, 'Brief Exposures: Commodification, Exchange Value, and the Figure of Woman in "Eumaeus"', *James Joyce Quarterly*, 30.4–31.1 (1993), 757–82

'Weddings', *Lady's Pictorial*, 23 February 1907, p. 545

Weir, David, 'Stephen Dedalus: Rimbaud or Baudelaire?' *James Joyce Quarterly*, 18.1 (1980), 87–91

Weir, Lorraine, 'Joyce, Myth and Memory', *Irish University Review*, 2.2 (1972), 172–88

Wells, Kentwood D., 'The Stereopticon Men: On the Road with John Fallon's Stereopticon, 1860–1870', *The Magic Lantern Gazette*, 23.3 (2011), 3–34

West, Nancy Martha, *Kodak and the Lens of Nostalgia* (Charlottesville: University Press of Virginia, 2000)

Wheatstone, Sir Charles, 'Contributions to the Physiology of Vision — Part the First. On Some Remarkable, and Hitherto Unobserved, Phenomena of Binocular Vision', *Philosophical Transactions of the Royal Society*, 128 (1838), 371–94

White, Jerry, *London in the Twentieth Century: A City and Its People* (London: Vintage, 2008)

Wicke, Jennifer, 'Joyce and Consumer Culture', in *The Cambridge Companion to James Joyce*, ed. by Derek Attridge, 2nd edn (Cambridge: Cambridge University Press, 2004), pp. 234–53

Wilkie, Edmund H., 'Optical Illusions', in *The Optical Lantern and Cinematograph Journal* (London: E. T. Heron, 1904), pp. 41–3

Williams, Keith, '*Dubliners*, "the Magic-Lantern Business" and Pre-Cinema', in *James Joyce in the Nineteenth Century*, ed. by John Nash (Cambridge: Cambridge University Press, 2013), pp. 215–33

Williams, Keith, *James Joyce and Cinematicity: Before and After Film* (Edinburgh: Edinburgh University Press, 2020)

Williams, Keith, 'Time and Motion Studies: Joycean Cinematicity in *A Portrait of the Artist as a Young Man*', in *Cinematicity in Media History*, ed. by Jeffrey Geiger and Karin Littau (Edinburgh: Edinburgh University Press, 2013), pp. 88–106

Winkenweder, Brian, 'Dada', in *Encyclopedia of Twentieth-Century Photography*, 3 vols, ed. by Lynne Warren (New York: Routledge, 2006), I, pp. 353–5

'Women Photographers', *Irish Society and Social Review*, 17 September 1921, p. 634

Woolf, Virginia, *Jacob's Room* (London: The Hogarth Press, 1960)

Wulz, Carlo, 'Wanda e Marion Wulz durante il bagno', 1905, AIM Alinari Image Museum, Trieste

Wulz, Wanda, 'Io + gatto', 1932, courtesy of Ford Motor Company Collection, The Metropolitan Museum of Art, http://www.metmuseum.org/ [accessed 25 November 2021]

Wulz, Wanda, 'Ritratto di Marion Wulz in costume egiziano', c. 1930 in Silvia Valisa, 'An Imaged Life: Wanda Wulz and the Familiar Archive', in *A Window on the Italian Female Modernist Subjectivity: From Neera to Laura Curino* (Newcastle upon Tyne: Cambridge Scholars Publishing, 2013), pp. 45–77

Zone, Ray, *Stereoscopic Cinema and the Origins of 3-D Film, 1838–1952* (Lexington: University Press of Kentucky, 2007)

Index

Abbott, Berenice
   photography of Barnacle, Nora 111
   photography of Joyce, James 14, 111, 148
   photography of Joyce, Lucia 20, 111, 133
   at Shakespeare and Company 15
Alacoque, Blessed Margaret Mary 29, 32
albumen print 5, 8, 29, 65
Alice's Adventures in Wonderland. See Carroll, Lewis
L'Amateur Photographe 94
The American Amateur Photographer 83
American Mutoscope and Biograph Company 40
anaglyph technology
   and cinema 54
   in *Finnegans Wake* 23, 56, 70, 78–9
   printed 79
   viewing-masks 52
Anastasi, William 120
animatograph 54
Anna Livia Plurabelle (ALP) 70, 72, 74, 107, 139
Aquinas, Thomas 57
Aristotle 55, 81. *See* pseudo-Aristotle
Art-Journal 78
'L'Arte fotografica' 91
Atget, Eugène 8
Atherton, James S. 19–20
audiences 2, 37, 42, 54, 66, 72, 82

Bannon, Alec. *See* Bloom, Milly
Barnacle, Nora
   absence 17
   and Joyce, James 10, 13, 31, 127, 139
   painted 16
   photography 112, 130
   receipt of photograph 10
Barthes, Roland 1, 27, 49
Bass, Richard K. 103

Baudelaire, Charles
   and Dedalus, Stephen 54–5
   'The Salon of 1859' 54–5, 82–3, 102
Beach, Sylvia. *See also* Shakespeare and Company
   and Carroll, Lewis 118, 146
   Papers at Princeton University Library 17
   and photography 14–15, 112, 134, 146
Bekker, Pieter 136
The Belfast News-Letter 123
Black Friars 140
Blanquart-Evrard, Louis Désiré 5, 29
Bloom, Leopold 40
   advertising 117
   as artist 23, 35, 49, 91, 96–8, 102
   and Bloom, Rudy 17, 49
   erotic photocards 96, 98, 101–3, 110
   and Gerty MacDowell 85, 99
   mutoscope 58, 96, 104, 128
   nude photography 108–9
   observation of women 61, 94
   photograph of Bloom, Molly 11, 17, 19, 24, 27, 35, 47, 65, 79, 82, 83, 90–4, 97–9
   photographs of celebrated figures 84, 96, 106, 114, 131
   on photography and art 1, 24, 55, 82, 96
   photography and family lineage 4, 23, 96, 112, 122–3, 131–2, 142
   sexual fantasies 82, 91, 93, 96–7, 99, 146
   stereoscope 55
Bloom, Milly. *See also* Mullingar
   and Alec Bannon 92, 96, 120, 126–8
   earnings 28, 122
   eroticised 104, 109, 128
   photographed 91, 114, 127
   professional role 18, 24, 43, 96, 112, 114, 120–6
   and Trieste 131–3

Bloom, Molly. *See also* Bloom, Leopold
   earnings 92
   and erotic postcards 102–3
   posing naked 108–10
   voyeurism 106–8
The Bohemian Girl 31, 32
The Book Buyer: A Monthly Review of American and Foreign Literature 99
Bowman, Isa 20, 118, 119, 121
Bragaglia, Anton Giulio 132. *See also* Photodynamism
Braslasu, Viviana Mirela 20, 118, 121
Breton, André 9
Brewster, David 51, 52, 65
British Journal of Photography 4, 6, 28, 39, 48, 60, 88, 99, 137
Broom, Christina 4
Bruno, Juliana 58
Budgen, Frank 12, 82, 91
Buenos Aires 32, 109. *See also* Mullin, Katherine
Butt and Taff 55, 73, 75, 77, 135
Byrne, John Francis 81
Byron, Lord George Gordon 26, 36

cabinet print 5, 10, 92
calotype 3, 73, 77, 81
camera obscura 2, 33, 82
Camera Work 1, 7, 8, 25, 87
Camerani, Marco 104
Cameron, Julia Margaret 7, 8, 9, 28, 118, 120
Carlin, Francis 140
Carroll, Lewis. *See also* Finnegans Wake
   Alice's Adventures in Wonderland 118, 119, 140
   Christ Church College, University of Oxford 7, 118, 140
   Joyce's reading of 118–19
   The Life and Letters of Lewis Carroll (with Stuart Collingwood) 118, 119
   photography (beginning) 7–8
   photography of children 7, 118–19, 120
   at Shakespeare and Company 119
   Sylvie and Bruno 20, 119
   writing on photography 8
cartes de visite 5, 10, 27, 28, 32, 34, 76, 92, 93
Carville, Justin 20–1, 46, 94
Catholicism 25, 28, 40, 41, 70

Chicago Exhibition 84
Cigarette cards 101
cinema
   colour technology 54
   in *Dubliners* 27–8, 38, 46
   early forms 6, 19, 67
   in *Finnegans Wake* 71, 73
   influence on Joyce, James 21, 70, 72, 133
   stereoscopy 55, 70
   in *Ulysses* 19, 58, 67, 69
cinematograph 32, 54
Circovich, Mario 129
Claris, Marcello 132
Clarke, J. J. 21
Clery, Emma 23, 55, 56, 60, 61
Clifford, Martha 93
Clongowes Wood College, County Kildare 5, 10, 45, 66, 92, 147
Conley, Tim 58
consumer culture 18, 24, 86, 101, 115, 117. *See also* Wicke, Jennifer
Conway, Mrs 'Dante' Hearn 11
Corelli, Marie 138
Cosgrave, Vince 81, 128
covert photography 88, 90, 94, 104, 138. *See also* detective cameras
Crispi, Luca 109, 131, 134
Curran, Constantine 11, 26, 31
Curran, Helen Laird 12, 111

Dada 9–10, 25
Daguerre, Louis-Jacques-Mandé 2, 52, 76, 77, 82, 102
daguerreotype 3, 76, 123
   in *Dubliners* 18
   exposure time 25
   in *Finnegans Wake* 23, 75, 77–8, 82
   in *Ulysses* 4, 92, 123, 130, 131, 132
Daily Express (Dublin) 137
dancing
   in *Finnegans Wake* 10, 20
   modelling 108–9
   in *The National Police Gazette* 103
   stereoscopy 65, 68
   in *Ulysses* 68, 85
Darby, Paul 11, 147
The Dead (film) 47
Detective cameras 105, 138
   as binoculars 90, 107–8
   as books and watches 105

and *Dubliners* 18. (*see also* Knowlton, Elouise)
for evidence 105
Kodak 135
privacy 94. (*see also* Phillips, Sandra, S.)
and *Ulysses* 94
Dettmar, Kevin J. H. 138
Devlin, Kimberly J. 104
diableries. *See* Williams, Keith
DiBattista, Maria 67
Dickens, Charles 52
divorce 105
documentary photography 8
Dodgson, Charles Lutwidge. *See* Carroll, Lewis
Doyle, Richard 99
'Drama and Life' 136
du Maurier, George
  illustrations 61, 89
  Trilby 89, 90
Dublin International Exhibition 5, 83
Dublin Photographic Convention (1894) 26
Dubliners 22, 25–8, 50
  'The Boarding House' 128
  'The Dead' 22, 25, 26, 28, 43–50, 93, 97. (*see also The Dead* (film))
  'Eveline' 22, 26, 28–34, 36, 37, 41, 45, 50, 109, 112. (*see also The Bohemian Girl*)
  'Grace' 22, 26, 27–8, 30, 39–43, 72. (*see also* Leo XIII, Pope)
  'A Little Cloud' 22, 34–9
  'The Sisters' 25, 27, 40, 41, 48
Duboscq, Jules 52
Ducos du Hauron, Louis Arthur 79. *See also* anaglyph
Duse, Eleanora 32, 93

Eastman, George. *See* Kodak Limited Company
Edis, Olive 4
Edison, Thomas Alva 101
Edison Manufacturing Company of America 101
Ehrenzweig, Alex 11
Ellmann, Richard 13, 66, 121
Empire Palace Theatre, Dublin
Encyclopaedia Britannica 105

The Era 59
ethnographic photography 22, 38, 114
Evening Standard (London) 139

Fables, William E. S. 126. *See also* Kodak Girls
Fellowes, Honorable Mrs. Reginald (Daisy) 13
Femmina, Quindicinale Femminile 130
Fenton, Roger 53, 76–8, 79. *See also* wars, Crimean War
  Agnew & Sons, Thomas 76
  and Barker, Thomas J. 76
Finnegans Wake
  Algy, Autist 109
  Buckley and the Russian General 75–8
  Carroll, Lewis 2, 8, 10, 19–20, 24, 112, 118–19, 121, 139–43
  and *Dubliners* 35, 37
  'The Hen' episode 20, 56, 72, 121
  'lady performers' 59
  Latouche, Luperca 107
  Liddell, Alice Pleasance 10
  nude female models 24, 82, 91, 109–10
  'Photoflashing it' 107
  'snapograph' 136
  stereopticon 70–4
  stereoscopic technology 22, 23, 51, 54–5, 56, 59
  technology 18–19. (*see also* Wicke, Jennifer and Williams, Keith)
flashback 140, 142
flashlight photography 14, 139
Flynn, Catherine 22
Flynn, Deidre 35
Freeman's Journal 7, 59, 66, 77, 78
French Academy of Fine Arts 2, 82
French Academy of Sciences 2, 6, 82
Freud, Sigmund 10, 141
Freund, Gisèle
  and Monnier, Adrienne 111
  photography of Joyce, James 6, 14–15, 17, 138–9
  photography of Joyce, James and family 111
  photography of Woolf, Virginia 118
  promotion for *Finnegans Wake* 14
  at Shakespeare and Company 15
futurism 130, 132–3

gelatin dry plate process 5–6, 9, 25, 29, 43, 48, 76, 105
Gibraltar 92, 103
Gleeson White, Joseph 87, 88
Gonne, Maud 38
Grafton Street, Dublin 83
   Kodak (89). (*see* Kodak Limited Company)
   Mutoscope Palace (29) 21
   Robinson's (65) 72
   Schroeder, Mr (28) 83
   Thornton's (63) 115, 135. (*see* Tulloch-Turnbull girl)
   in *Ulysses* 6, 115
The Graphic 123
Growth and the Structure of the English Language. *See* Jespersen, Otto

halftone printing process 85
Hamilton, Edwin 136
Hanaway-Oakley, Cleo 19, 55, 79
Harmsworth, A.C.W., Viscount Northcliffe 138
Harry Ransom Center, University of Texas 146
Hart, Clive 55
Hayman, David 72
Healy, Michael 12
heliography 2, 33, 82
hemiplegia 1, 21, 22, 26, 31, 121, 145
Hoey, Patrick J. 130
Holmes, Oliver Wendell 53, 57, 74
Homer 103
Hughes, Cornelius Jabez 122
Humphrey Chimpden Earwicker (HCE)
   and Buckley 135
   incestuous infatuation 20
   intercourse 107, 139, 141
   as Lewis Carroll 112, 142, 143
   politicized photography 75, 80
   rumours of sexual transgression 32, 72, 73, 74, 136, 140

Ibsen, Henrik 23, 108
The Illustrated London News 52, 79
L'Illustrazione Triestina 128, 130
'Ireland: Island of Saints and Sages' 145
Irish Animated Photo Company 32
Irish census records 108, 113, 115, 121
Irish Courts 105

Irish National Land League 40
Irish Society and Social Review 113
The Irish Times 63, 83, 84, 85, 100, 115, 127
Issy 91, 109, 116, 118, 134, 141, 142
Italian language 4, 112, 124, 131, 132

Jacob's Room. *See* Woolf, Virginia
James, Charles Augustus 58–9
Jarry, Alfred 117, 120
Jespersen, Otto 6, 135
Joyce, Giorgio 10, 12, 13, 15, 112–13, 128
Joyce, Helen 15
Joyce, James
   eyesight 14, 51, 112, 139
   and newspapers 7, 46
   painted 16, 17
   relationship with photography 10–17
Joyce, John Stanislaus 11, 12, 16, 17, 40
Joyce, Lucia
   absence 17
   dancing 20, 133
   exchange of photographs 12–13, 111–12
   Italian 112, 131
   and Jung, Carl 141
   photographically framed 33
   photography 12–13, 24, 111–14, 143, 147
Joyce, Mary Jane Murray 11, 44
Joyce, Stanislaus
   correspondence from Joyce, James 46, 50, 137, 146
   at *Cyrano de Bergerac* 32
   on photography 11, 89–90
   sending photograph 12

kalloscope 59, 60
Kendall, Marie 100–1, 103
Kendrick, Walter 85
through the keyhole motif
   in art 104
   in photography 103
   in *Ulysses* 104–6, 128, 134
Khan, Albert 114
Killeen, Terrence 148
kineticism 31, 36, 132
kinetoscope 19
Kitchin, Xie (Alexandra) 118
Knock apparitions 40. *See also Dubliners*, 'Grace'

Kodak Girl
    in advertising 117, 120, 123–4, 126, 135
    history 124
    in poetry 126
Kodak Limited Company
    brand etymology 135. (*see also Growth and the Structure of the English Language*)
    cameras 25, 36, 87, 113, 114, 135
    and cycling 117–18, 126
    in Dublin, Grafton Street (89) 115, 116
    and Joyce, James 2, 24, 36
    launch 114

Lady's Pictorial 24, 82, 85–6, 99. *See also* MacDowell, Gerty
Lafayette's
    cost of photographs 5–6, 10, 34, 92
    history 5–6, 26–7, 76, 83–5, 96, 99–100, 115
    influence on Joyce, James 24, 82, 84
    Lafayette, Jacques
    paintings 85, 100
    photographic artist 26–7, 84, 95, 99
    photography of Joyce, James 10, 27, 28, 43–4, 147
    photography of priests 28, 44
    in *Ulysses* 83–4, 91–2, 94–96, 98, 99
landscape photography 7, 33, 52, 133
Lartigue, Jacques Henri 93–4
Lauder, James Stack. *See* Lafayette's, Lafayette, Jacques
Lawrence, William 5, 27, 38
lectures (with photography) 4–5, 71, 84
Lenehan 97
Leo XIII, Pope
    cinematic form 21, 39–40
    photographed 40
    on photography 26, 39, 42, 91
Liddell, Alice Pleasance. *See also Finnegans Wake*
    and Carroll, Lewis 118, 140, 142
    photographed 7, 8
The Life and Letters of Lewis Carroll (with Stuart Collingwood). *See* Carroll, Lewis
lighting (electric) 40, 49, 115
limned 98, 99, 100
lithography 2, 18

Little Chandler. *See also Dubliners,* 'A Little Cloud'
    artistic ambitions 35, 37
    and poetry 26
London's 1851 Crystal Palace Exhibition 52
London's Camera Club 90, 108
Lowe-Evans, Mary 70
Lynch 64, 97

MacDowell, Gerty 24, 85–6, 99, 103, 107. *See also Lady's Pictorial*
Maddon, Richard Leach 5
magic lantern. *See also* stereopticon
    in *Dubliners* 26, 27–8, 40–1, 42, 72
    in *Finnegans Wake* 54, 72, 79–80
    influence on Joyce, James 19, 21, 38, 56
    shows 4–5, 54, 66
    slides 38, 40, 78, 113
    in *Stephen Hero* 27
    in *Ulysses* 69
man 'in the macintosh' 90–1
Marinetti, Filippo Tommaso 132, 133
Marsh, Tess 101
Maurisset, Théodore 3
McCourt, John 19, 128, 132
memento mori 47–8
The Memoirs of Vidocq (Vidocq, Eugène François) 29
Mespoulet, Marguerite 114
Mignon-Alba, Madeleine 114
Miller, Lee 148
modernism 18, 19, 33, 49
    and photography 1, 10, 14, 19–22, 25, 46, 55, 117, 132–3, 148
Monto (Dublin) 63
Moore, Thomas 26
Morley, F. V. 139
Moses, Belle 20, 118, 121, 140, 142
Mulligan, Buck 96, 100, 104, 128
Mullin, Katherine 19, 21, 32, 58, 104, 109, 120
Mullingar
    Joyce's visits to 120, 121
    in *Stephen Hero* 122
    in *Ulysses* 91, 109, 112, 120–3, 126–7, 131
Munro, Fred 139
Murphy, Niall 146
music 4, 48, 64, 84, 89, 92, 132

music hall 100, 101. *See also* Kendall, Marie
mutoscope 19, 21, 58, 96, 104, 128. *See also* Mullin, Katherine
Muybridge, Eadweard 18, 73

The National Police Gazette 103
Negretti & Zambra 53
newspapers
  colour photography 6
  in *Finnegans Wake* 107
  Ireland 6, 7, 77, 101, 127, 130, 137–8
  Italy 46, 130
  reproduction of photographs 7, 77, 107
  stereoscopes 59, 79
  in *Ulysses* 107
Niépce, Nicéphore 2, 33, 82
Norris, Harry B.
  'Seaside Girls' (song) 124–6
nude models
  appeal 61
  art photography 87–89, 120
  camera clubs 108–9
  in *Finnegans Wake* 24, 60, 82, 91, 109–10
  as illustrative tools 88–9, 108
  in *Stephen Hero* 89
  in *Ulysses* 24, 82, 91, 102–3

O'Brien, Peter 148
O'Shea, Katherine 'Kitty' 103, 138
Occasional, Critical and Political Writing
  drama 136
  epiphany 19
  photograph 1, 16, 24, 26, 35, 55, 81, 83, 91, 93 97, 132, 148
  sculpture 27
Osteen, Mark 86, 122
Ostend 12, 112, 130, 47

Pankhurst, Emmeline 138
panorama 37, 38, 56
paralysis
  and *Dubliners* 1, 22, 26, 27, 41, 121, 145
  in Joyce, James 21
  and photography 25–6
Paris
  ateliers 132
  correspondence from Joyce, James 7, 22
  in *Dubliners* 35
  and Irish photography 84, 85

photography of Joyce, James 11, 14, 81, 111, 138, 147
  Salons 82
  in *Stephen Hero* 60, 89
  in *Ulysses* 105
Paris and Pola Commonplace Book. *See Occasional, Critical and Political Writing*
Parnell, Charles Stewart 103, 138
Peeping Tom 104, 105
Pepper's Ghost 66, 67, 69
phantasmagoria 79
  in *A Portrait of the Artist as a Young Man* 64
  in *Dubliners* 41–2
  in *Finnegans Wake* 71
  in Joyce, James 23, 51, 65
  in *Ulysses* 56, 63, 67–8, 70, 123
Phantasmascope 59
phenakistoscope. *See* Phantasmascope
Phillips, Sandra S. 94
Photo Bits 11, 95, 98, 101, 105
Photodynamism 132–3. *See also* Bragaglia, Anton Giulio
photographic miniatures 85, 100, 126–7
The Photographic News 117
photographic retouching 6, 24, 82, 83, 99, 100–1, 130, 135
photography
  and art 77, 83, 87
  in court 7, 138
  humour 66, 68
  and nature 2, 26, 31, 33, 39, 43, 57, 76, 78, 82, 99
photo-secession 1, 8, 87. *See also* Stieglitz, Alfred
pictorialism 7–8
picture postcards
  erotic 18, 89
  in *Finnegans Wake* 79
  from Joyce, James 22, 81, 103, 146
  Lafayette's, of royalty 84
  religious 28
  in *Ulysses* 22, 84, 102
Pittoni, Anita 132
Pleyer, Wilhelm 11
Pola 146
pornography 2, 18, 35, 54, 61, 70, 102, 104, 109–11, 128
Portrait of the Artist as a Young Man (A)
  aestheticism 97

and eyesight 51
photographic marketing 13
prostitutes 75
stereoscopy 57–8, 61–5
Post Office Protection Act of 1908 90
Princess Novelette 85
professional photographers (women) 5, 18, 24, 120, 130, 139, 143, 146
pseudo-Aristotle 81
Punch 6, 89, 90, 99–100, 108, 123

The Queen 86

Ray, Man 8, 14–15, 22, 26, 148
realism 9, 8, 23, 52, 54, 57–8, 75
Reeve, Lovell 53. *See also* stereo cards, *The Stereoscopic Magazine*
Richards, Grant 27, 129
Roberts, Mary Ann 108
Rockett, Kevin and Emer 20, 21
Rome 46, 146
Rotunda, Dublin 32, 37, 66, 71
Rowley, Mr. Sydney 85, 100
royalty
    Albert, Prince 127
    Alexander of Teck, Princess 86
    Alexandra, Queen 84, 95–6, 106, 114, 131
    Arthur of Connaught, Prince 85
    Connaught, Duke and Duchess of 84–5
    Edward VII, King 84, 114
    Frederica of Hanover, Princess 114
    George V, King 84
    George of Greece, Prince 117
    Victoria, Queen 38, 47, 84–5, 126
Ruf, Camille 11–12

Sackville Street, Dublin 40, 53, 83
Saint Malo 12, 112
Sambourne, Edward Linley 90, 108. *See also* Punch
Sartor, Genevieve 20, 143
'Seaside Girls' (song). *See* Norris, Harry B.
Shackleton, Jane W. 113
Shakespeare and Company 8, 14–15, 87, 119
Shaun
    and Carroll, Lewis 142
    as Jaun 91, 109–10
    stereoscope 78–80
    and the Tulloch-Turnbull girl 118, 136–9

Shaw's, Phil (photographic shop, Mullingar) 121
Shem
    and Carroll, Lewis 141
    stereoscope 66, 79–80
    and the Tulloch-Turnbull girl 118, 120, 133–4, 136–9, 142
Sicker, Philip 19, 55
Simonton and Millard 52
'Skerry's School of Shorthand' 123, 137
The Sketch 138
Slote, Sam 134
Soleil, François 52
'Souvenir of the Twenty-Fifth Anniversary of the Opening of the Gaiety Theatre' 136, 139–40
Sparling, Marcus 76
The Speaker: The Liberal Review 113
The Spectator 59
The Sphere 123
Star Theatre of Varieties, Dublin 101
Stein, Gertrude 87
Stephen Hero
    art 55, 89
    Belvedere College, two photographs 23, 75
    consumer culture 117
    epiphany 27
    Ibsen's photograph 82
    Ireland 90, 122
    stereoscopic principles 55, 57–8
    supernatural stereoscopy 67
stereo cards
    erotically-charged 56, 61–2, 64
    Irish scenes 52–3
    and Joyce, James 18, 22, 51, 61
    mock supernatural 65–8
    nudes 54, 61
    popularity 51–2
    religious 28, 40
    in *The Stereoscopic Magazine* 53
stereoscope
    invention and reception 52–4, 57, 59, 60, 69–70
    and Joyce, James 19, 23, 51, 66, 148
    penny-in-the-slot 23, 51, 56, 58–61, 64, 69–70
Sterne, Laurence 126–7
Stieglitz, Alfred. *See Camera Work*

The Story of Lewis Carroll, Told for Young People by the Real Alice in Wonderland. See Bowman, Isa
straight photography 8
Strand, Paul 8
street photography 8, 19, 21, 38, 93
surrealism 8–10
Sylvie and Bruno. See Carroll, Lewis
Synge, John Millington 45–6, 71

Talbot, William Henry Fox 2–3, 52, 73, 81
Tatler 123
Tennyson, Alfred 78
This Quarter 134
Tindall, William York 75
Tóth, Endre 132
transition 119
Trieste
    amateur photographers 128–9
    and cinema 128–9
    Joyce, James, acquiring newspapers 103
    Joyce, James, photography on display (Meštrović, Ivan) 91
    Joyce, James, writing 127–8
    Joyce, Stanislaus, photographed 128
    newspapers 130
    photography 128, 132
    professional photographers in 128, 130
        Wulz, Marion 24, 120, 130–1, 148
        Wulz, Wanda 24, 120, 130–1, 132, 148
Trilby. See du Maurier, George
Trotter, David 55
Tulloch-Turnbull girl
    blackmail 136
    and Bloom, Milly 24, 112, 114, 120–1, 133, 143, 146
    Issy 118
    Kodak 6, 70
    military origins 134, 142
    and the 'national apostate' 13, 20, 121, 132–4, 139
    professional work 4, 120, 137–9
    Scottish clan 134

Ulysses
    Antichrist, Reuben J. 68
    Apjohn, Percy 97, 98
    'Calypso' 28, 61, 92, 101, 112, 114, 121, 122–5, 126–8, 131
    cigarette cards 101
    'Circe' 51, 64, 66–70, 89, 101–2, 104–6, 128, 134
    'Cyclops' 67, 103
    'Eumaeus' 1, 5, 11, 17, 23–4, 27, 35, 49, 55, 65, 79, 82–3, 91–103, 138, 143, 145
    'Hades' 22, 91, 93, 131, 145
    'Ithaca' 48, 58, 84, 91–3, 96–7, 102, 104–6, 114, 122, 123, 125, 131, 133
    'Lestrygonians' 4, 40, 66, 93, 102, 104–5, 109, 115, 117, 127, 130–2, 137, 142
    'Lotus Eaters' 93, 94
    'Nausicaa' 82, 85–7, 96, 99, 103–4, 128
    'Oxen of the Sun' 24, 65, 92, 98–100, 109, 126, 131
    photographic haunting 67, 69, 93
    'Penelope' 11, 23, 82, 92, 102, 106–8, 110, 122–4
    'Proteus' 51, 60, 74, 113
    'Sirens' 92–3, 99, 122
    Stephen's mother 67, 69–70
    stereoscope 51, 55–6, 74
    Sweets of the Sin
    'Telemachus' 24, 69, 70, 81, 96, 104, 112, 124, 141
    'Wandering Rocks' 36, 42, 97, 100–2, 115, 135
University at Buffalo's James Joyce Collection 146

Valente, Joseph 120
Valisa, Silvia 130
Virag, Sandor 132
Vogue 148
Volta Cinematograph 133
von Herkomer, Sir Hubert 85

Waggoner, Diane 120
Ward, William Humble, Earl of Dudley 100
wars
    Boer War 63
    Crimean War 4, 23, 56, 75–9
    Mexican-American War 4, 76
    Russo-Turkish War 37
Watson, W. W. and Sons of London 107

Weaver, Harriet Shaw 12–13, 15, 111, 118, 141
    British Library's Collection 146, 147
Weir, David 54
Weir, Lorraine 133
Weiss, Ottocaro 28
West, Nancy Martha 124
wet collodion process 7
Wheatstone, Charles 52, 69
Wicke, Jennifer 18, 120

Wilkie, Edmund H. 66
Williams, Keith 42, 19, 56, 65
Woolf, Virginia 14, 118

Zatzka, Hans 104
Zürich 146
    and photography 11–12, 16, 91
    and portraiture 16
Zürich James Joyce Foundation 146

www.ingramcontent.com/pod-product-compliance
Lightning Source LLC
Chambersburg PA
CBHW062226300426
44115CB00012BA/2235